Mauzy's *Depression* *Glass*

Barbara & Jim Mauzy

Revised & Expanded 2nd Edition

a Photographic Reference

with Prices

Schiffer Publishing Ltd®

4880 Lower Valley Road, Atglen, PA 19310 USA

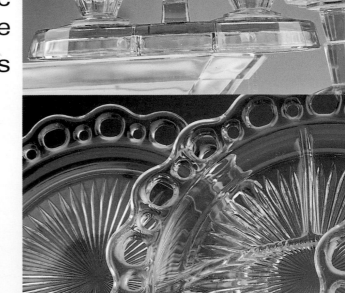

Library of Congress Cataloging-in-Publication Data

Mauzy, Barbara E.
(Depression glass)
Mauzy's depression glass / Barbara & Jim Mauzy.--Rev. & expanded
2nd ed.
p. cm.
ISBN 0-7643-1371-1
1. Depression glass--Collectors and collecting--Catalogs. I. Mauzy,
Jim. II. Title.
NK5439.D44 M37 2001
748.2913'075--dc21
2001000623

Revised price guide: 2001

Cover design by Bruce Waters
Book design by Blair Loughrey
Type set in Florens/Souvenir/Zurich

ISBN: 0-7643- 1371-1
Printed in China
1 2 3 4

Published by Schiffer Publishing Ltd.
4880 Lower Valley Road
Atglen, PA 19310
Phone: (610) 593-1777; Fax: (610) 593-2002
E-mail: Schifferbk@aol.com
Please visit our web site catalog at
www.schifferbooks.com

This book may be purchased from the publisher.
Include $3.95 for shipping. Please try your bookstore first.
We are always looking for people to write books on new and
related subjects. If you have an idea for a book please contact
us at the above address.
You may write for a free catalog.

In Europe, Schiffer books are distributed by
Bushwood Books
6 Marksbury Avenue
Kew Gardens
Surrey TW9 4JF England
Phone: 44 (0) 20-8392-8585; Fax: 44 (0) 20-8392-9876
E-mail: Bushwd@aol.com
Free postage in the UK. Europe: air mail at cost.

Dear Readers

It is with a sense of excited delight we present to you our second edition of *Mauzy's Depression Glass*. It has taken two years and scores of contributors to create this showcase of glassware created primarily from the 1920s to the 1940s. Some of the additions are in response to collectors and dealers who have been using our first edition book as well as the accompanying handbook, *Mauzy's Comprehensive Handbook of Depression Glass Prices*. You will find Forest Green, Royal Ruby, Moroccan Amethyst, National, and a greatly expanded Fire-King listing in this edition. We have even included Canadian Depression Glass! There are many new pieces and colors throughout this book and the very latest reproduction information. We hope you find this glassware as wonderful to see as we did while photographing it.

This is **your** book. Our format of showing reproduction information on the same page as the pattern, of providing a check-off tally column to inventory a collection, and of having a ruler in the inside back cover is simply to give **you** the most comprehensive and most useful Depression Glass book possible. If there are other patterns or features you would find helpful, please let us know as we create these books for you!

Mauzy's Depression Glass is an ongoing work in progress; we simply had to stop and get this second edition to press. We know there are patterns that still need better coverage and we are discovering that many of you collectors own elusive items that have never been pictured or listed elsewhere. We invite you to be a part of our third edition! The family of contributors has grown and we happily acknowledge these generous individuals throughout the book. If you find pleasure turning the pages that follow, it is totally due to their generous spirit as they shared both their glass and their knowledge.

We thank them and welcome your comments and additions!

Barbara & Jim Mauzy

About the Glass   **6**
About the Prices   **6**
Acknowledgments   **7**
Adam   **9**
American Pioneer   **11**
American Sweetheart   **13**
Anniversary   **16**
Aunt Polly   **18**
Aurora   **19**
Avocado   **19**
Beaded Block   **21**
Block Optic   **24**
Bowknot   **29**
Bubble   **29**
Cameo   **32**
Canadian Swirl   **38**
Cherry Blossom   **40**
Cherryberry   **45**
Chinex Classic   **46**
Christmas Candy   **47**
Circle   **48**
Cloverleaf   **49**
Colonial, "Knife and Fork"   **51**
Colonial Block   **54**
Colonial Fluted   **55**
Columbia   **56**
Corex   **58**
Coronation   **59**
Cremax   **60**
Crow's Foot   **62**
Crown   **64**
Cube   **65**
Cupid   **67**
Daisy   **68**
Della Robbia   **69**
Diamond Quilted   **71**
Diana   **73**
Dogwood   **74**
Doric   **76**
Doric and Pansy   **77**
Emerald Crest   **79**

English Hobnail   **81**
Fire-King Alice   **84**
Fire-King Breakfast Set   **85**
Fire-King Charm   **85**
Fire-King Jane Ray   **87**
Fire-King Laurel   **88**
Fire-King Miscellaneous Jade-ite **89**
Fire-King Restaurantware   **91**
Fire-King Sapphire Blue   **93**
Fire-King 1700 Line   **94**
Fire-King Sheaves of Wheat   **94**
Fire-King Shell   **95**
Fire-King Swirl   **96**
Fire-King Turquoise Blue   **96**
Floragold   **98**
Floral   **100**
Floral and Diamond Band   **105**
Florentine No. 1   **106**
Florentine No. 2   **108**
Flower Garden
   with Butterflies   **110**
Forest Green   **112**
Fortune   **114**
Fruits   **114**
Georgian Lovebirds   **115**
Harp   **117**
Heritage   **118**
Hex Optic   **118**
Hiawatha   **120**
Hobnail   **121**
Holiday   **122**
Homespun   **124**
Horseshoe   **126**
Indiana Custard   **127**
Iris   **128**
Jubilee   **131**
Katy   **133**
La Furiste   **134**
Lake Como   **135**
Laurel   **136**
Lincoln Inn   **138**

Contents

Lorain **139**
Madrid **140**
Manhattan **142**
Mayfair "Federal" **145**
Mayfair "Open Rose" **146**
Miss America **153**
Moderntone **157**
Moondrops **161**
Moonstone **164**
Moroccan Amethyst **166**
Mt. Pleasant **168**
National **169**
New Century **170**
Newport **171**
Normandie **173**
Old Cafe **174**
Old Colony **175**
Old English **177**
Orchid **178**
Ovide **179**
Oyster and Pearl **180**
Park Avenue **181**
Patrician **182**
Patrick **183**
Peacock and Rose **184**
Peacock Reverse **186**
Pebble Optic (was listed as
   Raindrops) **187**
Petalware **188**
Philbe **190**
Pie Crust **191**
Pineapple and Floral **192**
Pretzel **193**
Primo **193**
Princess **194**
Pyramid **196**
Queen Mary **196**
Radiance **199**
Ribbon **202**
Ring **202**

Rock Crystal Flower **205**
Romanesque **207**
Rose Cameo **208**
Rosemary **208**
Roulette **209**
Round Robin **210**
Roxana **211**
Royal Lace **211**
Royal Ruby **216**
"S" Pattern **218**
Saguenay **219**
Sandwich **220**
(Anchor Hocking)
Sandwich (Indiana) **223**
Sharon **224**
Sierra **226**
Spiral **228**
Starlight **229**
Stars and Stripes **230**
Strawberry **230**
Sunburst **231**
Sunflower **232**
Swirl **233**
Sylvan **235**
Tea Room **236**
Thistle **238**
Thumbprint **239**
Tulip **239**
Twisted Optic **241**
U.S. Swirl **242**
Vernon **243**
Victory **243**
Vitrock **245**
Waterford **246**
White Ship **248**
Windsor **250**
Bibliography **253**
Dealer Directory **254**
Index
   ... Names & Nicknames **255**

About the Glass

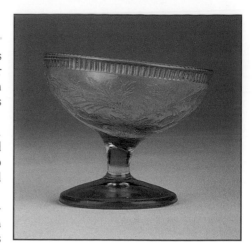

A few remarks need to be made regarding Depression Glass and its very nature. As poorer quality glassware that was often given away with the purchase of a product or service, Depression Glass is full of flaws. Newbies to this wonderful DG World often struggle with some of the characteristics that many know are expected. We hope this short presentation will help.

*A straw mark is a line on the surface of glassware that is a result of manufacture. A straw mark is not a crack and it will not get larger. A crack will have a dimensional look that will catch the light and often look silver or gray while a straw mark will show up only on the surface if the glassware is tilted just so in the right light. A straw mark should not negatively affect the value of an item.

*It is normal to find bumps of extra glass, especially along mold lines. We recommend the "fingernail test." Run your fingernail along exposed edges. If your nail feels a protruding bump look carefully for extra glass. This is normal, perfectly fine, and does not diminish the value of the item in any way. If your fingernail seems to go down it is time to stop and examine the spot in question. It may still be an imperfection and not a chip.

*You may find pieces that lean to one side, wobble on the counter top, and seem slightly misshapen. Two identical items may have slightly different dimensions. One pattern may have several shades of the same color. This is Depression Glass!

*We do offer a warning. Foggy, cloudy, and lime-deposited glass cannot be cleaned! Buyer beware. Likewise, buying outside on a dewy morning can cause one to inadvertently purchase "sick" glass. Dew can mask the real surface of the glassware leaving one with an unhappy surprise later in the day.

*When in doubt rely on a reputable dealer and our books! Together you can buy with confidence!

About the Prices

We have done everything possible to provide accurate prices. We have monitored the Internet, auctions, and trade papers, gone to shows, and consulted with collectors and dealers alike. We have also brought to this our years of buying, selling, and collecting glass.

This book is designed to be a tool and a reference for identification. Hopefully it is an invaluable one! Values vary immensely according to the condition of the piece, the location of the market, and the overall quality of the design and manufacture. Condition is always of paramount importance when assigning a value. The prices shown in this reference are for individual items that are in mint condition, but not packaged. Prices in the Midwest differ from those in the West or East, and those at specialty shows such as Depression Glass shows will vary from those at general shows. And, of course, being at the right place at the right time can make all the difference.

All of these factors make it impossible to create an absolutely accurate price list, but we can offer a guide. The values shown in this reference reflect what one could realistically expect to pay.

Neither the authors nor the publisher are responsible for any outcomes resulting from consulting this reference.

Acknowledgments

This book was a group effort and without the contributions and collaboration of the following individuals (and a few more who wish to be unnamed) this second edition would not exist. Most of the people added to the list were strangers who took the time to contact us. Some live in Canada, some shipped box after box to the studio, and some took vacation days and drove their collection to the studio in Pennsylvania to be photographed by our phenomenal photographer, Bruce Waters. In the truest sense, this book belongs to all of these wonderful people. It is entirely through their gift of time and information that we humbly offer you the second edition of *Mauzy's Depression Glass.*

Deborah D. Albright
Sherelyn A. Ammon
David G. Baker
Donald G. and Juanita M. Becker
Bob and Cindy Bentley
Helen & Edward Betlow
Sylvia A. Brown
Donna L. Cehlarik
Ardell & George Conn
Charles & Theresa Converse
Wes & Carla Davidson
Charlie Diefenderfer
Diefenderfer's Collectibles & Antiques
Carol L. Ellis
Corky & Becky Evans
Kyle & Barbara Ewing
Ruth Farrington
L.E. Fawber & Thomas Dibeler
Mark Fors / Marwig Glass Store
Scott & Rhonda Hackenburg / Blue Jay Antiques & Collectibles
Connie & Bill Hartzell
Dottie & Doug Hevener / The Quacker Connection
Rick Hirte / Sparkle Plenty Glassware
Fran & Tom Inglis
Bettye S. James
Brad and Tammy James
Bryan and Marie James
Janice Johnston / Behind The Green Door
Michael and Kathleen Jones
Stephen & Christine Krzanowsk
Vic & Jean Laermans
Walter Lemiski / Waltz Time Antiques
Kathy McCarney
Neil McCurdy - Hoosier Kubboard Glass
Maria McDaniel
Doris McMullen
Paula Apperson McNamara
Dave & Jamie Moriarty
Robert S. Newbrough
Jane O'Brien
Kelly O'Brien-Hoch
Lucille and Joseph Palmieri
Samantha Parish
Lorraine Penrod

Tanya Poillucci
Bill Quillen
Paul Reichwein
Michael Rothenberger / Mike's Collectibles
Verna Rothenberger
Staci and Jeff Shuck / Gray Goose Antiques
Jesse Speicher
Reta M. Stoltzfus
Marie Talone
Jo Timko / Snowflake58 Collectibles
Debora & Paul Torsiello, Debzie's Glass
Robert Tulanowski
Ian Warner & Mike Posegay
Steve Wasko & Jeaneen Heiskell
Kevin L. Weiss
Ruth Worthington
Eunice A. Yohn
Don & Terry Yusko

Special mention must be made of Walter Lemiski / Waltz Time Antiques for suggesting the inclusion of Canadian Depression Glass and for orchestrating the photo shoot. We are thrilled to share this glass and now a wonderful friendship as well. (Hugs to Kim, Nick, and "White Fang!") We also need to publicly thank Lorraine Penrod for shipping scores of packages to the studio! Lorraine's efforts and treasures will be a part of the next several books. Finally, a big thank you to Michael Rothenberger / Mike's Collectibles for being a diligent and faithful Internet observer. We also need to acknowledge the support and creative freedom given to us by Peter and Nancy Schiffer. We have taken picture after picture after picture in an effort to give you the most superior images possible. They were our cheerleaders who allowed us unlimited use of the studio, the equipment, and Bruce. Until the next edition, thank you very much!

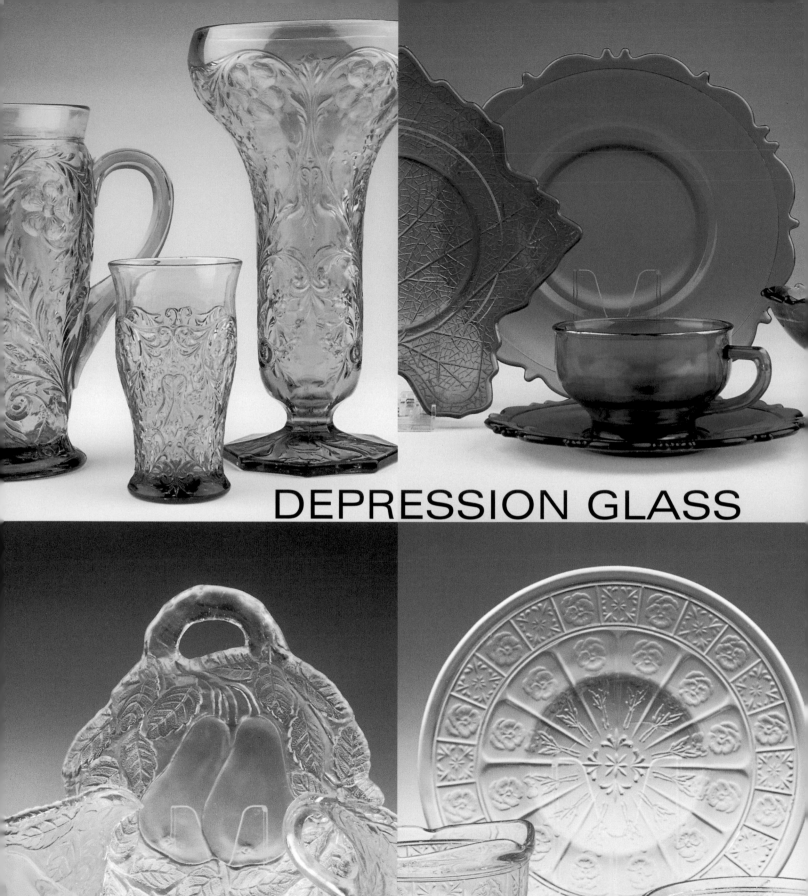

DEPRESSION GLASS

ADAM
Reproduced
(1932-1934 Jeannette Glass Company)

Adam is a pattern that is well received even by people who have limited knowledge of Depression Glass. The strong design features in terms of shape and style make it appealing to many.

This pattern also does well in terms of holding its value, or increasing in value. It is not found in great quantity and there is a strong demand for Adam in both pink and green. The 7.75" salad plate is getting difficult to find in either color. Likewise, the green pitcher with a round base is not often seen.

Three items need to be noted. First is the butter dish which has been reproduced; check our information pertaining to this matter prior to making a purchase. Second is the more elusive Adam-Sierra combination butter dish. On the bottom of the butter dish will be either Adam or Sierra. The key is the top which has both the Adam motif and the Sierra motif. The Adam pattern is on the outside of the lid and the Sierra pattern is on the inside of the lid. If you locate one of these consider yourself lucky indeed. Another piece worthy of your attention is the pitcher. It is most commonly seen with a square foot. The pricing reflects the fact that the round-footed pitcher is harder to locate, and we are pleased to present one here.

We purchased a set of Adam a few years ago that included cups and saucers. The cups were in a purplish-pink hue we had never seen before, and they didn't even look like they belonged on the pink saucers. We were relieved when the last set sold and now we wish we had saved one set to photograph.

Pitcher w/ round base. *Courtesy of Vic & Jean Laermans.*

Back row: 10" oval vegetable bowl, 4.5" ashtray; *front row:* creamer & sugar.

7.5" tumbler & 4.5" tumbler.

Back row: cake plate, 9" grill plate, 9" dinner plate, 7.75" salad plate; *front row:* 4.5" tumbler, platter, sherbet, candlesticks. *Courtesy of Marie Talone & Paul Reichwein.*

Back row: sugar w/ lid & creamer; *front row:* shaker, sugar w/ lid, creamer, salt & pepper. *Courtesy of Vic & Jean Laermans.*

9" bowl w/ lid. *Courtesy of Bryan & Marie James.*

ADAM	Pink	Green	Qty
Ash tray, 4.5"	34	34	____
Bowl, 4.75" berry	25	25	____
Bowl, 5.75" cereal	50	55	____
Bowl, 9" w/o lid	35	45	____
Bowl, 7.75" berry	30	30	____
Bowl, 9" w/lid	75	90	____
Bowl, 10" oval vegetable	40	35	____
Butter dish base *R*	30	150	____
Butter dish lid *R*	70	250	____
Butter complete	100	400	____
Butter w/Adam bottom & Sierra/Adam lid	trtp*		____
Cake plate	35	40	____
Candlestick, ea.	50	60	____
Candy jar w/lid, 2.5"	125	125	____
Coaster	23	21	____
Creamer, 3"	30	30	____
Cup	30	32	____
Lid for 9" bowl	40	45	____
Pitcher, round base	75		____
Pitcher, square base	50	65	____
Plate, 6" sherbet	12	12	____
Plate, 7.75" salad	22	22	____
Plate, 9" dinner	36	36	____
Plate, 9" grill	28	28	____
Platter, 11.75"	38	35	____
Relish, 8", 2-part	25	25	____
Salt & pepper	90	120	____
Saucer	7	7	____
Sherbet	32	37	____
Sugar base, 3.25"	30	30	____
Sugar lid	30	45	____
Tumbler, 4.5"	35	35	____
Tumbler, 5.5"	85	65	____
Vase, 7.5"	450	150	____

Reproduction information: New butter base: points aimed at corners rather than middle of side edges. New butter lid: leaf veins disjointed rather than touching center

Note: Delphite candlesticks: $150 each. Yellow cup: $100. **Round** 7.75" salad plate & saucer in pink or yellow: $120. *trtp = too rare to price

AMERICAN PIONEER
(1931-1934 Liberty Works)

This pattern is one of those that show how regional Depression Glass can be. American Pioneer is rare on the East Coast, but much more prevalent in the Midwest.

Collector Bill Quillen was kind enough to bring some wonderful pieces of American Pioneer to the studio. Both pitchers are shown on liners, however the larger one (7" batter pitcher) is missing the lid. In virtually all patterns and with all items having lids, the lids will have a greater value than the base. Simply put, lids were banged, bumped, and dropped making them more susceptible to damage and destruction.

Three new items have been added to the American Pioneer list. First is a 5" water tumbler that is shown in green. Let us know if you have one in another color. Second is the 6"

plate w/turned-up handles which is pictured in amber, but has been confirmed in green as well. (Thanks, Tress!) Finally, the list now includes the 8.5" plate, which is a liner for the batter pitcher. This is not the same plate as the 8" luncheon plate.

Here's a piece of information on the 9.25" bowl with a lid, pictured in pink. The lid and base seem to be about 1/4" 'off' from each other creating an ill-fitting combination. Without considerable care it would be easy for the lid to simply slide off and ultimately be chipped or broken. This poor fit lends itself to damage and lids are likely to be the piece of a two-part item to receive abuse anyway. If you are considering the purchase of this item, make note of the poor fit so you can rest assured that, yes, the top and bottom really do go together.

11" tray w/2 handles, 8.5" liner for pitcher, 8" luncheon plate, 6.25" liner for syrup pitcher or dessert plate. *Courtesy of Bill Quillen.*

Back row: ice bucket; *front row:* 4.25" mayonnaise bowl, 4" creamer, 4" sugar, cup & saucer. *Courtesy of Bill Quillen.*

7" Batter pitcher on liner & 5" syrup pitcher w/lid on liner. *Courtesy of Bill Quillen.*

8.75" lamp (note: the chimney is not original). *Courtesy of Bill Quillen.*

AMERICAN PIONEER	Pink	Green	Qty
Bowl, 4.25" mayonnaise	65	100	____
Bowl, 5" w/2 handles	25	25	____
Bowl, 8.75" w/lid	125	145	____
Bowl, 9" w/2 handles	30	40	____
Bowl, 9" w/lid & foot	125	145	____
Bowl, 10.5" console	65	80	____
Candlestick, 6.5", ea.	50	60	____
Candy jar w/lid, 1 lb.	110	130	____
Candy jar w/lid, 1.5 lb., 10"	130	160	____
Cheese & cracker 2-piece set	65	80	____
Coaster, 3.5"	35	35	____
Creamer, 2.75"	25	25	____
Creamer, 4"	25	25	____
Cup	15	15	____
Dresser set, 4-piece set	600	600	____
Cologne bottle, ea.	125	125	____
Powder jar w/indents	125	125	____
Tray, 7.5"	100	100	____
Goblet, 4" wine	50	50	____
Goblet, 6" water	50	50	____
Ice pail	60	75	____
Lamp, 5.5" round	80		____
Lamp, 8.75" tall (all glass)	150	150	____
Lamp, 9.5" tall (glass base, metal shaft)		75	____
Pitcher/urn, 5", syrup	100	125	____
Pitcher lid for 5" urn	140	140	____
Pitcher/urn, 7", batter	140	140	____
Pitcher lid for 7" urn	125	125	____
Plate, 6" w/turned-up handles	45	45	____
Plate, 6.25"	15	15	____
Plate, 6" w/2 handles	15	15	____
Plate, 8", luncheon	15	15	____
Plate, 8.5", liner for pitcher	20	20	____
Plate, 11" tray w/2 handles	25	25	____
Saucer	8	8	____
Sherbet, 3.5"	18	20	____
Sherbet, 4.75" w/stem	40	50	____
Sugar, 2.75"	25	25	____
Sugar, 3.5"	25	25	____
Tumbler, 2.25", 1 oz. whiskey	65	100	____
Tumbler, 5 oz. juice	55	65	____
Tumbler, 5 oz. water		50	____

Note: Crystal items half of pink. 8.5" plate, liner for pitcher in amber, $45.

Back row: 11" tray w/2 handles; *front row:* 10.5" console bowl, saucer, 8" luncheon plate. *Courtesy of Bill Quillen.*

6" plate w/turned-up handles, $45. *Courtesy of Bill Quillen.*

AMERICAN SWEETHEART
(1930-1936 Macbeth-Evans Glass Company)

The name says it all. This is definitely in the top five patterns that our customers enthusiastically love and collect, and it is equally popular in both pink and Monax. The delicate nature of both the glass and the design meld to create a truly appealing sweetheart of a pattern.

Ritz Blue and Ruby Red American Sweetheart pieces may be just as challenging to find as to afford. Presented is Lorraine Penrod's stunning Ruby Red collection, which she graciously shipped to the studio. Found on the Internet was a Ruby Red American Sweetheart Lazy Susan made with the 15.5" serving plate on a ball bearing base. The owner stated that it was an original Macbeth-Evans item.

Monax American Sweetheart has a tendency to "feather." (This is a term Barbara has been using for years!) Simply put, the glass on the outer edges seems to separate as barbs on a feather. Occasionally there is some chipping after the "feathering" develops. The feathering itself is not damage as the glass is conducive to this sort of aging effect. Obviously, each purchaser must make his or her own judgment on this matter, but keep in mind this glass is almost 70 years old. Of all the Monax pieces, the sugar lid is the most difficult item to find even though sugar bases are plentiful.

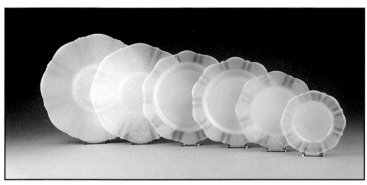

15.5" serving plate, 12" salver, 10.25" dinner plate, 9.75" dinner plate, 8" salad plate, 6" bread & butter plate. *Courtesy of David G. Baker.*

Back row: dinner plate, platter, 11" oval vegetable bowl; *front row:* 8.5" berry bowl, sugar, creamer, cup & saucer. *Courtesy of Kathy McCarney.*

Sugar w/lid. *Courtesy of Charlie Diefenderfer.*

Back row: sugar & creamer; *front row:* cup & saucer. *Courtesy of Lorraine Penrod.*

Dinner plate, cup, and saucer trimmed in gold. Dinner plate has rose motif painted in center & is signed, "EZ." *Courtesy of Kathy McCarney.*

2-tier tidbit. *Courtesy of Lorraine Penrod.*

8" salad plate, 12" salver, 15.5" serving plate. *Courtesy of Lorraine Penrod.*

18" console bowl. *Courtesy of Lorraine Penrod.*

Crystal sherbet in chrome base. *Courtesy of Jane O'Brien.*

3.5" juice tumbler, 4.25" tumbler, 4.75" tumbler, 7.5" pitcher. *Courtesy of Vic & Jean Laermans.*

Salt & pepper. *Courtesy of Vic & Jean Laermans.*

AMER. SWEET.	Pink	Monax	Red	Blue	Trimmed rim	Qty
Bowl, 3.75" flat berry	100					----
Bowl, cream soup, 4.25"	100	125				----
Bowl, 6" cereal	22	20			45	----
Bowl, 6.75"		trtp*				----
Bowl, 8.5" berry	60	70			250	----
Bowl, 9.5" flat soup	100	90			150	----
Bowl, 11" oval vegetable	75	95				----
Bowl, 18" console		600	1250	1400		
Creamer	22	22	200	200	125	----
Cup	20	12	110	165	100	----
Lamp shade, 8.5"		700				----
Plate, 6" bread & butter	8	8			35	
Plate, 8" salad	15	10	110	140	45	----
Plate, 9" luncheon		12			50	----
Plate, 9.75" dinner	40	28			120	----
Plate, 10.25" dinner		30				----
Plate, 11" chop plate		20				----
Plate, 12" salver	30	24	220	265	150	----
Plate, 15.5" server		300	425	500		----
Platter, 13"	70	70			250	----
Pitcher, 7.5", 60 oz	1200					----
Pitcher, 8", 80 oz.	900					----
Salt & pepper	700	500				----
Saucer	5	4	35	45	25	----
Sherbet, 3.75"	25					----
Sherbet, 4.25"	20	24			100	----
Sugar base	22	10	220	250	125	----
Sugar lid		600				----
Tid-bit, 2- tier (8" & 12" plates)	55	45	360	400		----
Tid-bit, 3-tier (8", 12", & 15.5" plates)		300	825	800		----
Tumbler, 3.5" juice	130					----
Tumbler, 4.25"	110					----
Tumbler, 4.75"	150					----

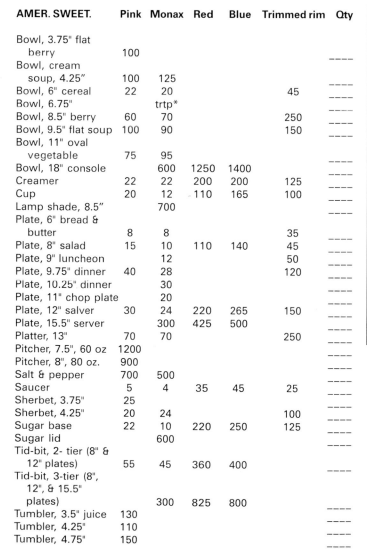

3.75" flat berry bowl, 9.5" flat soup bowl, 4.25" cream soup bowl. *Courtesy of Vic & Jean Laermans.*

Note: Crystal sherbet in chrome base: $5. Cremax: 6" cereal, $15; 9" berry, $45; cup, $500; lamp shade, $800.
*trtp = too rare to price

2.5 oz. wine goblet. *Courtesy of Diefenderfer's Collectibles & Antiques.*

ANNIVERSARY
(1947-1949 Pink...see note at bottom
Jeannette Glass Company)

There aren't many customers collecting this pattern, but those who do may be some of the more enthusiastic collectors around. Finding certain Anniversary pieces can be a REAL challenge. We have had the opportunity to buy many collections through the years, but we have never been offered a set of Anniversary.

As with other patterns having iridescent pieces, Anniversary is sometimes mistaken for Carnival Glass. It is really one of the more recent offerings shown in this book. In fact, a few pieces in crystal and iridescent weren't made until 1972.

Thanks to Stephen and Christine Krzanowski for sharing their square Anniversary cake plate and cover. The four-footed cake plate has two handles of plastic and metal that slide back and forth to securely lock the metal cover in place. This cake plate has now been added to the list.

Another change to the listing involves the tidbit. The first edition described the Anniversary tidbit as having a 4.75" berry above a 9" fruit bowl, but two other versions are now pictured.

It is always exciting to find original boxes of vintage glassware. The dinner set is numbered 2900/32 meaning the Jeannette Glass Company line of glassware was number 2900 and there are 32 items in this package.

The 6.5" wall pin-up vase has gone up in price. These are becoming very difficult to find and with a continued interest in creating retro kitchens they are quite desirable.

ANNIVERSARY	Pink	Crystal	Iridescent	Qty
Bowl, 4.75" berry	10	4	4	----
Bowl, 7.25" soup	20	8	8	----
Bowl, 9" fruit	27	12	14	----
Butter dish base	35	20		----
Butter dish lid	30	10		----
Butter complete	65	30		----
Candy jar w/lid	50	25		----
Cake plate, 12.5" round	20	8		----
Cake plate, 12.5" square		30		----
Cake plate cover, round (metal lid)	8			----
Cake plate cover, square (metal lid)	15			----
Candlestick, 4.75" ea.		10	14	----
Comport w/3 feet	18	5	8	----
Comport, ruffled w/3 feet		7		----
Creamer, 3.5"	14	5	8	----
Cup	8	3	4	----
Goblet, 2.5 oz. wine	20	8		----
Plate, 6.25" sherbet	5	1	2	----
Plate, 9" dinner	25	5	7	----
Plate, 12.5" sandwich	18	6	8	----
Relish, 8"	15	5	7	----
Relish, 4-part w/metal base		15		----
Saucer	4	1	2	----
Sherbet	10	3		----
Sugar base, 3.25"	12	5	8	----
Sugar lid	100	20	10	----
Tid-bit, 2-tier		20		----
Tray/pickle dish, 9"	20	5	8	----
Vase, 6.5"	75	15		----
Vase, wall pin-up, 6.5"	75	30		----

Note: Crystal and Iridescent pieces made in 1960s & 1970s. Shell pink: cake plate & pin-up vase, $200 ea.

Back row: 12.5" sandwich plate, 9" fruit bowl; *front row:* cup & saucer, 6.25" sherbet plate, 7.25" soup bowl, candlesticks.

Boxed 32-piece dinner set of pink Anniversary. *Courtesy of Janice Johnston / Behind The Green Door.*

2-tier tidbits. 7.25″ soup bowl above 12.5″ sandwich plate & 6.25″ sherbet plate above 9″ dinner plate. *Courtesy of Doris McMullen.*

Candy jar w/lid & butter dish. *Courtesy of Mike Rothenberger/Mike's Collectibles.*

Square cake plate with cover. *Courtesy of Stephen & Christine Krzanowski.*

AUNT POLLY

(Late 1920s U.S. Glass Company)

Once you own the 3.75" tumblers and sherbets, Aunt Polly becomes a challenge. The blue is a most appealing shade that many find attractive, while the green is much more difficult to locate.

U.S. Glass Company used the same blank for butter bottoms on Aunt Polly and other patterns including Cherryberry, Floral and Diamond Band, Strawberry, and U.S. Swirl. Other than a starburst pressed in the center of the base, the bottom is void of design, making the bases interchangeable.

Price increases are often seen in the items that are already the more expensive pieces in any given pattern. As a result of supply and demand these hard-to-find pieces continue to be desired and competition for ownership drives the prices. This is reflected in the value adjustments for the salt and pepper shakers and the 8" pitcher.

Back row: 6.5" vase, 8" luncheon plate, 6" sherbet plate, 7.75" berry bowl; *front row:* 3.75" tumbler, 4.75" bowl, 7.25" oval pickle w/ 2 handles, sherbet, sugar w/ lid. *Courtesy of Charlie Diefenderfer.*

4.5", 2.75" deep bowl.

7.25" oval pickle bowl.

AUNT POLLY	Blue	Green	Qty
Bowl, 4.5", 2.75" deep	65		____
Bowl, 4.75" berry, shallow	20	10	____
Bowl, 4.75", 2" deep		20	____
Bowl, 5.5" w/1 handle	28	18	____
Bowl, 7.25"oval pickle w/2 handles	45	18	____
Bowl, 7.75" berry	55	25	____
Bowl, 8.25" oval	145	60	____
Butter dish base	150	75	____
Butter dish lid	100	200	____
Butter complete	250	275	____
Candy base w/2 handles	50	25	____
Candy/sugar lid	200	75	____
Creamer	50	40	____
Pitcher, 8"	225		____
Plate, 6" sherbet	15	10	____
Plate, 8" luncheon	22		____
Salt & pepper	300		____
Sherbet	16	12	____
Sugar base	40	30	____
Sugar/candy lid	200	75	____
Tumbler, 3.5"	35		____
Vase, 6.5"	55	35	____

Note: Iridescent items ½ of Green EXCEPT for these: butter complete, $250; & pitcher, $200.

AURORA
(1937-1938 Hazel-Atlas Company)

Cobalt glass lovers are often drawn to Aurora—what a shame it is such a limited pattern! With a 6.5" plate as the only plate, this line is limited to desserts rather than meals.

The 4.5" bowl, sometimes referred to as "the deep bowl," is the most treasured item in Aurora, and its price has steadily risen through the years. Sometimes as prices increase the availability of an item may improve. Pieces perceived as more valuable have a way of showing up in the marketplace as individuals seek to take advantage of a higher price by selling something they own. Even with the upward pricing of the 4.5" bowl these items are no more available than they were ten years ago.

Cobalt is the easiest of all the colors to collect. Here is a case of supply and demand controlling the market. One would assume that since the other colors are more elusive they would be worth more. In some cases this would be true, but Aurora is primarily a cobalt collector's pattern and the color in most demand.

Back row: 6.5" plate, 4.75" tumbler; *front row:* cup & saucer, 5.25" cereal bowl, creamer.

AURORA	Cobalt & Pink	Qty
Bowl, 4.5" deep	80	____
Bowl, 5.25" cereal	20	____
Creamer	30	____
Cup	15	____
Plate, 6.5"	12	____
Saucer	8	____
Tumbler, 4.75"	28	____

Note: Green and Crystal items ½ those in Cobalt and Pink.

4.5" deep bowl. *Courtesy of Diefenderfer's Collectibles & Antiques.*

AVOCADO
Reproduced
(1923-1933...see note at bottom of page 20
Indiana Glass Company)

Avocado was made with a mold edge along the rim. This thin line of extra glass is frequently nicked, and some collectors agonize over the condition of a piece to the point of rejecting items with damage to the extra glass. As always, the decision to make a purchase is totally up to the buyer.

Another feature of Avocado is the plain glass inside each piece of fruit. Often there are scratches and wear marks within the avocados that negatively affect an item's value. Take the time to hold a piece of Avocado up to the light prior to making a purchase and examine the bottom carefully.

Be sure to pay special attention to the top of the 5" footed tumbler. Upon careful inspection one can see that there is a bit of a flare at the top. This is how to tell that this is an old tumbler. The newer Tiara tumblers are straight at the top.

The pitcher is a challenge to find accounting for why the price is much higher than most of the other pieces in this pattern.

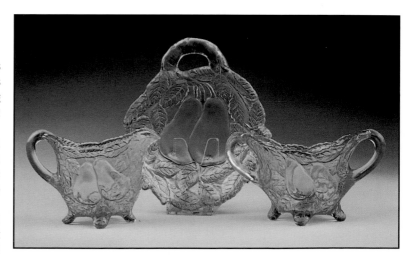

Creamer, 7" preserve bowl w/ 1 handle, sugar.
Courtesy of Diefenderfer's Collectibles & Antiques.

Avocado

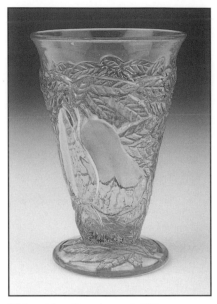

5" tumbler. *Courtesy of Mike Rothenberger / Mike's Collectibles.*

Back row: 10.25" cake plate w/ 2 handles, 9.5" salad bowl; *front row:* 5.25" olive bowl w/ 2 handles, 9" oval bowl w/ 2 handles, creamer & sugar. *Courtesy of Neil McCurdy - Hoosier Kubboard Glass.*

Sugar. *Courtesy of Vic & Jean Laermans.*

Back row: 6.25" cheese plate, 8.25" salad plate, 7" preserve w/ 1 handle; *front row:* cup & saucer, 6.25" bowl w/ 3 feet, 7.5" salad bowl. *Courtesy of Neil McCurdy - Hoosier Kubboard Glass.*

AVOCADO	Green	Pink	Crystal	Qty
Bowl, 5.25" olive w/2 handles	40	30	10	____
Bowl, 6.25" relish w/3 feet	40	30	10	____
Bowl, 7" preserve w/1 handle	45	35	10	____
Bowl, 7.5" salad	65	50	15	____
Bowl, 9" oval w/2 handles	35	28	12	____
Bowl, 9.5" salad	175	125	25	____
Creamer, 3.75"	40	40	15	____
Cup, 2 styles	42	37		____
Pitcher, 64 oz.	trtp*	1100	400	____
Plate, 6.25" cheese	30	20	10	____
Plate, 8.25" salad	30	20	10	____
Plate, 10.25" cake w/2 handles	75	55	15	____
Saucer	25	25		____
Sherbet/Sundae	65	65		____
Sugar, 3" at lowest pt.	40	40	15	____
Tumbler, w/foot 5"	300	350		____

Reproduction information: The following are new colors so everything in these colors is new: amethyst, blue, frosted pink, red, yellow, darker green, pink with an orange tint.

Note: Milk glass items made in 1950s. Milk white pitcher, $400; tumbler, $40; bowl, $30. Luncheon plate w/apple design, $15.

*trtp = too rare to price

Cup w/ foot.

BEADED BLOCK

(1927-1930s...see note bottom of page 22
Imperial Glass Company)

In the first edition of *Mauzy's Depression Glass* we discussed the changing market values of Beaded Block. We presented values that were very different from other price guides and we never heard a single word of disagreement on this pricing. Since the publication of that list, Beaded Block continues to sell for higher and higher prices. In March 2000 a 5.25" pitcher in white (milk glass) sold on the Internet for $457. We sold a 7.75" square plate in ice blue for $107 in June 2000. We need to repeat ourselves here: if you are an owner of a collection of Beaded Block congratulations on making an excellent investment.

Six-inch "go along" vases continue to be very popular. Shown is a grouping of three vases that is quite interesting. First, two of these vases are opalescent, something rarely seen on vases. Second, these have a flare and scallop at the rim. Normally the vases come straight up with a smooth rim.

Added to the listing is a 9" plate!

Here's a helpful hint on finding Beaded Block at bargain prices. Dealers selling a general line of antiques and collectibles often fail to recognize Beaded Block as a Depression Glass pattern as it is different in shape, color, and design from most other patterns. Experience has shown if you look at the wares of these generalists, particularly those who only have a few offerings of glassware or are selling primitives you may find a grossly under-priced piece of Beaded Block.

As for colors, presently it seems as though ice blue is the most popular choice of collectors, but this may pass. To put it simply, Beaded Block is hot!

Back: 7.75" plate; front: 4.75" jelly w/ 2 handles, creamer. Courtesy of Michael Rothenberger/Mike's Collectibles.

Center right: 5.5" square bowl, 5.25" pitcher, 6" "go along" vase. *Courtesy of Michael Rothenberger/Mike's Collectibles.*

Left: Assortment of creamers & sugars. *Courtesy of Neil McCurdy - Hoosier Kubboard Glass.*

Assortment of jelly bowls. *Courtesy of Neil McCurdy - Hoosier Kubboard Glass.*

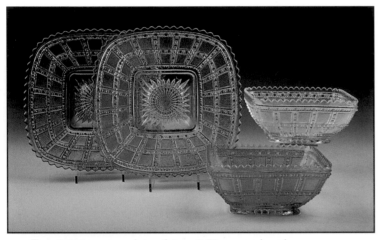

Two 7.75" square plates & two 5.5" square bowls.

Back: lily bowl—3" tall w/ 5" opening & 3.5" base; *front:* lily bowl—2.5" tall w/ 3" base, lily bowl—3" tall w/ 4.5" opening & 3.5" base. *Courtesy of Neil McCurdy - Hoosier Kubboard Glass.*

BEADED BLOCK	All Colors	Opalescent	Crystal	Qty
Bowl, lily, 2.5" tall, 3" base	50	50	50	____
Bowl, lily, 3" tall, 3.5" base, 4.5" opening	50	50	50	____
Bowl, lily, 3" tall, 3.5" base, 5" opening	50	50	50	____
Bowl, 4.5" round lily	35	50	20	____
Bowl, 4.75-5" jelly w/2 handles (looks like a cream soup)	35	45	20	____
Bowl, 5.25" round lily			35	____
Bowl, 5.5" square	70	80	20	____
Bowl, 5.5" w/1 handle	35	45	20	____
Bowl, 6" round	50	60	20	____
Bowl, 6" square w/ ruffled rim			75	____
Bowl, 6.25" round	50	60	20	____
Bowl, 6.5" round	50	60	20	____
Bowl, 6.5" pickle w/2 handles	60	70	20	____
Bowl, 6.75" round	50	60	20	____
Bowl, 7.25" round & flared	60	70	20	____
Bowl, 7.5" round	60	70	20	____
Bowl, 7.75" round w/fluted rim	60	70	20	____
Bowl, 8.5" celery	80	90	25	____
Candy jar, pear-shaped	300	300	300	____
Comport, 4.5" tall, 5" diam.			50	____
Comport, 4.75" tall, 4.5" diam.	50		50	____
Creamer	25	35	15	____
Jelly, 4.5" stemmed	65	75	20	____
Jelly, 4.5" stemmed & flared	65	75	20	____
Pitcher, 5.25"	175	200	100	____
Plate, 7.75" square	50	60	25	____
Plate, 8" round	45			____
Plate, 8.75" round	65	75	50	____
Plate, 9" round	45			____
Sugar, 4.25"	25	35	15	____
Syrup, 4.25"			150	____

Note: White made in 1950s. Later issued pieces in other colors from 1970s & 1980s marked "IG" for Imperial Glass. Yellow pear-shaped candy jar, $300. 6" vase (go along) pink and cobalt, $38. Cobalt items twice prices found in first column.

Back row: 8.5" celery bowl, 8.75" round plate, 8" round plate; *front row:* 6.5" pickle bowl w/ 2 handles, 8.5" celery bowl. *Courtesy of Neil MᶜCurdy - Hoosier Kubboard Glass.*

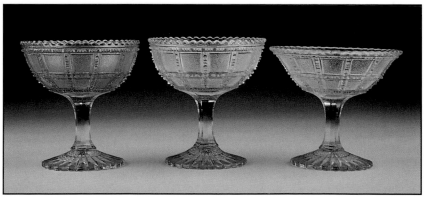

3 "go-along" vases. *Courtesy of Neil MᶜCurdy-Hoosier Kubboard Glass.*

Back row: 6.25" round bowl, two 5.25" pitchers; *front row:* square 6" bowl w/ ruffled rim, 7.75" round bowl w/ fluted rim. *Courtesy of Neil MᶜCurdy - Hoosier Kubboard Glass.*

Two 4.75" comports w/ 4.5" diameters & one 4.5" comport w/ 5" diameter. *Courtesy of Neil MᶜCurdy - Hoosier Kubboard Glass.*

Back row: 9" plate; *front row:* 6.25" square bowl w/ ruffled rim & 6" round bowl. *Courtesy of Mike Rothenberger / Mike's Collectibles.*

BLOCK OPTIC
(1929-1933 Hocking Glass Company)

Among the most popular of the green patterns is Block Optic. The clean lines, subtle design, and huge assortment of pieces make it fun to collect and easy to use. But it must be stated, yellow

Above: *Back row:* 11.75" console bowl w/ rolled edge, 6.25" candy jar w/ lid; *front row:* mayonnaise comport, sherbet on 6" sherbet plate. *Courtesy of Reta M. Stoltzfus*

Below: *Back row:* 12.75" plate, ice bucket w/ metal handle; *front row:* sugar & creamer in 2 styles. *Courtesy of Reta M. Stoltzfus*.

Block Optic is becoming more and more popular. To this end, it is great to present the chunky Block Optic sherbet found in yellow.

There are two other items shown for the first time. There are five styles of cups; four are green with variations in the handles, thickness of glass, and amount of liquid held. The fifth cup has a black foot as found on several footed tumblers. The ice bucket was actually a container for High Boy Peanut Butter. We have no confirmation if this was true for the colored ice buckets, but pictured is a crystal (clear) peanut butter pail. Also found is the 7.5" pitcher in crystal.

The 6" sherbet plate is often used as a saucer, but there are saucers with real cup rings. They are a bit harder, but not impossible to find. This is a pattern that provides options. There are many bowls, goblets, tumblers, pitchers, and plates from which to choose. Block Optic even has two styles of shakers, four styles of sherbets (counting the chunky sherbet), five creamers, and three sugars. Many of these pieces are quite reasonably priced providing a pattern that is easy to find and afford. What a winning combination!

A word of caution: new collectors seem to have trouble distinguishing Block Optic from Circle, especially when considering the bowls. Be sure to use the measurements provided on the lists and work with a knowledgeable seller.

BLOCK OPTIC	Green	Pink	Yellow	Qty
Bowl, 4.25", 1.25" deep	12	12		____
Bowl, 4.5", 1.5" deep	30	30		____
Bowl, 5.25" cereal	18	35		____
Bowl, 7.25" salad	175	175		____
Bowl, 8.5" berry	35	35		____
Bowl, 11.75" console w/rolled edge	100	100		____
Butter dish base	50			____
Butter dish lid	25			____
Butter complete, 3" x 5" rectangle	75			____
Candlestick, ea.	60	50		____
Candy jar w/lid, 2.25" tall	65	65	65	____
Candy jar w/lid, 6.25" tall	70	140		____
Creamer, 5 varieties	14	14	16	____
Cup, 4 styles	8	8	8	____
Cup, black foot	25			____
Goblet, 3.5" wine	trtp*		trtp*	____
Goblet, 4" cocktail	45	45		____
Goblet, 4.5" wine	45	45		____
Goblet, 5.75"	35	35		____
Goblet, 7.25"			45	____
Ice bucket w/metal handle	60	85		____
Ice/butter tub w/2 tab handles	80	120		____
Mayonnaise comport, 4" across	80	80		____
Mug	65			____
Pitcher, 7.5", 54 oz.	85	150		____
Pitcher, 8", 80 oz.	100	100		____
Pitcher, 8.5", 54 oz.	70	70		____
Pitcher, 9".	100			____
Plate, 6" sherbet	4	4	4	____
Plate, 8" salad	6	6	7	____
Plate, 9" dinner	30	40	40	____
Plate, 9" grill	70	70	70	____
Plate, 10.25" sandwich	25	25		____
Plate, 12.75"	30		30	____
Salt & pepper, short	130			____
Salt & pepper, tall w/foot	50	85	100	____
Sandwich server w/center handle	75	75		____
Saucer, 5.75"	10	10		____
Saucer, 6.25"	10	10		____

BLOCK OPTIC (Cont.)	Green	Pink	Yellow	Qty
Sherbet, chunky, 3.5" diam., 2.5" deep			15	____
Sherbet, cone-shaped	8			____
Sherbet, 3.25" round	9	8	10	____
Sherbet, squared low foot, 3.5" diam., 2.5" deep			25	____
Sherbet, 4.75" stemmed sundae	20	20	24	____
Sugar, 3 styles	14	14	16	____
Tumbler, 1.5", 1 oz. whiskey	45	45		____
Tumbler, 2.25", 2 oz. whiskey	38	38		____
Tumbler, 2.5", 3 oz.	25	25		____
Tumbler, 3.25", 3 oz. w/foot	30	30		____
Tumbler, 3.5", 5 oz. 3.75"	25	25		____
Tumbler, 3.75", 9.5 oz. flat	18	18		____
Tumbler, 4.75", 12 oz. flat	30	30		____
Tumbler, 4.75", w/foot		25		____
Tumbler, 5", 10 or 11 oz. flat	25	20		____
Tumbler, 5.25", 15 oz. flat	45	40		____
Tumbler, 6", 10 oz. w/foot	35	35		____
Tumbler, 9 oz. w/foot	20	18	28	____
Tumble-up night set	130			____
Bottle	30			____
Tumbler, 3"	100			____
Vase, 5.75"	350			____

*trtp = too rare to price

Note: Amber: 11.75" rolled edge console bowl, $75; candlesticks, $40 ea. Rectangular butter: green clambroth, $300; blue, $500; crystal, $100. Crystal ice bucket with metal handle, $40, pitcher, $35

5.75" goblet, 4.75" stemmed sherbet/sundae, 9 oz. footed tumbler w/ gold rim, two 10 oz. footed tumblers, one w/ black foot. *Courtesy of Reta M. Stoltzfus.*

3" x 5" rectangular butter, 9" dinner, 2.25" candy jar w/ lid, ice/ butter tub w/ 2 tab handles. *Courtesy of Reta M. Stoltzfus.*

Back row: 10.25" sandwich plate, 4.25" bowl; *front row:* 5.25" cereal bowl, 8.5" berry bowl, 7.25" salad bowl. *Courtesy of Reta M. Stoltzfus.*

Sandwich server w/ center handle, cup & saucer, 8" salad plate, candlesticks, cup. *Courtesy of Reta M. Stoltzfus.*

Salt & pepper in both styles. *Courtesy of Reta M. Stoltzfus.*

Mug.

7.5" 54 oz. pitcher & 8" 80 oz. pitcher.
Courtesy of Reta M. Stoltzfus.

Ice bucket (peanut butter pail) w/
label advertising "High Boy Peanut
Butter."

Cup w/black foot.

9" pitcher &
8.5" 54 oz. pitcher.
*Courtesy of Reta M.
Stoltzfus.*

3.75" flat tumbler, 5.25" flat tumbler, tumble-up night set. *Courtesy of Reta M. Stoltzfus*.

3 different cup styles.

An assortment of creamers & sugars. *Courtesy of Vic & Jean Laermans*.

7.25" goblet. *Courtesy of Diefenderfer's Collectibles & Antiques*.

Chunky sherbet.

BOWKNOT
(Late 1920s ? Manufacturer ?)

For what Bowknot lacks in the number of pieces made, it makes up for in its delicate and charming design. As there is no dinner plate, this pattern is relegated to luncheons and desserts, but what a lovely table setting it presents!

The 5.5" cereal bowl has become scarce. The footed tumbler is found more frequently than the flat one as reflected in the price difference. Interestingly, there is no saucer for the cup.

Back row: 5.5" cereal bowl & 7" salad plate; *front row:* sherbet, 4.5" berry bowl, cup, 5" tumbler w/foot, 5" flat tumbler.

BOWKNOT	Green	Qty
Bowl, 4.25" berry	20	____
Bowl, 5.5" cereal	30	____
Cup	9	____
Plate, 6.75" salad	14	____
Sherbet	20	____
Tumbler, 4.75" flat	28	____
Tumbler, 4.75" w/foot	25	____

BUBBLE
(1934-1965 Hocking Glass Company)

First it was Fire-King jade-ite, next it became Fire-King in general, and then it became anything Anchor Hocking. Bubble collectors are on the rise due to this phenomenon, specifically sapphire blue collectors. Even the Japanese are getting into the act as crystal Bubble was recently featured in one of their publications. The result is that dealers who once shied away from keeping Bubble in their inventory have changed their minds, and those who always had Bubble in stock are finding their reserves disappearing. As Bubble is still plentiful the prices haven't changed much, but if the current demand continues or increases this will surely change.

Bowls are the most difficult pieces to find in perfect condition. Be sure to go over the edges and bumps carefully using a fingernail. The 4" berry bowl is the most difficult bowl to find, but it is getting to the point that none are common anymore. It used to be easy to stumble into piles of Bubble. Even at "half of book" many passed it by. No more! Throughout *Mauzy's Depression Glass* you will find original boxes of glassware due to the generous sharing of Janice Johnston. Janice had a box of the Bubble 8.25" bowls. These were marked as "Vegetable" bowls so we have changed our wording to provide accuracy.

Canadians Ian Warner and Mike Posegay shared the fabulously unique blue plate and cup. They are not the sapphire blue commonly seen, but a turquoise blue. Often really interesting shades of glassware ended up in England and Canada. Aren't they lucky?

Back row: 8.25" pitcher, 9.25" dinner plate; *front:* 4.5" 12 oz. iced tea tumbler, 4.5" fruit bowl, cup & saucer. *Courtesy of L. E. Fawber & Thomas Dibeler.*

The Inspiration stems have been moved to Forest Green and Royal Ruby, two of the new listings in this book in an effort to make this easier for you.

Now for some trivia for you hard-core glass enthusiasts: Anchor Hocking prefixed all sapphire blue glassware with a "B." This included both blue Bubble and Fire-King Sapphire Blue Ovenware. So, did the coding for crystal Bubble begin with a "C?" No, it did not. Anchor Hocking use only numbers

(text continues on page 31)

4.5" fruit bowl, 9.25" dinner plate, 4" berry bowl, 7.75" flat soup bowl. *Courtesy of Donald G. & Juanita M. Becker.*

5.25" cereal bowl, 4.5" fruit bowl, 9.25" dinner plate, cup. *Courtesy of Donald G. & Juanita M. Becker.*

8.25" berry bowl in 3 colors. *Courtesy of Donald G. & Juanita M. Becker.*

Back: 5.25" cereal bowl in hammered aluminum rim ($25); *front:* candlestick, 4" fruit bowl.

Bubble

with no letters of any kind when coding crystal Bubble.

Here are a few numbers to throw around as we have had the good fortune to use information from original boxes:

Anchor Hocking marking	listed as
B1630 salad plate	Plate, 6.75" pie or salad
B1641 dinner	Plate, 9.25" dinner
B1665 cereal bowl	Bowl, 5.25" cereal
B1667 flat soup	Bowl, 7.75" flat soup

Anchor Hocking sticker.

BUBBLE	Blue	Green	Red	White & Crystal	Qty
Bowl, 4" berry	34			5	____
Bowl, 4.5" dessert *R*	15	10	12	5	____
Bowl, 5.25" cereal	16	16		5	____
Bowl, 7.75" flat soup	20			10	____
Bowl, 8.25" vegetable *R*	24	25	22	7	____
Bowl, 9" flanged	trtp*				____
Candlestick, ea.		30	30	8	___
Creamer	35	14		7	____
Cup	5	8	10	3	____
Lamp, 3 styles				40	____
Pitcher, 8.25"			60	75	____
Plate, 6.75" pie or salad	4	18		2	____
Plate, 9.25" dinner	9	30	25	5	____
Plate, 9.25" grill	20				____
Plate, 9.75" dinner		40			____
Platter, 12"	18			12	____
Saucer	1	5	5	1	____
Sugar	20	14		7	____
Tidbit, 2-tier			50	50	____
Tumbler, 3.75" juice			12	3	____
Tumbler, 3.25", 8 oz. old fashioned			16	3	____
Tumbler, 4.5" water			12	3	____
Tumbler, 5.75", 12 oz. iced tea			18	6	____
Tumbler, 6", 16 oz. lemonade				8	____

Note: Pink: 8.25" berry bowl, $28; cup, $100; saucer, $50. Jade-ite 8.25" berry bowl, $30. Dark blue: cup & saucer, $125 for set; 6.75" bread & butter plate, $45. Iridescent: 8.25" berry bowl, $10.

Reproduction information: In Ruby only 4.5" and 8" bowls with Anchor trademark on bottom are reissues.

*trtp = too rare to price

6" lemonade tumbler, 4.5" iced tea tumbler, 4" juice tumbler, 3.25" old-fashioned tumbler.

Rare teal/ice blue color! 6.75" bread & butter plate & cup.
Courtesy of Ian Warner & Mike Posgay.

CAMEO
Reproduced
(1930-1934 Hocking Glass Company)

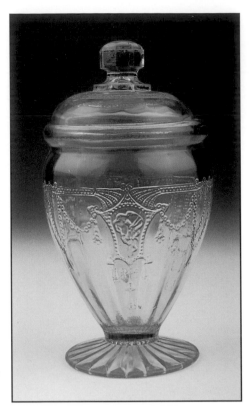

6.5" candy
jar w/ lid.
*Courtesy
of David
G. Baker.*

One of the most popular patterns of 2000 was Cameo. Anything and everything seemed in demand, especially hollowware. If you aren't familiar with this term it refers to candy jars, cookie jars, pitchers, and other items that are "hollow" inside allowing one to store food or liquid.

Cameo is sometimes confused with Rose Cameo or Georgian Lovebirds. The "cameo" or medallion on this pattern has a ballerina on one foot, with the other leg and both arms extended. If you look carefully you can see why this pattern is also called "Ballerina" or "Dancing Girl."

Early pieces of Cameo came from Block Optic molds. Examining the creamer, sugar, candy jar with lid, and additional items verifies their connection. Hocking Glass Company further developed Cameo with additional pieces such as the cookie jar and console bowl, and then used the Cameo mold in 1940 to create the "Philbe" line, which is also presented in this book.

There is one new item added to the Cameo list. The 8.5" water pitcher can be found with a plain rim and a rope rim, which is now shown. The rope design is a signature of Hocking glassware.

Back row: 9" soup bowl, 10" cake plate; *front row:* salt & pepper, candlestick, 5" mayonnaise comport. *Courtesy of David G. Baker.*

Back row: 7.5" 3-part relish, 12" platter w/ tab handles; *front row:* 11" console bowl w/ 3 feet, 4" candy jar w/ lid. *Courtesy of David G. Baker.*

Back row: 10" sandwich plate, 8.5" square plate; *front row:* cup & saucer, cream soup bowl, jam jar w/ lid. *Courtesy of David G. Baker.*

Back row: 10.5" plate w/ tab handles, 10" oval vegetable bowl; *front row:* 3.25" sugar, 4.25" sugar, 3.25" creamer. *Courtesy of David G. Baker.*

5.5" cereal bowl, 7.25" salad bowl, 8.25" berry bowl.
Courtesy of David G. Baker.

3.75" juice tumbler, 4" water tumbler, 5" tumbler.
Courtesy of David G. Baker.

CAMEO	Green	Yellow	Pink	Crystal (Platinum trim)	Qty
Bottle, water/Whitehouse Vinegar (dark green)	20				____
Bowl, 4.25" sauce				8	____
Bowl, cream soup	170				____
Bowl, 5.5" cereal	35	35	200	8	____
Bowl, 7.25" salad	75				____
Bowl, 8.25" berry	45		200		____
Bowl, 9" soup	100		150		____
Bowl, 10" oval vegetable	45	55			____
Bowl, 11" console w/3 feet	90	120	65		____
Butter dish base	100				____
Butter dish lid	150				____
Butter dish complete	250	trtp*			____
Cake plate, 10" w/ 3 feet	40				____
Cake plate, 10.5" no feet (same as rimmed 10.5" dinner)	125		250		____
Candlestick, ea.	80				____
Candy jar w/lid, 4" tall	100	120	500		____
Candy jar w/lid, 6.5" tall	225				____
Cocktail shaker w/metal lid, 11.25"				1000	____
Comport, 5" mayonnaise	65		250		____
Cookie jar/lid	75				____
Creamer, 3.25"	25	25			____
Creamer, 4.25"	30		150		____
Cup, styles	15	8	100	8	____
Decanter w/stopper, 10.25"	200		225		____
Decanter w/stopper, 10.25" frosted	50				____
Domino tray, 7" w/ 3" indent	200				____
Domino tray, 7" no indent			350	200	____
Goblet, 3.5" wine	1500		1000		____
Goblet, 4" wine	90		250		____
Goblet, 5.75" water	65		200		____
Ice bowl/Open butter, 3" tall x 5.5" wide	200		850	300	____
Jam jar w/lid	200		175		____
Pitcher, 5.75" milk or syrup, 20 oz.	375	trtp*			____
Pitcher, 6" juice, 36 oz.	85				____
Pitcher, 8.5" water, 56 oz., plain rim	75	trtp*		500	____

8.5" pitcher with plain rim, 8.5" pitcher with "rope" rim, 6"
juice pitcher. *Courtesy of David G. Baker & Marie Talone.*

Creamer & sugar. *Courtesy of Vic & Jean Laermans.*

CAMEO	Green	Yellow	Pink	Crystal (Platinum trim)	Qty
Pitcher, 8.5" water, 56 oz., rope rim	85				----
Plate, 6" sherbet	6	5	100	4	----
Plate, 7" salad				5	----
Plate, 8.25" luncheon	14	12	35	4	----
Plate, 8.5" square	75	300			----
Plate, 9.5" dinner	25	15	100		----
Plate, 10" sandwich	20		50		----
Plate, 10.5" dinner, rimmed (same as 10.5" cake plate)	125		250		----
Plate, 10.5" grill no handles	20	15	50		----
Plate, 10.5" grill w/tab handles	75	10			----
Plate, 10.5" w/tab handles	20	15			----
Platter, 12" w/tab handles	30	45			----
Relish, 7.5", 3-part w/3 feet	30			160	----
Salt & pepper *R*	100		1000		----
Sandwich server w/center handle	trtp*				----
Saucer	250				----
Sherbet, 3.25", blown	25		75		----
Sherbet, 3.25" molded	18	40	80		----
Sherbet, 4.75" w/tall stem	35	50	100		----
Sugar, 3.25"	25	25			----
Sugar, 4.25"	30		150		----
Tray, Domino sugar, 7" w/indent	200				----
Tray, Domino sugar, no indent			350	200	----
Tumbler, 3 oz. juice w/foot	75		150		----
Tumbler, 3.75" juice, 5 oz.	60		100		----
Tumbler, 4" water, 9 oz.	40		80	10	----
Tumbler, 4.75", 10 oz. no foot	40		100		----
Tumbler, 4.75", 9 oz., w/foot	40	20	120		----
Tumbler, 5", 11 oz., no foot	50	60	100		----
Tumbler, 5.25"	90		140		----
Tumbler, 5.75"	80		140		----
Tumbler, 6.25"	750				----
Vase, 5.75"	400				----
Vase, 8"	65				----

Reproduction information: All miniatures are new. Salt & pepper reproduced in blue, green, & pink; glass is too thick, green is too dark.

*trtp = too rare to price

Cookie jar, 8" vase. *Courtesy of David G. Baker.*

5.75" water goblet, 4.75" sherbet w/ tall stem. *Courtesy of Charlie Diefenderfer.*

7" domino tray w/ 3" indent. *Courtesy of Vic and Jean Laermans.*

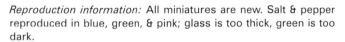

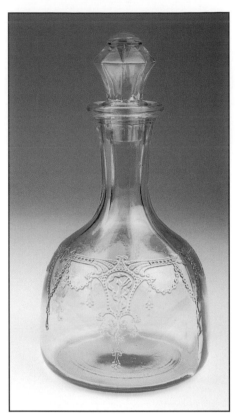

Above: 3.25" molded sherbet, 4" wine goblet, 5" footed tumbler, 6" water goblet. *Courtesy of David G. Baker.*

Right: 10.5" decanter. *Courtesy of Charlie Diefenderfer.*

Back row: 8.25" berry bowl, 8.25" luncheon plate; *front row:* 3.25" molded sherbet, 4" 9 oz. water tumbler, 3.75" 5 oz. juice tumbler. *Courtesy of Staci & Jeff Shuck/Gray Goose Antiques.*

Back row: 9.5" dinner, 10.5" grill w/ no handles; *front row:* 3.25" molded sherbet, 3.25" sugar, cup & saucer.

Cocktail shaker, 4" 9 oz. water tumbler. *Courtesy of Neil McCurdy - Hoosier Kubboard Glass and Staci & Jeff Shuck/Gray Goose Antiques.*

11" console bowl w/ 3 feet. *Courtesy of Donna L. Cehlarik & Jane O'Brien.*

CANADIAN SWIRL
(late 1930s-1940s   Dominion Glass Company Limited)

From the Wallaceburg plant of the Dominion Glass Company Limited comes this Swirl pattern, which has been listed as Canadian Swirl to avoid confusion with Jeannette Glass Company's Swirl. A full array of tableware is available in clear (crystal). As the production of Swirl continued some of the molds began to show wear. In an effort to extend the life of these molds and camouflage the worn mold marks, Dominion added a stippled design to every other swirl in the mold. The pieces that were manufactured on these molds are now called "stippled" and the others are "plain." The vast majority of Canadian Swirl is plain in label but not in appearance. The design is pleasing and the pieces are well finished.

Only Plain Swirl is available in all 21 pieces as this was the original line, and Stippled Swirl is found in 10 pieces (counting the butter as two pieces, and the salt and pepper as one). Fired-on Canadian Swirl is also found in vivid colors that would brighten any table. Dinner plates, cups, and saucers have been found in blue, green, red, and yellow. So far the sugar has been found only in red and the creamer only in yellow. The shakers have been found in dark green, gray, and gold and may have metal or plastic lids.

Until our visit to Canada to photograph this glassware we had never seen or at least paid attention to this pattern. Several months later we found a variety of Plain Swirl and Stippled Swirl in Oregon. Be on the look out as this is still a bargain and you will really find it pleasing!

Back row: 6" sherbet plate, 8" salad plate, 9.75" dinner plate; *front row:* sherbet, butter dish, cup & saucer, salt & pepper. *Courtesy of Walter Lemiski / Waltz Time Antiques.*

Back row: 7.5" berry bowl w/silver overlay & 7.5" soup bowl; *front row:* 7.5" berry bowl & 4.5" berry bowl. *Courtesy of Fran & Tom Inglis and Ian Warner & Mike Posegay and Walter Lemiski / Waltz Time Antiques.*

Back row: 7.75" pitcher & sugar w/ lid; *front row:* 4.5" pitcher, creamer, 3.75" tumbler w/out foot, 4" footed tumbler, 5" footed tumbler. *Courtesy of Ian Warner & Mike Posegay and Walter Lemiski / Waltz Time Antiques.*

Stippled sherbet & plain sherbet. *Courtesy of Ian Warner & Mike Posegay and Walter Lemiski / Waltz Time Antiques.*

Fired-on colors. *Back row:* 9.75" dinner plates in three different colors; *middle row:* saucers in three colors & sugar; *front row:* salt & peppers in two colors & cup. *Courtesy of Fran & Tom Inglis, Ian Warner & Mike Posegay, and Walter Lemiski / Waltz Time Antiques.*

Creamer & sugar. *Courtesy of Ian Warner & Mike Posegay.*

Canadian Swirl	Plain	Stippled	Qty
Bowl, 4.5" small berry	4	6	____
Bowl, 7.5" large berry	8	8	____
Bowl, 7.5" soup	13		____
Butter dish base	5	5	____
Butter dish lid	5	5	____
Butter dish complete	10	10	____
Creamer	6	6	____
Cup	4		____
Pitcher, 4.5", 20 oz.	12	12	____
Pitcher, 7.75", 60 oz.	18		____
Plate, 6" sherbet	4	4	____
Plate, 8" salad	6		____
Plate, 9.75" dinner	8		____
Salt & pepper	10		____
Saucer	2		____
Sherbet	4		____
Sugar base	6	6	____
Sugar lid	18		____
Tumbler, 3.75" flat, 9 oz.	8		____
Tumbler, 4" w/foot, 5 oz.	8		____
Tumbler, 5" w/foot, 9.5 oz.	20		____

Note: Fired-on colors: Dinners, cups, saucers are found in blue, green, red, & yellow. Creamer found in yellow, sugar found in red. Salt & pepper found in dark green, gray, and gold. Add 50% for fired-on colors. Cobalt (not fired-on) creamer & sugar, $35 ea.

CHERRY BLOSSOM
Reproduced
(1930-1939 Jeannette Glass Company)

Here is one pattern collected equally in all colors with universal appeal. The strong, attractive design is recognizable even to a novice collector, lending itself to selection by someone just entering the world of Depression Glass. Cherry Blossom must have had a large distribution area when introduced in the 1930s as people from all over the country tell us how they remember Cherry Blossom in Grandma's house.

The earliest footed pieces have round bases. Later changes to molds include creating scalloped bases. Pink was made throughout Jeannette's production of Cherry Blossom, but green was terminated around 1935, which leaves us with more pink than green.

A sure sign of a pattern's popularity is when it is reproduced. The list of items that fall under this category is long, so

do take care to review our explanations prior to purchasing a piece that has been reproduced. Look for an R to determine the pieces that need this extra attention.

The following Cherry Blossom pieces exist, but there are only one or two of each: cookie jar, 4.5" ruffled bowl, 7" ruffled bowl, 5-part relish, violet bowl, 12-sided 8.25" plate, 10.25" plate, and 9" plate with flowers around the one-inch rim. There are also frosted pieces (which we have never personally seen) and there is a 9" opalescent plate. Thanks to the Wagoners for sharing this information! As for the salt and pepper shakers, we have been told the following: the original box of shakers was shipped from Jeannette Glass Company and due to poor packaging all but a few arrived broken. Rather than redesigning the package, Jeannette opted to discontinue their manufacture. As you build your collection you must assume all shakers you see are reproductions.

Robert Newbrough brought his wonderful collection of Jade-ite Cherry Blossom to the studio. Note that there is no cherry pattern on the very bottom of the bowls, and there is a plain rim at the edges and on the front or top. Jade-ite is popular, Cherry Blossom is popular, and this combination is a real winner!

Cherry Blossom 4.75" berry bowls and 5.75" cereal bowls were made with a "hard edge." This definitive line where the rim interfaces with the curve of the bowl is subject to damage when stacking the bowls or using them. Most Cherry Blossom collectors are a bit forgiving of this rim. Actually, 100% perfect rims may have been repaired. These bowls are just prone to imperfections after the passage of time.

Prices on the "Child's Junior Dinner Set" have been lowered due to a glut of boxed sets offered on line. So many sets in both pink and Delphite are being offered that the supply is beginning to outdistance the demand. Child's pieces sold individually are still doing well as collectors often need a piece or two to complete a set. It is a shame that this is the case as sets that have survived in tact for sixty-five years are now going to be taken apart to for the sake of a few dollars.

Above: 7 oz. mug. *Courtesy of Marie Talone.*

Right: *Back row:* 7" salad plate, 10.25" cake plate, 9" dinner plate; *middle row:* 8" flat pitcher w/ pattern only at top, 8.5" berry bowl, 4.25" tumbler w/ no foot, sherbet, 6.75" pitcher w/ round base; *front row:* 11" platter, sugar w/ lid, creamer. *Courtesy of Marie Talone & Paul Reichwein.*

Butter dish, 4.75" berry bowl, 4.5" tumbler w/ scalloped foot. *Courtesy of Diefenderfer's Collectibles & Antiques.*

Back row: 10.25" cake plate & sherbet; front row: sugar, 10.5" fruit bowl, 3.75" tumbler, 4.5" tumbler w/ scalloped foot. *Courtesy of Charlie Diefenderfer.*

Delphite Cherry Blossom. 3.75" tumbler, 4.5" tumbler w/ round foot, 4.5" tumbler w/ scalloped foot. *Courtesy of Robert S. Newbrough.*

Back row: 9" grill plate, 10.5" sandwich tray w/ 2 handles, 13" divided platter; *middle row:* 5.75" cereal bowl, 3.5" tumbler w/ no foot, cup & saucer, 9" oval vegetable bowl; *front row:* 3.75" tumbler w/ foot, 4.75" berry bowl. *Courtesy of Marie Talone & Paul Reichwein.*

Delphite Cherry Blossom. *Back row:* 11" platter, 6.75" pitcher w/ scalloped foot; *front row:* 4.75" berry bowl, 9" bowl w/ 2 handles. *Courtesy of Bob & Cindy Bentley.*

Delphite Cherry Blossom. *Back row:* 9" dinner plate, 6" sherbet plate; *front row:* cup & saucer, sherbet. *Courtesy of Bob & Cindy Bentley.*

Delphite Cherry Blossom. *Back:* 10.5" sandwich plate w/ 2 handles; *front:* 4.5" tumbler w/ round foot, sugar, 9" oval vegetable bowl, creamer. *Courtesy of Bob & Cindy Bentley.*

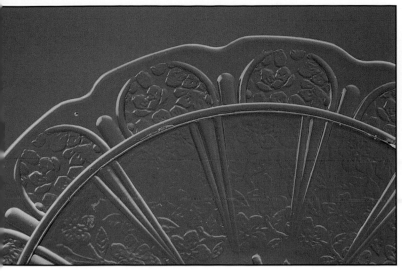

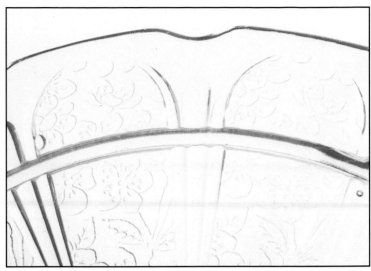

Close-up of edge of reproduction cake plate. Note that the design along the outside rim does not accurately line up with the rest of the design along the plate. *Courtesy of Charlie Diefenderfer.*

Close-up of edge of original cake plate. Compare this to the repro cake plate and see how much more closely the design lines up as it crosses the outside rim. *Courtesy of Charlie Diefenderfer.*

CHERRY BLOSSOM	Pink	Green	Delphite	Qty
Bowl, 4.75" berry	28	28	20	____
Bowl, 6" cereal *R*	65	50		____
Bowl, 7.75" flat soup	95	95		____
Bowl, 8.5" berry *R*	55	55	65	____
Bowl, 9" oval vegetable	65	55	65	____
Bowl, 9" w/2 handles	55	70	40	____
Bowl, 10.5" fruit w/3 feet	100	100		____
Butter dish base *R*	20	30		____
Butter dish lid *R*	80	90		____
Butter complete *R*	100	120		____
Cake plate, 10.25" *R*	35	45		____
Coaster, 3.25"	20	18		____
Cookie Jar	trtp*			____
Creamer	25	24	30	____
Cup *R*	22	22	20	____
Mug, 7 oz.	600	400		____
Pitcher, 6.75", scalloped base w/pattern all over *R*	65	65	90	____
Pitcher, 6.75", round base w/pattern all over	80	80		____
Pitcher, 8" footed w/pattern only at top	80	75		____
Pitcher, 8" flat w/pattern only at top	80	70		____
Plate, 6" sherbet *R*	10	12	12	____
Plate, 7" salad	30	30		____
Plate, 9" dinner *R*	30	30	28	____
Plate, 9" grill	35	30		____
Plate, 10" grill		120		____
Platter, 9"	1000	1200		____
Platter, 11"	60	60	50	____
Platter, 13" & 13" divided *R*	100	100		____
Salt & pepper *R*	trtp*	trtp*		____
Saucer *R*	6	6	6	____
Sherbet, 2.75" tall	24	28	24	____
Sugar base, 3"	25	24	30	____
Sugar lid	28	30		____
Tray, 10.5" sandwich w/2 handles *R*	45	45	35	____
Tumbler, 3.5" no foot, pattern only at top	25	30		____
Tumbler, 3.75" w/foot, pattern all over *R*	20	25	30	____
Tumbler, 4.25" no foot, pattern only at top	25	28		____
Tumbler, 4.5" w/round foot, pattern all over *R*	42	42	38	____
Tumbler, 4.5" scalloped foot, pattern all over *R*	40	40	38	____
Tumbler, 5" no foot, pattern only at top	125	100		____

Note: Yellow: 10.5" 3-footed fruit bowl, $450. Translucent Green: grill plate, $400. Jade-ite: grill plate, $400; 10.5" 3-footed fruit bowl, 6' cereal bowl, 11" platter, 8.5" berry bowl, 10.25" cake plate, & dinner plate, $450 each.

Reproduction information: New colors: blue (transparent, cobalt, & delphite), iridescent, & red. Also reproduced in pink & green. 5.75" cereal bowl: *new* - 2" mold ring on bottom; *old* - 2 ½" mold ring on bottom. 8.5" round berry bowl: *new* - smooth edges to leaves, veins same size; *old* - irregular veins, realistically shaped leaf. Butter dish lid: *new* - 1 molded line in smooth area near base; *old* - 2 molded lines. Butter dish base: *new* - branches without texture and end about 1/4" from outer edge, leaves unrealistic; *old* - textured branch that ends very close to outer edge, realistic leaves. *New* cake plate: from underside of plate the design along the outside rim does not accurately line up with the rest of the design inside the rim. Cup: *new* - pattern is sparse on bottom; *old* - 4 cherries w/ pattern all over & many leaves on bottom. 6.75" pitcher: *new* - 7 cherries on smooth bottom; *old* - 9 cherries on textured bottom. 9" dinner plate, 6" sherbet plate, & saucer: *new* - crudely finished at outer edges so one can feel a ridge; *old* - smooth edges. 13" divided platter: *new* - too heavy & too thick, VERY DIFFICULT TO DISCERN; *old* - leaves still have more realistic design upon close examination. Salt & pepper: assume what you have found is new! 10.5" sandwich tray w/ 2 handles: *new* - if handles are at 9:00 & 3:00 center branch lines up horizontally; *old* - if handles are at 9:00 & 3:00 center branch with textures will be vertical. Tumblers with scalloped feet and pattern all over: *new* - 1 or 3 weak lines dividing pattern and smooth rim at top; *old* - 3 clearly distinct lines between pattern and rim at top and Cherry Blossom design entirely covers bottom of foot.
Delphite scalloped-foot tumbler reproduced with a crude pattern, wrong color, and the line separating the pattern is incomplete.

Jade ite Cherry Blossom. Back row: 10.25" cake plate; front row: 11" platter, 6" cereal bowl, 8.5" berry bowl. Courtesy of Robert S. Newbrough.

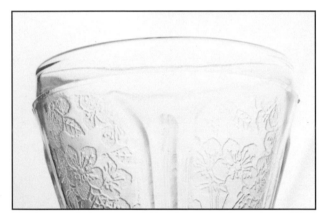

Reproduction tumblers do not have three distinct lines between the pattern design and the smooth rim at the top. *Courtesy of Charlie Diefenderfer.*

CHILD'S JUNIOR DINNER SET (Reproduced)	Pink	Delphite	Qty
Creamer	55	50	____
Cup *R*	55	45	____
Plate, 6"	20	15	____
Saucer *R*	12	8	____
Sugar	55	50	____
14-piece set	458	372	____

Box (for pink)
  in fairly reasonable condition: $35,
  mint condition: $50

Reproduction information: Butter dish: all are new regardless of color! Cup: lopsided handle, cherries may be upside down & off-color. Saucer: design not centered.

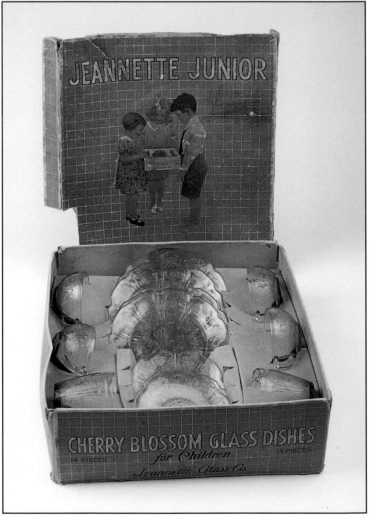

"Child's Junior Dinner Set" in original box. *Courtesy of Charlie Diefenderfer.*

CHERRYBERRY
(1928-1931 U.S. Glass Company)

Cherryberry is a pattern that is growing in popularity. Despite the fact that there are no dinner plates, the charming design and usable serving pieces are gaining favor with increasingly larger numbers of collectors. Sherbets are plentiful but beyond them, this pattern becomes a challenge to find, and more individuals are rising to the challenge.

Many of the rims on Cherryberry pieces have a ridged texture susceptible to damage. The rims need particular attention when choosing a piece to buy. An area that may appear to have damage might also be roughness from the time of manufacture.

If you like this pattern, you may want to consider the Strawberry pattern, which is also by U.S. Glass Company. The molds are the same and the designs are quite similar. Pieces from the two patterns mix and match nicely.

7.5" salad plate.

CHERRYBERRY	Pink & Green &	Crystal & Iridescent	Qty
Bowl, 4" berry	12	6	____
Bowl, 6.25"	120	50	____
Bowl, 6.5" salad	30	15	____
Bowl, 7.5" berry	30	15	____
Butter dish base	75	40	____
Butter dish lid	150	85	____
Butter complete	225	125	____
Comport, 3.5" tall, 5.5" dia.	35	18	____
Creamer, small	25	14	____
Creamer, large, 4.5"	40	16	____
Olive dish, 5" w/1 handle	25	14	____
Pickle dish, 8.25" oval	25	14	____
Pitcher, 7.75"	200	120	____
Plate, 6" sherbet	10	5	____
Plate, 7.5" salad	20	6	____
Sherbet	12	5	____
Sugar, small	25	14	____
Sugar base, large	35	14	____
Sugar lid (fits large)	65	36	____
Tumbler, 3.25"	45	20	____

Comport.

6" sherbet plate, sherbet, 6" sherbet plate.

Above: 3" creamer. *Courtesy of Vic & Jean Laermans.*

CHINEX CLASSIC

(Late 1930s-1942 Macbeth-Evans
Division Corning Glass Works)

Chinex Classic is most often collected with the castle design. We have met many men who particularly enjoy this pattern. The castle design was actually marketed as the Windsor design on Cremax, a line by Corning.

Condition, condition, condition. Most collectors of Chinex are looking for the "Castle" design. If the blue trim is worn or the center decorations faded these are pieces that will receive little interest.

Plain Chinex Classic continues to have few collectors; the Floral design is getting increased interest. Again, the designs should be as if the item had never been used.

Castle decoration dinners with two distinctly different shades of blue, values the same. *Courtesy of Charlie Diefenderfer.*

Castle decoration creamer & sugar.
Courtesy of Vic & Jean Laermans.

CHINEX CLASSIC	Castle decoration	Floral decoration	Plain	Qty
Bowl, 5.75" dessert	15	10	5	____
Bowl, 6.75" salad	13	20	10	____
Bowl, 7" vegetable	35	25	10	____
Bowl, 7.75" coupe soup	35	25	10	____
Bowl, 9" vegetable	35	25	10	____
Bowl, 11"	40	30	20	____
Butter dish base	30	20	15	____
Butter dish lid	120	60	35	____
Butter complete (actually a covered utility dish)	150	80	50	____
Creamer	15	10	5	____
Cup	12	7	5	____
Plate, 6.25" bread & butter	8	4	3	____
Plate, 9.75" dinner	25	10	6	____
Plate, 11.5" salver	25	15	8	____
Saucer	6	4	3	____
Sherbet	20	10	7	____
Sugar	15	10	5	____

Castle decoration.
Back: 9" vegetable bowl, 7.75" coupe soup bowl; *front:* 6" dessert bowl.

Castle decoration. *Back row:* 11.5" salver, 9.75" dinner plate, 6.25" bread & butter plate; *front:* cup & saucer.

CHRISTMAS CANDY

(Late 1930s-early 1950s Indiana Glass Company)

Take note of the name change in the pricing list. Having had the opportunity to examine the Davidson's boxed set of Christmas Candy we can confirm that the color "teal" is actually "Terrace Green." It is this color that captivates collectors and non-collectors alike. It is an uncommon color and the simplicity of the design allows it to make a bold statement.

Once you make the connection between the pattern names and the designs, it becomes relatively easy to remember the names, as they are exemplified by the pattern. The outer rim of the glassware is reminiscent of the hard ribbon candy associated with Christmas lending itself to the name "Christmas Candy." Because the design is only on the rim and feet, there is a vast expanse of undecorated glass, making scratches easy to detect. Scratches do negatively impact the value of any glassware.

Here are some specifics on the boxed set that is pictured. Dated 4/2/52, it was shipped to Zale Jewelry in Springfield, Missouri. On a side of the box not shown reads the message, "Complimentary Luncheon Set Terrace Green" and "Glassware for Gracious Living." One can surmise that this was a gift to a customer whom had made another purchase of some kind. People occasionally comment negatively on the quality (or lack) of Depression Glass. Remember, much of it was free, so a great deal of care may not have been given to create perfection.

Top: Boxed "Complimentary Luncheon Set Terrace Green" dated 1952. *Courtesy of Wes & Carla Davidson.*
Bottom: Contents of boxed 15-piece luncheon set of "Terrace Green" Christmas Candy. *Courtesy of Wes & Carla Davidson.*

CHRISTMAS CANDY	Terrace Green	Crystal	Qty
Bowl, 5.75" fruit		5	____
Bowl, 7.25" soup	75	10	____
Bowl, 9.5" vegetable	trtp*		____
Creamer, 3.5"	35	10	____
Cup	35	5	____
Mayonnaise 3-pc. set		35	____
Mayo. comport		20	____
Mayo. ladle		10	____
SMayo. under plate		5	____
Plate, 6" bread & butter	15	5	____
Plate, 8.25" luncheon	30	8	____
Plate, 9.5" dinner	50	12	____
Plate, 11.25" sandwich	80	18	____
Saucer	15	5	____
Sugar, 3.25"	35	10	____
Tidbit, 2 tier		20	____

*trtp = too rare to price

CIRCLE

(1930s Hocking Glass Company)

New collectors sometimes have problems discerning the difference between Circle, Ring, and Block Optic. Circle has one grouping of ridges encircling each piece. Block Optic has a geometric block design, and Ring has multiple groupings of four rings each. Hocking Glass Company made all, so the colors and shapes do blend together well.

Green is much more prevalent than pink and is also the primary color sought by collectors. Items made with two colors of glass, e.g., the crystal sherbet with a green foot, are especially popular at this time.

Like Block Optic that has five cup styles, Circle has two. Hocking Glass Company was wonderful at providing options for their customers, but there is a difference between these items worth noting. One cup has a smaller bottom that fits the saucer. The other cup tapers in toward a base too wide to fit in the ring of the saucer and it will only work resting on the 6" sherbet plate like Princess, another Hocking pattern.

Prices of bowls and pitchers are on the increase as these are items that have become difficult to find.

6" sherbet plate, 8.25" luncheon plate, cup.

3" sherbet, 5" flat iced tea tumbler.

3" sherbet w/ green foot, crystal bowl ($10).

Circle	Green	Pink	Qty
Bowl, 4.5"	12		____
Bowl, 5" w/flared rim	20		____
Bowl, 5.25"	12		____
Bowl, 8"	30		____
Bowl, 9.25"	30		____
Creamer	12	15	____
Cup, 2 styles	6	6	____
Decanter, handled w/ stopper	75	75	____
Goblet, 4.5" wine	15	15	____
Goblet, 8 oz., water	15	15	____
Pitcher, 60 oz.	60		____
Pitcher, 80 oz.	60		____
Plate, 6" sherbet	5	5	____
Plate, 8.25" luncheon	8	8	____
Plate, 9.5" dinner	40	40	____
Plate, 10" sandwich	15	15	____
Reamer (fits top of 80 oz. pitcher)	25	25	____
Saucer	8		____
Sherbet, 3" w/stem	8	8	____
Sherbet, 4.75" w/ stem	10	10	____
Sugar	12	15	____
Tumbler, 3.5" juice, flat	12		____
Tumbler, 4" water, flat	10		____
Tumbler, 5" iced tea, flat	18		____
Tumbler, 15 oz., flat	25		____

Note: Crystal items ½ of those in green. Vase w/ shape similar to pitcher: crystal & iridescent, $35.

Left: 8 oz. water goblet. *Courtesy of Charlie Diefenderfer.*

Below: Creamer & sugar. *Courtesy of Vic & Jean Laermans.*

CLOVERLEAF

(1930-1936 Hazel-Atlas Glass Company)

Green, yellow, and black Cloverleaf continue to be popular among new collectors and confirmed Depression Glass addicts. The pieces are relatively affordable with a shape and style that are quite pleasant. Pink is the color receiving minimal attention and that may be in part to the limited number of items available in pink.

Bowls are the most difficult pieces to amass. If this is a pattern intended for use, it may take some diligent hunting to acquire a desired quantity. (Be sure to check our Dealer Directory in the back of the book as these reputable people may be of help in any of your collecting needs.) The candy jar and smaller tumblers are also getting harder to find and the values of all these pieces reflects their elusiveness.

Some Cloverleaf pieces have the clover design on the inside, and some have the design on the outside. There is no difference in the value between the two. You may want to make careful note of what you own if consistency is important to you.

Above: *Back:* 8" luncheon plate; *front row:* salt & pepper, cup & saucer, candy jar w/ lid. *Courtesy of Paula Apperson McNamara.*

Left: 3.75" tumbler, 4" tumbler, 5.75" tumbler w/ foot. *Courtesy of Paula Apperson McNamara.*

Back: 10.25" grill plate; *front row:* sherbet w/ pattern on outside, sherbet w/ pattern inside, creamer & sugar. *Courtesy of Paula Apperson MᶜNamara.*

Cup & saucer. *Courtesy of Charlie Diefenderfer.*

Back: 7" salad bowl; *front:* 5" cereal bowl, 4" dessert bowl, 8" bowl. *Courtesy of Paula Apperson MᶜNamara.*

Back row: sugar & creamer; *front row:* salt & pepper, sugar & creamer. *Courtesy of Vic & Jean Laermans.*

Cloverleaf	Green	Yellow	Black	Pink	Qty
Ash tray, 4"	65		65		____
Ash tray, 5.75"	85		85		____
Bowl, 4" dessert	30	32		25	____
Bowl, 5" cereal	60	70			____
Bowl, 7" salad	55	55			____
Bowl, 8"	85				____
Candy jar w/lid	85	120			____
Creamer	15	20	25		____
Cup	10	12	22	10	____
Plate, 6" sherbet	8	8	40		____
Plate, 8" luncheon	10	15	20	10	____
Plate, 10.25" grill	35	35			____
Salt & pepper	50	120	120		____
Saucer	5	5	8	5	____
Sherbet	10	12	25	8	____
Sugar	15	20	25		____
Tumbler, 3.75" flat	75				____
Tumbler, 4" flat	55			30	____
Tumbler, 5.75" w/foot	35	35			____

COLONIAL, "KNIFE & FORK"

(1934-1938 Hocking Glass Company)

Colonial is one of the few patterns with a huge array of pieces made in multiple colors. At the time of our first edition, pink and green were the overwhelming colors of choice, but this trend seems to be in transition. Crystal (clear) Colonial is receiving great attention, and is performing well on Internet auction sites with an increase in demand.

Colonial has a very distinctive look that is not easily mixed with other patterns as there are no other patterns having a similar design. The green is not the same shade as many other green Depression Glass patterns. Green Colonial has a definite yellow tint to it.

Grill plates, divided dishes that separate the food on the plate, are much easier to find than dinner plates. We have never had a mug in any color and would love to photograph one—Hint!

Here is a clarification on the tumblers and stems as this pattern has an assortment of both. Flat tumblers are like drinking glasses that have no foot and rest flat on a surface. Footed tumblers have a ball of glass and then a circular base or foot of glass. Just as it sounds, stems have a stem of glass separating the circular foot from the rest of the glass.

Keep in mind the sugar and spoon holder/celery are similar in design. The sugar base is 4.25" tall and the spoon holder is 5.5" tall. If you are shopping with *Mauzy's Comprehensive Handbook of Depression Glass Prices* you can use the measure provided on the back cover of the book to verify what you are looking at.

Hopefully the printing process will not alter the color of the cup shown on the purple background. This cup is not white, it is Cremax. It may have little interest in terms of collectibility or usefulness, but it is another oddity that has recently been discovered.

Back row: 3" goblet w/platinum trim, 4" cocktail goblet, 10" dinner plate, sugar; *front* row: 2.5" whiskey tumbler, cup & saucer, creamer or milk pitcher. *Courtesy of Charlie Diefenderfer.*

Back row: 5.5" celery/spoon holder, 12" platter; *middle row:* 4.25" sugar base, 5.75" water goblet, 3" goblet, 7" pitcher; *front row:* 2.5" whiskey tumbler, 4" water tumbler. *Courtesy of Charlie Diefenderfer.*

5.75" water goblet, 4" water tumbler, 3" juice tumbler, 2.5" whiskey tumbler. *Courtesy of Charlie Diefenderfer.*

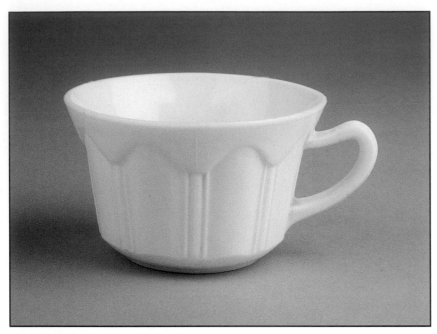

White cup.

5.25" claret, 4" cocktail, 3.75" cordial, 3" goblet.
Courtesy of Charlie Diefenderfer.

4.75" cream soup bowl.

Colonial, "Knife & Fork"	Pink	Green	Crystal	Qty
Bowl, 3.75" berry	65			____
Bowl, 4.75" berry	20	20	10	____
Bowl, 4.75" cream soup	75	75	50	____
Bowl, 5.5" cereal	70	110	25	____
Bowl, 7.25" low soup	70	70	20	____
Bowl, 9" berry	35	35	20	____
Bowl, 10" oval vegetable	40	40	20	____
Butter dish base	500	40	25	____
Butter dish lid	200	20	15	____
Butter complete	700	60	40	____
Celery/spoon holder, 5.5"	135	135	60	____
Cheese dish		260		____
Creamer, 5" (same as 5" milk pitcher)	70	35	20	____
Cup	14	12	5	____
Goblet, 3", 2 oz., 2" diam.	30	30	10	____
Goblet, 3.75" cordial, 1 oz.		30	10	____
Goblet, 4" cocktail, 3 oz.		28	8	____
Goblet, 4.5" wine, 2.5 oz.		28	8	____
Goblet, 5.25" claret, 4 oz.		28	8	____
Goblet, 5.75" water, 8.5 oz.		32	15	____
Mug, 4.5"	600	800		____
Pitcher, 5" milk/creamer	70	35	20	____
Pitcher, 7" w/or w/out ice lip	60	60	30	____
Pitcher, 7.75" w/or w/out ice lip	75	85	30	____
Plate, 6" sherbet/saucer	8	8	4	____
Plate, 8.5" luncheon	10	10	4	____
Plate, 10" dinner	65	70	25	____
Plate, 10" grill	30	25	10	____
Platter, 12"	40	35	15	____
Salt & pepper	160	160	60	____
Saucer/sherbet plate	8	8	4	____
Sherbet, 3"	25			____
Sherbet, 3.25"	14	15	5	____
Spoon holder/celery, 5.5"	135	135	60	____
Sugar base, 4.25"	28	18	10	____
Sugar lid	60	30	15	____
Tumbler, 2.5" whiskey, 1.5 oz., flat	18	20	12	____
Tumbler, 3" juice, 5 oz., flat	25	25	10	____
Tumbler, 3.25", 3 oz. w/foot	22	27	10	____
Tumbler, 4" water, 9 oz., flat	25	25	10	____
Tumbler, 4", 5 oz. w/foot	35	45	15	____
Tumbler, 5", 11 oz., flat	36	45	15	____
Tumbler, 5.25", 10 oz. w/foot	50	50	20	____
Tumbler, 12 oz. iced tea, flat	55	55	20	____
Tumbler, 15 oz. lemonade, flat	70	80	40	____

Note: Beaded top pitcher, $1300. Ruby tumblers, $150.
White: cup, $5; saucer, $2. Creamex: cup, $5.

Back row: 10" grill plate, 10" dinner plate, 8.5" luncheon plate; *front row:* 4.75" berry bowl, cup & saucer, 5.5" cereal bowl, 7.75" pitcher. *Courtesy of Charlie Diefenderfer.*

Back row: 2.5" whiskey tumbler, 4" water tumbler, 10" oval vegetable bowl; *front row:* butter, 9" berry bowl. *Courtesy of Charlie Diefenderfer.*

Back row: 5" creamer/milk pitcher, 12" platter; *front row:* sugar w/ lid, shaker, 5.5" spoon holder/celery. *Courtesy of Charlie Diefenderfer.*

Goblet, butter dish, candy jar.

COLONIAL BLOCK
(1930s, White in 1950s Hazel-Atlas Glass Company)

Many dealers believe that generally pink is the most popular color of Depression Glass. Colonial Block is one of those patterns to dispel that myth. Pink is not easily found, but not many are looking for it either, so the pink prices haven't risen . . . yet.

Hazel-Atlas advertised Colonial Block as having a "modernistic design." Colonial Block may have been a response to the Cubist movement in design and art; however, many collectors looking for a retro style lean toward Manhattan and Moderntone. Once again here is a pattern lacking dinner plates and for that matter plates of any kind. There are no cups and no saucers. Practically speaking it is necessary to mix this with other patterns in order to serve a meal.

Some Colonial Block pieces are marked with the Hazel-Atlas Glass Company H with an A inside. New collectors sometimes confuse this mark with Anchor Hocking when seeing the initials A and H.

Sherbets continue to be easily found and remain a bargain at $10 each. We are finding an increased interest in them by people looking for sherbets, dessert dishes, or ice cream dishes that are vintage yet inexpensive. Between their availability and low price, many are opting for a set of these to mix and match with other glassware and china.

Above: *Back row:* creamer, 7" bowl, butter; *front row:* sugar w/ lid, 7" bowl, sherbet. *Courtesy of Debora & Paul Torsiello, Debzie's Glass.*

Right: Creamer & sugar w/ lid.

Colonial Block   **Pink & Green Qty**

Colonial Block	Pink & Green	Qty
Bowl, 4"	10	____
Bowl, 7"	20	____
Butter dish base	20	____
Butter dish lid	40	____
Butter complete	60	____
Butter tub	60	____
Candy jar w/lid, 8.75"	45	____
Creamer	15	____
Goblet	15	____
Pitcher	75	____
Powder jar w/lid	40	____
Sherbet	10	____
Sugar base	15	____
Sugar lid	15	____
Tumbler, 5.25" sm. stem & foot	30	____

Note: White creamer, sugar base, $7; sugar lid $8. Black powder jar w/lid, $40. Crystal items half of those in pink and green.

4" bowl. *Courtesy of Michael Rothenberger/Mike's Collectibles.*

COLONIAL FLUTED

(1928-1933 Federal Glass Company)

In 1928, Federal Glass Company entered the world of manufacturing the colored glass now referred to as Depression Glass with this pattern. The design was simple and later patterns with greater detail became more popular. Colonial Fluted was removed from production in 1933 before many pieces were created.

Shown are an 8" luncheon plate, cup, and saucer in crystal (clear) with black trim that were found in Virginia. If these are part of "The Bridgette Set" made in 1930 there are sherbets, creamers, and sugars with lids to go along. Glassware for this set was available with red or black trim and would have had the four suits as additional decorations. These may have been worn away or deliberately removed.

You can recognize Colonial Fluted, nicknamed "Rope," by the distinctive rope-like design near the outer rim of each piece.

Back row: 8" luncheon plate, 6" sherbet plate; *front row:* sherbet, creamer.

8" luncheon plate, cup & saucer.

Above: Sugar w/ lid. *Courtesy of Vic & Jean Laermans.*

COLONIAL FLUTED	Green	Qty
Bowl, 4" berry	10	____
Bowl, 6" cereal	14	____
Bowl, 6.5" salad (deep)	25	____
Bowl, 7.5" berry	25	____
Creamer	10	____
Cup	5	____
Plate, 6" sherbet	5	____
Plate, 8" luncheon	8	____
Saucer	3	____
Sherbet	8	____
Sugar base	10	____
Sugar lid	25	____

Note: Crystal items worth 1/2 of those in green.

COLUMBIA
Reproduced
(1938-1942 Federal Glass Company)

Only a few patterns are more popular in crystal (clear) than another color and Columbia is one of them. In all fairness to pink lovers, there are only four Columbia items made in pink and they are very difficult to find.

Often butter dishes are one of the most challenging items to locate in a given pattern. Columbia butter dishes are very common and remain an inexpensive commodity.

Pieces of Columbia can be found with gold trim. This is not as popular as the plain pieces and must be in pristine condition for collectors to show any real interest in them.

Shown is the Columbia pitcher. As with the snack plate, its unique design almost makes it seem to not belong to this pattern.

Back: 11" chop plate; *front:* butter, cup & saucer.
Courtesy of Marie Talone & Paul Reichwein.

Snack plate, cup. *Courtesy of Michael Rothenberger/ Mike's Collectibles.*

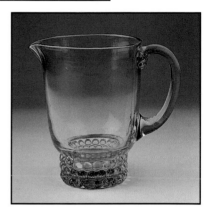

Pitcher. *Courtesy of Mike Rothenberger / Mike's Collectibles.*

9.5" luncheon plate, saucer, 6" bread & butter plate. *Courtesy of Debora & Paul Torsiello, Debzie's Glass.*

COLUMBIA	Crystal	Pink	Qty
Bowl, 5" cereal	20		____
Bowl, 8" soup	26		____
Bowl, 8.5" salad	20		____
Bowl, 10.5" fruit w/ruffled rim	20		____
Butter dish base	6		____
Butter dish lid	14		____
Butter complete	20		____
Cup	8	25	____
Pitcher	100		____
Plate, 6" bread & butter	6	20	____
Plate, 9.5" luncheon	10	35	____
Plate, 11" chop	14		____
Saucer	3	10	____
Snack plate	25		____
Tumbler, 2.75" 4 oz. juice *R*	30		____
Tumbler, 9 oz. water, 4"	35		____

Note: Ruby flashed butter, $25. Other flashed or satinized butters, $20.

Reproduction information: Juice glasses marked "France" on bottom are new.

4" tumbler, 8" soup bowl, 11" chop plate w/ decorative trim, 5" cereal w/ decorative trim, 6" plate. *Courtesy of Kathy McCarney.*

COREX
(1948 Corning Glassworks of Canada)

Here is another treasure tucked away in Canada: Corex. It is very similar to Cremax which is also presented in this book. In fact they are almost like cousins as both are products of Corning Glass Works. Corex was manufactured at the Leaside, Toronto plant of Corning Glassworks of Canada with all pieces marked, "COREX TM REG MADE IN CANADA." Corex offers a mug but has no serving pieces. One could supplement with the Cremax vegetable bowl and salver. Simply add some Bakelite flatware and a vintage tablecloth and the table would be stunning!

Corex	Ivory	Qty
Bowl, 5" berry	5	____
Bowl, 7.75" soup	8	____
Creamer	6	____
Cup	4	____
Mug, 8 oz.	18	____
Plate, 6.75" sherbet	4	____
Plate, 7.5" salad	6	____
Plate, 9.25" dinner	10	____
Saucer	2	____
Sherbet, 4.5"	5	____
Sugar	6	____

Back row: 9.25" dinner plate, 7.75" soup bowl; *middle row:* 6.75" sherbet, 7.5" salad plate; *front row:* sugar, creamer, cup & saucer, 5" berry bowl. *Courtesy of Walter Lemiski / Waltz Time Antiques.*

CORONATION
(1936-1940 Hocking Glass Company)

Ruby Coronation is very popular with Royal Ruby collectors. We have sold many a "berry set" of either a 6.5" bowl or an 8" bowl with four, six, or eight 4.25" bowls. These bowls are always easier to sell when grouped together especially when approaching the Christmas season.

Take note of the 5" tumbler. It is very similar to the Old Colony tumbler. Both have a scalloped foot; however Coronation has a vertical band of ribs above the middle of the tumbler. Old Colony tumblers have wider ribs in the bottom half of the tumbler. Recently collectors have begun to mix and match patterns and pieces based on availability and cost. The Coronation tumbler is a very acceptable substitute for Old Colony with a substantial savings.

The pink 8" berry bowl with handles continues to go up in price, although at $20 it is still quite affordable. It is attractive and useful and the simple design blends nicely with other patterns. For a collector needing a reasonably priced serving bowl this is a great choice.

We have never owned a piece of green Coronation. If there is a collector willing to get their green pieces to the studio we would love to include them in our third edition.

Sherbet & 7.75" pitcher. *Courtesy of Kyle & Barbara Ewing.*

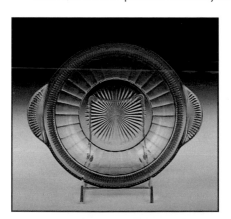

8" berry bowl w/2 handles. *Courtesy of Neil McCurdy-Hoosier Kubboard Glass.*

6" sherbet plate/saucer, sherbet, 5" tumbler.

CORONATION	Pink	Ruby	Green	Qty
Bowl, 4.25" berry w/2 handles	8	8		____
Bowl, 4.25" with no handles	80		50	____
Bowl, 6.5" w/2 handles	15	15		____
Bowl, 8" berry w/2 handles	20	20		____
Bowl, 8" with no handles	150		180	____
Cup	5	9		____
Pitcher, 7.75"	700			____
Plate, 6" sherbet/saucer	6			____
Plate, 8.5" luncheon	15	15	50	____
Saucer/6" sherbet plate	5			____
Sherbet	8		80	____
Tumbler, 5"	35		180	____

Note: Crystal saucer, $1.

CREMAX

(Late 1930s-early 1940s Macbeth-Evans
Division Corning Glass Works)

Corning created a line of tableware called Cremax. The opaque glass was given dark fired-on rims and named "Bordette" and pastel rims and named "Rainbow." The Windsor design on Cremax is also known as Chinex Classic. When referring to this ivory color, Corning used the term "Chinex," as used on certain pieces of Dogwood Depression Glass. This glassware was created to compete with china and pottery. Advertisements touted the fact that this amazing dinnerware would not craze and would be difficult to chip.

Overall transparent glass has had the greatest following, but Cremax seems to be gaining in popularity. Perhaps the pastel colors of Rainbow are pleasing to those seeking to create a pastoral look. This will be a pattern worth watching as increased demand may result in higher prices.

Be sure to look at the Corex pattern. This is similar to Cremax and was also made by Corning. Cremax offers a few more choices than Corex including serving pieces and demitasse cups and saucers. If you find a piece marked

"COREX TM REG MADE IN CANADA" it is Corex.

Demitasse pieces have become extremely popular, perhaps with many people's increased love affair with Espresso and other exotic coffees.

Above: Cup & saucer, demitasse cup & saucer.

Below: *Back row:* 12" salver, 6" dessert/cereal bowl; *front row:* 2 cups & saucers, 6" bread & butter plate.

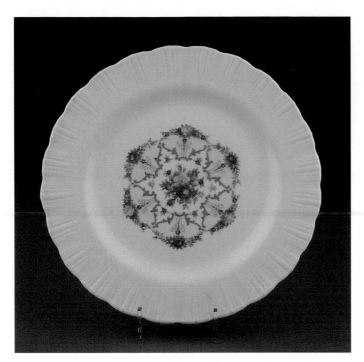

CREMAX	Cremax	All other colors w/or w/out decorations	Qty
Bowl, 6" dessert/cereal	5	8	____
Bowl, 7" bowl	8	16	____
Bowl, 7.75" coupe soup	8	16	____
Bowl, 9" vegetable	8	16	____
Creamer	6	10	____
Cup	5	6	____
Cup, demitasse	15	15	____
Plate, 6" bread & butter	5	7	____
Plate, 9.75" dinner	8	12	____
Plate, 12" salver	8	10	____
Saucer	5	6	____
Saucer, demitasse	5	5	____
Sugar	6	10	____

Above: Princess decoration on 9.75" dinner plate.

Right: 7.75" coupe soup bowl. *Courtesy of Charlie Diefenderfer.*

CROW'S FOOT
(1930s Paden City Glass Company)

Paden City Glass Company produced wonderful pieces of excellent quality as exemplified by this pattern. The colors are brilliant and the shapes distinctive.

No pieces of Crow's Foot are common and the choices are many so collecting the entire set will be a hunt. Fortunately this is not a pattern prone to chipping, so if there is an absence of scratching, the item is probably in good condition.

Many people who collect Crow's Foot are interested in any piece, not a particular color as is the norm with most collectors of other patterns. Some collectors of Crow's Foot are actually Paden City Glass Company collectors and this is part of a larger search.

Red is a bit more common than black or blue. Don't misinterpret this comment as no color is easily found. The Internet has proven to be a good source for this pattern.

Many variations are available as Paden City used Crow's Foot blanks with other patterns and with silver overlays. Pieces with a decorative overlay in good condition would be worth about 20% more than their plain counterparts.

The red comport is an interesting transitional piece. The bowl is #895 "Lucy" and the stem is Crow's Foot (#890).

Crow's Foot molds were used to create Peacock Reverse.

Cup & saucer. *Courtesy of Kathy McCarney.*

11" oval bowl, 11.5" bowl w/ 3 feet, 11" square console bowl w/ rolled edge. *Courtesy of Debora & Paul Torsiello, Debzie's Glass.*

Back row: lid w/ silver overlay for 6.25" candy dish, 4.25" tumbler; *front row:* "mushroom" candlestick, base for 6.25" candy dish, pair of candlesticks, 6.5" bowl. *Courtesy of Debora & Paul Torsiello, Debzie's Glass.*

11.75" vase & 10.25" vase. *Courtesy of Debora & Paul Torsiello, Debzie's Glass.*

6.5" comport. *Courtesy of Debora & Paul Torsiello, Debzie's Glass.*

Creamer. *Courtesy of Vic & Jean Laermans.*

CROWSFOOT	Red	Black, Blue & Amethyst	Other colors	Qty
Bowl, 4.75" square	32	37	15	____
Bowl, cream soup	28	32	14	____
Bowl, 6" round	30	35	15	____
Bowl, 6.5" round	50	60	25	____
Bowl, 8.5" square w/ 2 handles	50	60	30	____
Bowl, 8.75" square	50	60	30	____
Bowl, 10" w/foot	80	80	35	____
Bowl, 10" square w/2 handles	65	75	35	____
Bowl, 11" oval	35	45	20	____
Bowl, 11" round			35	____
Bowl, 11" square	65	75	35	____
Bowl, 11" square w/rolled edge	70	80	35	____
Bowl, 11.5" round w/3 feet	90	120	50	____
Bowl, 11.5" console	85	100	45	____
Bowl, Nasturtium w/3 feet	200	225	100	____
Bowl, whipped cream w/3 feet	60	70	30	____
Cake plate, square	85	100	45	____
Candlestick, round base, ea.	50	55	25	____
Candlestick, square "mushroom", ea.	20	25	15	____
Candlestick, 5.75" tall, ea.	20	25	15	____
Candy w/lid, 6.25" across	170	200	90	____
Candy w/ lid, 6.5" 3-sections, 2 styles	75	90	40	____
Cheese stand, 5"	30	40	20	____
Comport, 3.25" tall	30	40	18	____
Comport, 4.75" tall	60	75	40	____
Comport, 6.5" tall	70	90	40	____
Creamer, flat or footed	18	20	10	____
Cup, flat or footed	10	15	5	____
Gravy boat, flat	100	120	50	____
Gravy boat, pedestal	150	175	75	____
Mayonnaise, 3 feet	50	65	30	____
Plate, 5.75"	10	15	5	____
Plate, 8"	15	20	5	____
Plate, 8.5" square	15	20	8	____
Plate, 9.25" small dinner	40	50	20	____
Plate, 9.5" 2 handles	70	80	40	____
Plate, 10.25" round w/2 handles	55	65	25	____
Plate, 10.25" square w/2 handles	45	55	25	____
Plate, 10.5" dinner	100	125	50	____
Plate, 11" cracker	50	60	30	____
Plate, 12"	30	45	20	____
Relish, 11", 3 sections	100	120	50	____
Sandwich server, round w/center handle	70	80	40	____
Sandwich server, square w/center handle	50	60	20	____
Saucer, round	10	15	5	____
Saucer, square	12	17	7	____
Sugar, flat or footed	18	20	10	____
Tumbler, 4.25"	80	100	40	____
Vase, 4.5"	60	75	40	____
Vase, 10.25", curved in	110	130	50	____
Vase, 10.25", curved out	95	110	40	____
Vase, 11.75"	150	185	70	____

CROWN

(1940s Pyrex, Macbeth-Evans Division of Corning Glass Works)

There is no other pattern of Depression Glass with the unique color of Corning Glass Works' Crown. The turquoise blue color is deeper than, but reminiscent of Chalaine.

Manufactured by Pyrex, Macbeth-Evans Division of Corning Glass Works in the 1940s, this line of dinnerware features a rim of alternating Piecrust-type ridges and three-pointed crowns. However, it is not the design that makes this an awesome pattern, it is the color. When we saw Crown we immediately fell in love with it and started a personal collection!

There are four different bowls and three different plates; just enough choices to set a complete table, less shakers, a butter dish, and tumblers. Crown is one of the few patterns with a mug, and this is the most elusive piece.

Crown your own table with this really lovely set that our friends in Canada have been enjoying for years!

CROWN	Turquoise	Qty
Bowl, 4.75" small berry	6	____
Bowl, 6" oatmeal	8	____
Bowl, 7.75" soup	12	____
Bowl, 9" large berry	25	____
Creamer	10	____
Cup	5	____
Mug	20	____
Plate, 6.75" sherbet	5	____
Plate, 9" dinner	10	____
Plate. 12" salver	18	____
Saucer	2	____
Sugar	10	____

Back row: 12" salver; *middle row:* 3.5"mug & 9.25" dinner plate; *front row:* cup & saucer and 6.75" sherbet plate. *Courtesy of Walter Lemiski / Waltz Time Antiques.*

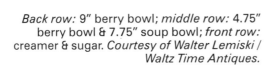

Back row: 9" berry bowl; *middle row:* 4.75" berry bowl & 7.75" soup bowl; *front row:* creamer & sugar. *Courtesy of Walter Lemiski / Waltz Time Antiques.*

CUBE

(1929-1933 Jeannette Glass Company)

The Cube or Cubist 2.5" creamer and 2.5" sugar may be among the most recognizable pieces of Depression Glass. Although common, dealers report that they consistently sell! On the other end of the spectrum is the 8.75" pitcher. This is the most challenging Cube piece to locate, but equally easy to sell.

Coloring inconsistencies are very evident within this pattern. The greens run from dark to medium green and the pink is found in pale shades, medium shades, and orangish pink. Both green and pink are equally collected; however green was discontinued prior to the end of production, so less green is now available.

The 7" 3-footed relish pictured is reportedly only one of two known to exist. If you have one, congratulations!

Shown is the newly listed crystal custard cup on a crystal sherbet plate. These were found on a tray lot at a Pennsylvania auction house. It is amazing that new pieces are constantly being discovered. This set would be great for desserts, salad dressings and other condiments, or a floating candle.

If you locate an item that doesn't match the measurements on the list you might have one of the dozens of pieces of American by Fostoria Glass Company.

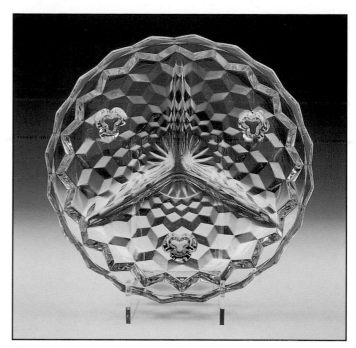

7" relish w/ 3 feet. *Courtesy of Staci & Jeff Shuck/Gray Goose Antiques.*

Back: 6.5" salad bowl; *front:* 4.5" dessert bowl, butter.
Courtesy of Diefenderfer's Collectibles & Antiques.

CUBE	Pink	Green	Qty
Bowl, 4.5" dessert, pointy rim	12	10	____
Bowl, 4.5" deep	12		____
Bowl, 6.5" salad	18	22	____
Butter dish base	40	40	____
Butter dish lid	60	60	____
Butter complete	100	100	____
Candy jar w/lid	45	55	____
Coaster, 3.25"	12	12	____
Creamer, 2.5"	5		____
Creamer, 3.75"	10	12	____
Cup	10	12	____
Pitcher, 8.75"	260	260	____
Plate, 6" sherbet	12	10	____
Plate, 8" luncheon	15	15	____
Powder jar w/lid, 3 feet	35	40	____
Relish, 7" w/3 feet (like Windsor)	trtp*		____
Salt & pepper	60	60	____
Saucer	4	4	____
Sherbet	10	12	____
Sugar, 2.5"	5		____
Sugar base, 3"	10	12	____
Sugar lid/candy lid	22	22	____
Tumbler, 4"	90	90	____

Back row: 3" sugar, 6" sherbet plate, candy jar w/ lid; *middle row:* 4" tumbler, powder jar w/ lid, 4.5" deep bowl; *front row:* cup, sherbet, 4.5" dessert. *Courtesy of Marie Talone & Paul Reichwein.*

*trtp = too rare to price

Note: Ultramarine: 4.5" bowl, $50; 6.5" bowl, $85. Amber: small cream & sugar, $10 ea. White: small cream & sugar, $3 ea. Crystal: tray for larger cream & sugar, $5; 6" sherbet plate, $5; 2.5" tall, 3.25" custard cup, $10; other items, $1.

Custard cup & sherbet plate.

Above: Salt & pepper. *Courtesy of Michael Rothenberger/Mike's Collectibles.*

Left: *Back:* 6.5" salad bowl; *front:* powder jar w/ lid, candy jar w/ lid. *Courtesy of Diefenderfer's Collectibles & Antiques.*

CUPID
(1930s Paden City Glass Company)

Cupid is another example of the fine quality of glassware manufactured by Paden City Glass Company. The distinctive etched design always shows two cupids facing one another.

The blue samovar is the rarest Cupid item and one of the most rare pieces of Depression Glass overall. Please note that the metal handles and spout are missing, but the glass is in perfect condition and clearly exhibits the beautiful Cupid design.

Cupid shapes and sizes are the same as Peacock and Rose by Paden City. Once again a glass company is able to get additional mileage from molds by utilizing them in more than one way.

We would love to feature a Cupid collection in our third edition. If you have one that can be brought in we thank you from the bottom of our hearts. Shoot an arrow, er, send a note our way! Thanks!!

11.25" cake stand, 8.5" oval bowl w/ foot. *Courtesy of Neil McCurdy - Hoosier Kubboard Glass.*

CUPID	Green & Pink	Qty
Bowl, 8.5" oval w/foot, 4.25" deep	300	____
Bowl, 9.25" fruit w/foot	300	____
Bowl, 9.25" w/center handle	300	____
Bowl, 10.25" fruit	225	____
Bowl, 10.5" w/rolled edge	225	____
Bowl, 11" console	225	____
Cake plate, 11.75"	200	____
Cake stand, 2" tall, 11.25" dia.	200	____
Candlestick, ea.	100	____
Candy jar w/lid, 5.25" tall	400	____
Candy dish w/lid, 3-part flat	300	____
Casserole w/lid	400	____
Comport, 6.25"	200	____
Creamer, no foot	175	____
Creamer, 4.25" w/foot	150	____
Creamer, 5" w/foot	150	____
Ice bucket, 6"	300	____
Ice tub, 4.75"	300	____
Lamp w/silver overlay	500	____
Mayonnaise, 3-piece set	250	____
Mayo. comport	150	____
Mayo. ladle	50	____
Mayo. under plate	50	____
Plate, 10.5"	175	____
Samovar	1000	____
Sugar, no foot	175	____
Sugar, 4.25" w/foot	150	____
Sugar, 5" w/foot	150	____
Tray, 10.75" w/center handle	200	____
Tray, 10.75" oval w/foot	250	____
Vase, 10.75" elliptical	600	____
Vase, fan-shaped	425	____
Vase, 10"	325	____

Note: Black: covered casserole, $650. Peacock blue: comport, $250; mayonnaise, $375; 10.5" plate, $250; samovar, $2000.

Samovar.

Back row: 9.25" dinner plate, 10.25" grill plate, 7.5" 3-part relish; *front row:* creamer, sugar, 9.25" berry bowl, sherbet. *Courtesy of Vic & Jean Laermans.*

DAISY

(1933 crystal, 1940 amber, others till 1980s Indiana Glass Company)

Crystal Daisy was introduced in 1933. Today it is neither common nor particularly popular except among a handful of enthusiasts. Amber followed in 1940 and today is the more popular and more often seen color. Daisy's amber is a deeper, browner color than most other amber Depression Glass making it very difficult to mix and match.

The green sugar is actually an avocado color that was popular in the 1960s and 1970s. This color has yet to be revived and therefore is not in any real demand at this time. Indiana Glass Company wasn't the only manufacturer to use this shade of glass and virtually none of the other avocado glassware from this period of time is enjoying any kind of a resurgence.

4.75" berry bowl. *Courtesy of Charlie Diefenderfer.*

DAISY	Amber & Fired-on red	Green	Crystal	Qty
Bowl, 4.75" berry	10	8	5	____
Bowl, cream soup	12	6	5	____
Bowl, 6" cereal	35	15	8	____
Bowl, 7.25" berry	15	10	8	____
Bowl, 9.25" berry	35	18	14	____
Bowl, 10" oval vegetable, w/tab handles	18	15	10	____
Creamer, 4.25"	14	10	8	____
Cup	6	5	4	____
Plate, 6" sherbet	5	4	2	____
Plate, 7.25" salad	7	5	4	____
Plate, 8.5" luncheon	7	5	4	____
Plate, 9.25" dinner	10	10	6	____
Plate, 10.25" grill	9	8	5	____
Plate, 10.25" grill w/indent (fits cream soup)	20	20		____
Plate, 11.5" cake/sandwich	18	10	7	____
Platter, 10.75"	15	10	7	____
Relish, 7.5" 3-part w/3 feet	35		10	____
Saucer	5	4	2	____
Sherbet, 3"	10	8	5	____
Sugar, 4"	14	10	8	____
Tumbler, 9 oz., 4.75"	20	12	10	____
Tumbler, 12 oz., 6.5"	40	25	20	____

Note: White sugar, $10.

Back row: 9.25" berry bowl, 11.5" cake/sandwich plate; *front row:* 7.25" berry bowl, 10" oval vegetable bowl on 10.75" platter. *Courtesy of Sherelyn A. Ammon.*

Above: Sherbet, 7.25" salad plate, 6" sherbet plate, creamer, sugar. *Courtesy of Sherelyn A. Ammon.*

Right: Sugar. *Courtesy of Vic & Jean Laermans.*

DELLA ROBBIA
(1928-1940s Westmoreland Glass Company)

Della Robbia is a unique pattern due to the applied colors of the apples, grapes, and pears. In order for a piece to be worth the price shown on the list these colors must be free from wear even though they were very susceptible to damage. Also prone to deterioration are the lids to the shakers, particularly to the salt shaker. The price provided assumes these lids to be in excellent condition.

Three pieces of the 1067 line are now shown. They are not easy to find, but in general they are in less demand than the fruit decorated Della Robbia.

Also presented for the first time are the white creamer and white sugar. We suspect that these pieces never had applied colors and surmise that there may be additional white Della Robbia.

As with all Depression Glass there is a pretty good correlation between availability and price. The pitcher and punch bowl will be difficult to find and are so reflected in their values.

If you are interested in a dramatic accent piece consider Della Robbia. This glassware stands alone with its special surface treatments and intricate detail and would look particularly stunning at a Thanksgiving table.

Close-up of pattern.

6.5" bowl w/one handle.

12" 3-footed 1067 bowl, 14" 1067 salver, pair of 1067 pyramid style candlesticks. *Courtesy of Dave & Jamie Moriarty.*

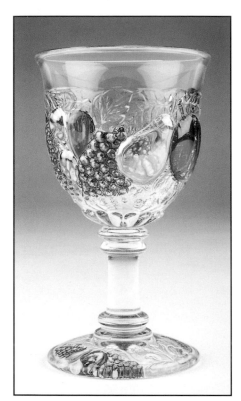

8 oz. 6" water tumbler.

DELLA ROBBIA	Crystal w/applied colors	Qty	DELLA ROBBIA	Crystal w/applied colors	Qty
Basket, 9"	100	____	Plate, 6.25" bread & butter	8	____
			Plate, 7.25" salad	18	____
Basket, 12"	125	____	Plate, 9" luncheon	20	____
Bowl, 4.5"	20	____	Plate, 10.5" dinner	75	____
Bowl, 5" finger	25	____	Plate, 14" torte	50	____
Bowl, 6"	25	____	Plate, 14" salver/cake		
Bowl, 6.5" w/1 handle	25	____	w/foot	85	____
Bowl, 7.5"	30	____	Plate, 18"	100	____
Bowl, 8"	35	____	Plate, 18" liner for punch		
Bowl, 8" w/handles	40	____	bowl w/upturned rim	150	____
Bowl, 8" heart w/1 handle	60	____	Platter, 14"	100	____
Bowl, 9"	45	____	Punch bowl	250	____
Bowl, 11.5", no. 1067	75	____	Punch bowl 15-piece set	600	____
Bowl, 12" w/foot	120	____			
Bowl, 13" w/rolled edge	80	____	Salt & pepper	60	____
Bowl, 14" oval	100	____	Saucer	8	____
Bowl, 14" punch	250	____	Stem, 3 oz. wine	25	____
Bowl, 15"	100	____	Stem, 3.25 oz. cocktail	25	____
Candlestick, no. 1067,			Stem, 5 oz. sherbet, 4.75"	20	____
pyramid style, ea.	40	____	Stem, 5 oz. champagne	25	____
Candlestick, 4" 1-light, ea.	20	____	Stem, 6 oz. champagne	25	____
Candlestick, 4" 2-light, ea.	35	____	Stem, 8 oz. water, 6"	25	____
Candy, chocolate,			Sugar	18	____
round & flat	50	____	Tumbler, 5 oz.		
Candy jar w/lid,			ginger ale, flat	25	____
scalloped edge	80	____	Tumbler, 8 oz. w/foot	25	____
Comport, 6.5" mint,			Tumbler, 8 oz. water, flat	25	____
3.5" tall	50	____	Tumbler, 11 oz. iced		
Comport, 8" sweetmeat	25	____	tea w/foot	30	____
Comport, 12"	80	____	Tumbler, 12 oz. iced		
Comport, 13"	80	____	tea, flat	30	____
Creamer	18	____	Tumbler, 12 oz. iced		
Cup	15	____	tea, w/foot	35	____
Cup, punch	12	____	Tumbler, 12 oz. iced tea,		
Pitcher	250	____	5.25" without usual		
Plate, 6" liner for 5"			"bell" or flare at rim	35	____
finger bowl	8	____			

Note: White creamer & sugar, $14 each.

Creamer & sugar.

Creamer. *Courtesy of Vic & Jean Laermans.*

DIAMOND QUILTED

(Late 1920s-early 1930s Imperial Glass Company)

Thinking rainbows of color? Think Diamond Quilted. If you like green, we've got you covered! How about pink, or amber, or even black? Yes, to them all. But the real favorite of this assortment has become ice blue. This is a color not used in the vast majority of Depression Glass patterns, but there are many options in Diamond Quilted.

There is a following of ice blue Depression Glass collectors and many of them are grabbing every piece of blue Diamond Quilted available. We sold a pair of low candlesticks for more than $100 on an Internet auction site.

Diamond Quilted is not easily found on the East Coast; however, it is fairly abundant in the Midwest in pink, green, and amber. Different colors and patterns were originally distributed in different regions and this may be an example of that phenomenon. Red and black are the most difficult colors to find.

For those of you shopping on eBay, Diamond Quilted is sometimes incorrectly listed as English Hobnail so you may want to increase your search.

Back row: 6.5" sherbet plate, 8" luncheon plate; *front row:* 2 sherbets, 7" bowl, 6" tall compote.

Left: *Back row:* cup & saucer, 6.75" ruffled bowl, creamer; *front row:* sherbet, pair of low candlesticks, sugar. *Courtesy of Vic & Jean Laermans.*

Back row: 6.5" sherbet plate, 8" luncheon plate, 5.5" bowl w/ 1 handle; *front row:* 3.5" tall sherbet, 7" bowl. *Courtesy of Charlie Diefenderfer.*

Creamers & sugars in a variety of colors.
Courtesy of Vic & Jean Laermans.

DIAMOND QUILTED	Pink, Green, & Amber	Blue & Black	Qty
Bowl, cream soup	20	20	____
Bowl, 5" cereal	10	18	____
Bowl, 5.5" w/1 handle	10	18	____
Bowl, 6.25" footed w/cover (resembles a stemmed candy)	50	50	____
Bowl, 7"	20		____
Bowl, 7" w/ crimped rim	15	20	____
Bowl, 7" footed, rolled edge (resembles a comport)	50	50	____
Bowl, 7.5" footed, straight rim (resembles a comport)	50	50	____
Bowl, 10.5" console w/rolled edge	30	60	____
Candlesticks, high and low, each	15	30	____
Candy jar w/lid, low w/3 feet	125		____
Compote, 3.5", 6.5" dia.	50	50	____
Compote, 6" tall, 7.25" across	50		____
Compote w/lid, 11.25"	120		____
Creamer	10	18	____
Cup	10	18	____
Goblet, 1 oz. cordial	15		____
Goblet, 2 oz. wine	15		____
Goblet, 3 oz. wine	15		____
Goblet, 9 oz. champagne, 6"	12		____
Ice bucket	60	90	____

DIAMOND QUILTED (Cont.)	Pink, Green, & Amber	Blue & Black	Qty
Mayonnaise, 3-pc. set	45	65	____
Mayo. comport	15	25	____
Mayo. ladle	20	30	____
Mayo. under plate	10	10	____
Pitcher	60		____
Plate, 6.5" sherbet w/indent	8	8	____
Plate, 7" salad	10	10	____
Plate, 8" luncheon	12	14	____
Plate, 14" sandwich	20		____
Punch bowl	400		____
Punch bowl foot (base)	250		____
Salver, 8.25" (resembles a pedestal cake plate)	50	50	____
Salver, 10" (resembles a pedestal cake plate)	50	50	____
Sandwich server w/center handle	30	50	____
Saucer	5	5	____
Sherbet, 3.5"	10	15	____
Sugar	10	18	____
Tumbler, 1.5 oz. whiskey	15		____
Tumbler, 6 oz. w/foot	10		____
Tumbler, 9 oz. water, flat	15		____
Tumbler, 9 oz. water w/foot	15		____
Tumbler, 12 oz. iced tea, flat	18		____
Tumbler, 12 oz. iced tea w/foot	18		____
Vase	60	80	____

Note: Red items twice those in pink. Basket with metal bail in a variety of sizes, $25-65. Larger baskets command higher prices.

DIANA
(1937-1941 Federal Glass Company)

Diana is a pattern that is rising in its level of popularity. It stood unnoticed by collectors for years and now dealers are finding sales of this pattern on the increase. It is a straight-forward pattern having all the important pieces to set a table in a design that is neither particularly feminine nor masculine. The glass is not thin and delicate like some patterns, giving many new collectors a sense of security when handling it.

Pink continues to be the most popular color of Diana, but amber also sells well. The 12.5" console bowl and 11" sandwich plate are the most common pieces in any color. The candy dish and shakers are getting more difficult to find. The salt and pepper shakers in Diana are the same dimensions as the Sharon shakers. Federal Glass Company incorporated the Diana mold and the Sharon mold. This was a common practice with glass manufacturers.

The demitasse cups and saucers are not child's dinnerware because there are no child's pieces in this pattern. Six demitasse cups and saucers fit on a circular rack for display, but we were unable to photograph this arrangement. Demitasse cups and saucers are not common in Depression Glass dinnerware. You will, however, find other examples in Fire-King.

Many of you thanked us for clearly showing the Diana sherbet. (You're welcome!) Do look at the tumbler shown in the amber grouping as it, too, is an item that is often confused by inexperienced dealers and new collectors.

Back row: 11.5" sandwich plate; *front row:* 12.5" console bowl w/scalloped rim. *Courtesy of Charlie Diefenderfer.*

Back row: creamer, 9.5" dinner plate, 4.25" tumbler; *front row:* cream soup bowl, sugar, cup & saucer.

Sherbet.

9" salad bowl, demitasse cup & saucer, 5" cereal bowl.

Above: Shakers in two colors. *Courtesy of Michael Rothenberger/ Mike's Collectibles.*

Right: Candy jar w/ lid. *Courtesy of Marie Talone.*

DIANA	Pink	Amber	Crystal	Qty
Ash tray, 3.5"	5		5	____
Bowl, 5" cereal	12	12	5	____
Bowl, cream soup	25	20	5	____
Bowl, 9" salad	30	20	10	____
Bowl, 11" console	40	30	10	____
Bowl, 12.5" console w/scalloped rim	35	25	18	____
Candy jar w/lid	50	50	15	____
Coaster, 3.5"	10	10	2	____
Creamer	12	12	5	____
Cup	20	10	3	____
Cup, demitasse, 2" tall	40		8	____
Plate, 6" bread & butter	8	5	2	____
Plate, 9.5" dinner	20	14	5	____
Plate, 11.5" sandwich	25	20	10	____
Platter, 12"	35	25	10	____
Rack (metal) to hold 6 demitasse sets	25			____
Salt & pepper	90	110	35	____
Saucer	8	5	2	____
Saucer, demitasse, 4.25"	10		4	____
Sherbet	12	12	3	____
Sugar	12	12	5	____
Tumbler, 4.25"	45	30	10	____

Note: Green ash tray, $10. Red demitasse cup, $12; saucer, $8.

Reproduction Information: 13.25" scalloped-edge bowl is new.

DOGWOOD

(1930-1934 Macbeth-Evans Glass Company)

Dogwood is among the oldest and most popular of all the Depression Glass patterns. The design is appealing, and a wide variety of items were made. The dogwood blossom is the state flower for several states contributing to its popularity among collectors. Pink is the most desired color and the easiest to find; although, some items are quite elusive. Less people collect green and less green Dogwood is found. The green 8" luncheon plate is common, but beyond that most anything else becomes a challenge. Fortunately few collectors are looking for Monax and Cremax as pieces in these colors are few and far between.

There are two creamers, two sugars, and two cups. The thick versus thin shapes are a bit different from each other beyond just the gauge of the glass. The thin ones are more difficult to find, seem to blend more consistently with other Dogwood pieces, and are in greater demand as reflected in the pricing.

Macbeth-Evans Glass Company used the same molds for both Dogwood and Thistle. More and more collectors are combining patterns to create an eclectic table setting. These two patterns do compliment each other.

Cup & saucer, 4.75" tumbler, 8" almost straight-sided pitcher. *Courtesy of Diefenderfer's Collectibles & Antiques.*

DOGWOOD	SPink	Green	Monax & Cremax	Qty
Bowl, 5.5" cereal	35	45	10	____
Bowl, rolled edge cereal	65	65		____
Bowl, 8.5" berry	65	130	40	____
Bowl, 10.25" fruit	600	300	150	____
Cake plate, 11"	1250			____
Cake plate, 13"	150	150	200	____
Coaster, 3.25"	trtp*			____
Creamer, 2.5" thin, no foot	30	50		____
Creamer, 3.25" thick, footed	22			____
Cup, thin	22	45		____
Cup, thick	18		45	____
Lamp shade (10.25" bowl w/hole)	125	125	50	____
Pitcher, 8", almost straight sided	275	575		____
Pitcher, 8", "fat" w/ice lip (similar to American Sweetheart pitcher)	650			____
Plate, 6" bread & butter	10	10	24	____
Plate, 8" luncheon	12	12		____
Plate, 9" dinner	40			____
Plate, 10.5" grill w/ pattern only on rim	25	25		____
Plate, 10.5" grill with pattern all over plate	30			____
Plate, 12" salver	45		20	____
Platter, 12"	800			____
Saucer	8	8	20	____
Sherbet, 2 styles	40	150		____
Sugar, 2.5" thin, no foot	30	45		____
Sugar, 3.25" thick, footed	22			____
Tumbler, 3.5"	400			____
Tumbler, 4"	50	120		____
Tumbler, 4.75"	60	125		____
Tumbler, 5"	95	140		____
Tumbler, molded w/decorated band near top	30			____

*trtp = too rare to price

Note: Yellow cereal and luncheon plate, $75 each. Crystal 8" luncheon plate, $10.

Back row: 9" dinner plate, 8" luncheon plate, 4.75" tumbler; *front row:* thick cup & saucer, sherbet on 6" bread & butter plate. *Courtesy of David G. Baker.*

Monax 12" salver, Cremax 8.5" berry bowl.

Back row: 13" cake plate, 12" salver; *front:* 8.5" berry bowl, 5.5" cereal bowl, 3.25" sugar, 3.25" creamer, 2.5" creamer, thin cup. *Courtesy of David G. Baker.*

10.25" fruit bowl.

DORIC
(1935-1938 Jeannette Glass Company)

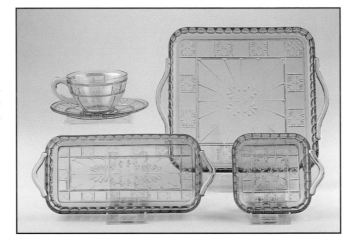

3-part candy dishes with 8.5" hammered aluminum tray. *Courtesy of Kevin L. Weiss.*

Close-up of mark on aluminum tray. *Courtesy of Kevin L. Weiss.*

Only a handful of Depression Glass patterns are equally popular in green and in pink. Doric is one of these patterns. It is hard to find any quantity of Doric and even harder for a dealer to keep in stock because of its tremendous demand.

Shown are the three-part candy dishes with the Everlast hammered aluminum tray. The candy dishes are available in iridescent (marigold, from the 1970s), green, Delphite, pink, and ultramarine which is shown in the tray. They measure about 6" x 7" and the tray is about 8.5" in diameter. These candy dishes are void of design except for the Doric motif found in the very center. Many people do not recognize these as Depression Glass, or particularly as Doric, so stumbling into an inexpensive candy dish is quite possible.

Care needs to be taken prior to buying the 4.5" berry bowls. The glass along the rim is often nicked from use. A moment taken to run a fingernail along the edge may save one from purchasing a damaged item. Another item to watch is the salt shaker. Salt is notorious for damaging the original metal shaker lids on old glass. However, Doric is a softer glass and the salt shaker is often permanently cloudy, and we do mean permanently. Don't buy a cloudy shaker with the expectation of taking it home, washing it, and returning it to its original shine. This just won't happen.

If the Doric pattern appeals to you, be sure to check Doric and Pansy.

Back row: cup & saucer, 8" x 8" relish tray; *front row:* 4" x 8" relish tray, 4" x 4" relish tray. *Courtesy of Don & Terry Yusko.*

Back row: 9" dinner plate, 10.25" cake plate, 4.5" berry bowl; *front row:* cup & saucer, salt & pepper. *Courtesy of Charlie Diefenderfer.*

DORIC	Pink	Green	Delphite	Qty
Bowl, 4.5" berry	12	12	50	____
Bowl, 5" cream soup	500	500		____
Bowl, 5.5" cereal	80	100		____
Bowl, 8.25" berry	35	35	150	____
Bowl, 9" w/2 handles	25	25		____
Bowl, 9" oval vegetable	35	40		____
Butter dish base	25	35		____
Butter dish lid	55	65		____
Butter complete	80	100		____
Cake plate, 10.25"	30	30		____
Candy dish, 3 parts	15	15	18	____
Candy dish, 3 parts in				
Hammered aluminum tray	75	75	75	____
Candy jar w/lid, 8"	40	40		____
Coaster, 3"	20	20		____
Creamer	18	18		____
Cup	10	10		____
Pitcher, 5.5", flat	50	65	1400	____
Pitcher, 7.5", footed	700	1200		____
Plate, 6" sherbet	8	8		____
Plate, 7" salad	28	28		____
Plate, 9" dinner	25	25		____
Plate, 9" grill	25	28		____
Platter, 12"	30	30		____
Relish tray, 4" x 4"	10	10		____
Relish tray, 4" x 8"	12	20		____
Relish tray, 2-tier, 4" x 4"				
over 4" x 8"	75	75		____
Relish tray, 8" x 8"	40	40		____
Salt & pepper	45	40		____
Saucer	5	5		____
Sherbet	14	18	5	____
Sugar base	18	18		____
Sugar lid	22	32		____
Tray, 10" w/handles	20	20		____
Tumbler, 4", footed (foot is				
barely more than a ring				
of extra glass)	75	100		____
Tumbler, 4.5", flat	75	120		____
Tumbler, 5", footed (foot is				
barely more than a ring				
of extra glass)	90	150		____

Note: Yellow 7.5" pitcher, too rare to price. 3-part candy dish, iridescent from 1970s, $10. Ultramarine, $30. Serrated 9" dinner, $200.

Top: 7" salad plate, 9" bowl w/2 handles, 5" tumbler. *Courtesy of Charlie Diefenderfer.*

Bottom: Butter dish. *Courtesy of Charlie Diefenderfer.*

DORIC AND PANSY

(1937-1938 Jeannette Glass Company)

Ultramarine Doric and Pansy was predominantly distributed in England and Canada, so for years it was difficult for Americans to find. Collectors in "the States" had to depend on dealers traveling, buying, and bringing into their area these elusive pieces. Then came the Internet and suddenly there were no more geographic constraints. Doric and Pansy is one of several patterns that has suffered from Internet exposure, or more aptly put, Internet overexposure. There has been such a glut of offerings of the "Pretty Polly Party Dishes" that the prices are actually falling, at least for now. Remember, supply and demand dictate the prices. In an effort to accurately indicate the values of all pieces it is necessary for us to share these lower values. The current supply is simply too high to support previously published prices. This is also true of the salt and pepper shakers. These used to be a rare commodity, but they have also been showing up in greater numbers on the Internet.

Doric and Pansy is most collected in ultramarine and in pink, but crystal (clear) is becoming increasingly popular.

Jeannette Glass Company manufactured this as well as Doric. These patterns work very well together, and Doric has offerings unavailable in Doric and Pansy. You may want to supplement your collection of pink with easier-to-find, generally less expensive Doric. If you are building an ultramarine collection, the tumblers will be the most difficult items of all. The 4.25" tumbler is very hard to find, and the 4.5" tumbler is virtually impossible to find.

Cup. *Courtesy of Neil McCurdy-Hoosier Kubboard Glass.*

Back: 9" bowl w/ handles; *middle:* butter & 6" sherbet plate; *front:* 8" berry bowl & 4.5" berry bowl. *Courtesy of Charlie Diefenderfer.*

Sugar, salt & pepper, creamer. *Courtesy of Vic & Jean Laermans.*

DORIC AND PANSY	Ultramarine	Pink	Qty
Bowl, 4.5" berry	25	15	____
Bowl, 8" berry	100	35	____
Bowl, 9" w/handles	40	25	____
Butter dish base	100		____
Butter dish lid	400		____
Butter complete	500		____
Creamer	130		____
Cup	25	15	____
Plate, 6" sherbet	20	13	____
Plate, 7" salad	50		____
Plate, 9" dinner	40		____
Salt & pepper	300		____
Saucer	10	8	____
Sugar	130		____
Tray, 10" sandwich w/2 open handles	40		____
Tumbler, 4.25", 10 oz.	125		____
Tumbler, 4.5", 9 oz.	trtp*		____

*trtp = too rare to price

Note: Crystal items 1/2 of ultramarine.

"Pretty Polly Party Dishes" Child's Set

"PRETTY POLLY PARTY DISHES" Child's Set	Ultramarine	Pink	Qty
Creamer	65	50	____
Cup	50	40	____
Plate	18	12	____
Saucer	13	10	____
Sugar	65	50	____
14-piece set	454	348	____

"Pretty Polly Party Dishes."

EMERALD CREST
called "GREEN CREST" in 1949
(1949-1955 Fenton Art Glass Company)

Emerald Crest was part of a series of "Crest" glassware. Aqua Crest was introduced in 1940, Crystal Crest in 1942, and then Emerald Crest. Later offerings included Ivory Crest and Peach Crest in 1940, Silver Crest in 1943, Rose Crest in 1944, and Snow Crest in 1950. One can see how successful these lovely pieces from the Fenton Art Glass Company were.

We were delighted to add some of Doris McMullen's treasures to our book. Her 5" crimped bowl is hand painted with ivy and signed with the initials "EZ." The candlesticks have an unusual shape that collectors of Emerald Crest will detect right away. The 6.5" relish (handled leaf) was an eBay purchase that cost $135. Remember, for every winning bidder there was at least one under bidder, so we feel the previously listed value of $80 is conservative.

The larger-sized plates are getting very difficult to find. If this is a pattern you are just beginning to collect it will take some patience and perseverance.

Some collectors specialize in one color, such as Emerald Crest, while others enjoy all versions. Still other collectors so appreciate Fenton's quality in craftsmanship and design that they buy anything Fenton. If it's Fenton glassware, they are interested!

Measurements were carefully made at the time of photographing these pieces in an attempt to accurately document this pattern. Prices reflect the availability of respective items. Baskets have delicate handles that are subject to damage. Those in perfect condition are worth considerably more than small plates. The green mayonnaise ladle is much harder to find than the crystal one. Candle holders are simply difficult to find.

10.25" crimped bowl, 6.5" relish (handled leaf), 5" candle holders. *Courtesy of Doris McMullen.*

Back: 10.25" dinner plate; *front row:* 3" sugar, 6" beaded melon pitcher, 3.25" creamer. *Courtesy of Vic & Jean Laermans.*

5" crimped bowl w/hand painted ivy. *Courtesy of Doris McMullen.*

5.5" vase w/1 turned up side, 4.5" flowerpot w/attached saucer, 8" vase. *Courtesy of Doris McMullen.*

EMERALD/GREEN CREST	White w/green rim	Qty
Basket, 5"	90	____
Basket, 6"	90	____
Basket, 7" w/smooth sides	120	____
Basket, 7" w/beaded sides	175	____
Bottle w/ stopper, 5.5"	140	____
Bowl, 4" low dessert	25	____
Bowl, 5" finger	25	____
Bowl, 5" crimped bonbon	30	____
Bowl, 5.5" soup	50	____
Bowl, 7" w/crimped rim	40	____
Bowl, 8.5" w/flared rim	50	____
Bowl, 9.5"	60	____
Bowl, 10.25", crimped	80	____
Bowl, 10.5" low salad	80	____
Cake plate, 13" w/foot	95	____
Candle holder, ea.	90	____
Comport, 3.75" w/5.5" dia.	45	____
Comport, 3.75" w/7" dia.	45	____
Comport, 6"	45	____
Creamer, 3.25" w/green twisted handle	50	____
Cup	40	____
Flower pot w/attached saucer, 4.5" tall	70	____
Mayonnaise, 3 pieces w/green ladle	100	____
Mayonnaise bowl	35	____
Ladle, crystal	10	____
Ladle, green	40	____
Under plate	25	____
Pitcher, 6" "beaded melon" w/twisted handle	75	____
Plate, 6.5" sherbet	20	____
Plate, 7"	25	____
Plate, 8"	35	____
Plate, 10.25" dinner	45	____
Plate, 11.5"	55	____
Plate, 12"	75	____
Plate, 13" cake w/foot	95	____
Plate, 16" torte	75	____
Relish, handled leaf, 6.5"	100	____
Saucer	15	____
Sherbet	30	____
Sugar, 3" w/twisted handles	50	____
Tidbit, 2-tier w/plates	60	____
Tidbit, 3-tier w/bowls	125	____
Tidbit, 3-tier w/plates	85	____
Top hat	45	____
Vase, 4" w/crimped rim	45	____
Vase, 4.5" fan	25	____
Vase, 5.5" w/1 turned up side	50	____
Vase, 6" w/crimped rim	45	____
Vase, 6" w/1 turned up rim	65	____
Vase, 6.5" fan	40	____
Vase, 8" w/crimped rim	60	____
Vase, bud w/ beaded sides	50	____

12" plate, 3 baskets. *Courtesy of Vic & Jean Laermans.*

3-tier tidbit using 12" plate, 8" plate, & 6.5" plate and 13" cake plate. *Courtesy of Doris McMullen.*

ENGLISH HOBNAIL

(1928-1950, Crystal & Amber until 1983 Westmoreland
Glass Company)

We are humbled. We thought we had listed all of the English Hobnail in our first book, but we have more, yes more, to show and to tell you about.

From Maine comes a wonderful jade-ite sherbet. Here are some measurements: square foot, 2-3/8" (simplified to 2.25"); height, 2.25"; diameter, 4.5". There are 24 rays on the foot in the signature design that is identical to a Miss America goblet so a rule has been broken!

Found with an original sticker is a pink 5.25" bowl. We don't know if it is available in other colors.

The Master Candy is flashed in red with gold trim. It was pictured in the front of the first edition, but it was not priced.

We stumbled across two crystal (clear) pieces with black trim, a 6.5" plate with a depressed center and a 3.5 oz. cocktail. Experience tells us that there must be more like these.

A collector in Pennsylvania sent us a picture of a previously unlisted green comport that is 9" tall and 6.5" in diameter with a round foot. Have you seen one in pink?

The longest list of Depression Glass has just gotten longer.

3 oz. cocktail w/ round foot, cup & saucer, 5.5" plate,
sherbet w/ tall stem & round foot, pair of 9" candlesticks.

Back: sherbet w/ short stem & round foot; *front row:* creamer
w/ hexagonal foot, 4.5" finger bowl, 5 oz. claret w/ round foot.

2 oz. oil cruet w/ stopper.

Merely a guess, but we suspect this will only continue to grow!

Back to a few particulars for those of you new to this pattern. Many a beginning collector will confuse Miss America and English Hobnail. They are similar, but there are a few differences that may provide some clarification. For the most part the starburst in the center of English Hobnail pieces is neither circular nor even. There are longer and shorter rays as seen in the picture of the easeled saucer. The points on English Hobnail are rounder and a bit stretched. English Hobnail plates often have indents while Miss America plates are smooth and level until the rim. Learning the difference may help you detect an error or find a bargain.

ENGLISH HOBNAIL	Pink & green	Turquoise/ Ice blue	Amber & Crystal	Qty
Ash tray, 3"	20		5	____
Ash tray, 4.5" round or square		25	5	____
Basket, 5" w/handle			30	____
Basket, 6" w/ handle			40	____
Bon bon, 6.5" w/1handle	25	40	15	____
Bottle, 5 oz. toilet	35	60	25	____
Bowl, 3" cranberry	20			____
Bowl, 4" rose (curves inward)	50		15	____
Bowl, 4.5" finger	18		10	____
Bowl, 4.5" round nappy	15	30	10	____
Bowl, 4.5" square finger w/foot	18	35	10	____
Bowl, 5" round nappy	18	40	10	____
Bowl, cream soup			15	____
Bowl, 5.25" round	35			____
Bowl, 5.5" bell nappy			12	____
Bowl, 6" crimped dish, flat	20		14	____
Bowl, 6" rose (curves inward)			20	____
Bowl, 6" mayonnaise, flat w/flared rim	20		10	____
Bowl, 6" round nappy	17		10	____
Bowl, 6" square nappy	17		10	____
Bowl, 6.5" grapefruit w/ inner rim	25		12	____
Bowl, 6.5" round nappy	22		14	____
Bowl, 6.5" square nappy			14	____
Bowl, 7" w/6 points (pinched and crimped)			25	____
Bowl, 7" oblong spoon			20	____
Bowl, 7" preserve			15	____
Bowl, 7" round nappy	25		15	____
Bowl, 7.5" bell nappy			18	____
Bowl, 8" cupped nappy (curves inward)	30		25	____
Bowl, 8" w/foot	50		30	____
Bowl, 8" 2-handled hexagonal w/foot	75	125	50	____
Bowl, 8" pickle, flat *R*	30		15	____
Bowl, 8" round nappy	35		25	____
Bowl, 8"w/6 points (pinched and crimped)			25	____
Bowl, 9" bell nappy			30	____
Bowl, 9" celery, flat	35		18	____
Bowl, 9.5" round, crimped			30	____
Bowl, 10" flared, flat	45		35	____
Bowl, 10" crimped oval			35	____
Bowl, 11" bell			35	____
Bowl, 11" rolled edge	50	100	30	____
Bowl, 12" celery, flat				
w/outward roll	35		20	____
Bowl, 12" flanged console	60		30	____
Bowl, 12" w/flare			35	____
Bowl, 12" crimped oval			40	____
Candelabra, each			20	____
Candlestick, each, 3.5"	15	20	10	____
Candlestick, each, 5.5"			10	____
Candlestick, each, 9"	25		10	____
Candy dish w/lid, 6" w/3 feet	60		30	____
Candy jar w/lid, ½ lb., diamond shaped	65	120	35	____
Candy jar w/lid, master	250		150	____
Chandelier, 17" shade w/prisms			500	____
Cheese and cover, 6"			40	____
Cheese and cover, 8.75"			60	____
Cigarette box w/cover, 4.5" x 2.5"	35	60	25	____
Cigarette Jar w/cover (round)	35	70	25	____
Coaster 3"			8	____
Compote, 5", round & square foot	25		15	____
Compote, 5.5" sweetmeat (ball at base of stem)			25	____
Compote, 5.5" bell, round & square foot			20	____
Compote, 6" honey, flat w/ round foot	30		18	____
Compote, 6" honey, flat w/square foot			18	____
Compote, 8" sweetmeat	60		40	____
Compote, 9"	100			____
Creamer, w/foot, 4", hexagonal *R*	25	50	10	____
Creamer, low & flat			10	____
Creamer, square w/foot	50		10	____
Cup	20	30	10	____
Cup, demitasse	60		30	____
Cup, punch			8	____
Decanter w/stopper, 20 oz.			70	____
Egg cup			18	____
Hat dish, high			20	____
Hat dish, low			18	____
Ice tub, 4"	50	80	25	____
Ice tub, 5.5"	75	100	50	____
Icer, square base			50	____
Ladle for punch bowl			30	____
Lamp, candlestick (several styles)			40	____
Lamp, 6.25" (electric)	75		40	____
Lamp, 9.25" (electric)	150		50	____
Lamp, 9.25" (oil)			110	____
Lampshade			200	____
Marmalade w/cover	50	75	30	____
Mustard w/cover, square			28	____
Nut, individual, w/foot	15		8	____
Oil cruet w/stopper, 2 oz. (1 handle)			20	____
Oil cruet w/ stopper, 6 oz. (1 handle)			30	____
Oil-vinegar combination bottle, 6 oz. (no handles)			40	____
Parfait, round foot			15	____
Pitcher, 23 oz., round	150		60	____
Pitcher, 32 oz., straight sides	200		70	____
Pitcher, 38 oz., round	250		80	____
Pitcher, 60 oz., round	320		90	____
Pitcher, 64 oz., straight sides	350		100	____
Plate, 5.5"	10	10	5	____
Plate, liner for cream soup			8	____

Item				
Plate, 6" square liner for finger bowls	10		5	____
Plate, 6", square			5	____
Plate, 6.5"	10		7	
Plate, 6.5" round liner for finger bowls	10		7	____
Plate, 6.5" w/ depressed center			7	____
Plate, 8"	14		8	____
Plate, 8.5"	14	30	15	____
Plate, 8.5", plain edge			10	____
Plate, 8.5" w/ 3 feet			10	
Plate, 8.75"			10	
Plate, 10"	40	70	15	____
Plate, 10" square			15	
Plate, 10.5" grill			15	____
Plate, 12" square			25	____
Plate, 14" torte	65		30	____
Plate, 12" square			35	____
Plate, 20.5" torte			65	____
Puff box w/lid, 6" round	50	80	30	____
Punch bowl			225	____
Punch bowl stand, 4.75" tall			75	____
Relish, 8" w/3 sections			18	____
Salt & pepper, flat	150	225		____
Salt & pepper, round foot, 4.5"	85		30	____
Salt & pepper, square foot			30	____
Saucer	5	8	3	____
Saucer, square			3	____
Saucer, demitasse	15		10	____
Saucer, demitasse, square			10	____
Sherbet, low w/ 1 glass ball on stem			8	____
Sherbet, short stem, round foot		15	8	____
Sherbet, short stem, square foot	12		8	____
Sherbet, tall stem, round foot	18		10	____
Sherbet, tall stem, square foot	18	40	10	____
Sherbet, tall, 2 balls of glass on stem, round foot			10	____
Stem, 1 oz. cordial, round foot			15	____
Stem, 1 oz. cordial, glass ball on stem, round foot			15	____
Stem, 1 oz. cordial, square foot			15	____
Stem, 2 oz. wine, square foot	30	60	10	____
Stem, 2 oz. wine, round foot			10	____
Stem, 2.25 oz. wine, glass ball on stem, round foot			10	____
Stem, 3 oz. cocktail, round foot	20	40	10	____
Stem, 3 oz. cocktail, square foot			10	____
Stem, 3.5 oz. cocktail, glass ball on stem			8	____
Stem, 5 oz. claret, round foot			15	____
Stem, 5 oz. oyster cocktail, square foot	20		10	____
Stem, 8 oz. water, square foot	30	50	10	____
Stem, champagne, 2 glass balls on stem, round foot			10	____
Sugar, w/foot, 4", hexagonal *R*	25	50	10	____
Sugar, low, flat			10	____
Sugar, square foot	50		10	____
Tid-bit, 2 tier	50	80	30	____

Item			
Tumbler, 1.5 oz. whiskey		15	____
Tumbler, 3 oz. whiskey		13	____
Tumbler, 5 oz. ginger ale, flat		10	____
Tumbler, 5 oz. old fashioned		10	
Tumbler, 5 oz. ginger ale, round foot		10	
Tumbler, 5 oz. ginger ale, square foot		10	
Tumbler, 7 oz. juice, round foot		10	
Tumbler, 7 oz. juice, square foot		10	
Tumbler, 8 oz. water, glass ball on short stem, round foot		10	____
Tumbler, 8 oz. water, flat	25	10	____
Tumbler, 9 oz. water, glass ball on short stem, round foot		10	____
Tumbler, 9 oz. water, round foot		10	____
Tumbler, 9 oz. water, square foot		10	____
Tumbler, 10 oz. iced tea, flat	30	15	____
Tumbler, 11 oz. iced tea, glass ball on short stem, round foot		10	____
Tumbler, 11 oz. iced tea, square foot		14	____
Tumbler, 12 oz. iced tea, flat	33	12	____
Tumbler, 12.5 oz. iced tea, round foot		10	____
Urn, 11" (w/lid 15")	400	50	____
Vase, 6.5" ivy bowl, square foot, crimped rim		35	____
Vase, 6.5" flower holder, square foot		25	____
Vase, 7.5" flip	100	30	____
Vase, 7.5", flip jar w/ cover	120	70	____
Vase, 8" w/square foot		35	____
Vase, 8.5", flared top	125	275	40	____
Vase, 10", Straw jar	110	75	____

Note: Cobalt and Black items 30% higher than Turquoise prices. Milk glass cigarette lighter, $25. Jade-ite sherbet, $300. Pieces with crystal with black trim, half of crystal. Master candy with red flash too rare to price.

Reproduction Information: New hexagonal creamers and sugars have Westmoreland circular marks on bottom; old are unmarked. 8" flat pickle bowl new marked with Westmoreland mark; old unmarked. Individual nut with foot new made in other colors and may have "S" on bottom.

Creamers & sugars w/ hexagonal feet. *Courtesy of Michael Rothenberger/Mike's Collectibles.*

Jade-ite sherbet measuring 2.25" tall & 4.5" in diameter. *Courtesy of Ruth Farrington.*

5.25" bowl w/ original sticker.

Master candy jar. *Courtesy of Mike Rothenberger / Mike's Collectibles.*

6.5" plate w/depressed center & 3.5 oz. cocktail with black trim.

FIRE-KING ALICE
(1945-1949 Anchor Hocking Glass Corporation)

Jade-ite continues to be extremely popular, and due to this ongoing trend jade-ite Alice is in great demand. There are no bowls; Alice was made only in cups, saucers, and 9.5" dinner plates. Packing cups and saucers in oatmeal, jade-ite being distributed in the greatest quantity, Anchor Hocking Glass Company introduced Alice in 1945. Dinner plates could be purchased at five and dime stores. As dinners didn't sell that well, Anchor Hocking added no other pieces to the Alice line. Even though there are few options, jade-ite lovers love Alice.

There are no manufacturer marks on most pieces of Alice but rather a series of concentric circles. New collectors of Fire-King mistakenly expect to buy "marked" pieces.

As for the other colors, these are actually harder to find than jade-ite. However, collectors are shying away from them at this time.

Above: Cup & saucer, 9.5" dinner w/ blue trim.

Right: Cup & saucer, 9.5" dinner in jade-ite.

FIRE-KING ALICE	Jade-ite	Blue trim	Red trim	Vitrock	Qty
Cup	10	15	35	7	____
Plate, 9.5" dinner	35	35	50	15	____
Saucer	2	5	15	3	____

FIRE-KING BREAKFAST SET

(1954-1956 Anchor Hocking Glass Corporation)

The pieces that make up this Fire-King line are not easy to find. Here is a breakdown of each item. The 5" cereal bowl is just a challenge to locate! The St. Denis cup is the easiest thing to find, even easier than the St. Denis saucer. Interesting to note, Anchor Hocking used the same St. Denis mold to create cups and saucers for Lake Como. Egg cups are available, but the $45 price is a far cry from the $7 price of 1994. The milk pitcher is very popular especially in variations not part of the Breakfast Set. Finally, the dinner plate is sometimes confused with a Restaurantware dinner plate. The rim of this plate is broader and turns up slightly. A Breakfast Set dinner plate is more valuable, so take care.

Any piece in this line is a worthwhile investment as availability continues to decrease and interest continues to grow.

It is very important to note that there is a line of "jade" glass from China being sold in gift shops that is meant to look like the Breakfast Set and the 1700 Line. These pieces are the wrong color, shape, and weight. We know for a fact that unscrupulous sellers have been placing Fire-King stickers and prices on these pieces that actually sell for only a few dollar apiece in gift shops. You need to be an informed and educated consumer. These new pieces are shown and their measurements provided, so buyers buy smart!

FIRE-KING BREAKFAST SET	Jade-ite	Qty
Bowl, 5" cereal, 2.5" deep *R*	125	____
Cup, 9 oz. St. Denis cup w/round handle *R*	10	____
Egg cup, 4" tall	45	____
Pitcher, milk, 4.5" tall, 20 oz.	105	____
Plate, 9.25" dinner *R*	50	____
Saucer, 6" St. Denis *R*	10	____

Note: 5" cereal bowl with red ivy trim: Azurite, $60; Jade-ite, $150. 5" cereal with green ivy trim, $60.

Reproduction Information: Cup, too heavy, unmarked, 2.75" tall. Saucer, too heavy, unmarked, 5.25" diameter; base is almost a .25" pedestal. Dinner plate, too heavy, unmarked, has a double rim on the underside, 10"; original plate is 9.25". Note: this glass is made in China. The color is a bit light and on the yellow side. The glass has minute ripples or lines that resemble sedimentary rock.

Reproduction jade-ite.

Back row: dinner plate, cup & saucer; *front row:* milk pitcher, egg cup, cereal bowl.

FIRE-KING CHARM

(1950-1956 Anchor Hocking Glass Corporation)

Jade-ite Charm continues to be popular among jade-ite collectors, but Azurite Charm has become the most popular color. This swing in taste may be due to collectors frustrated with the high prices and low availability of jade-ite Charm. If you have been updating your information with *Mauzy's Comprehensive Handbook of Depression Glass Prices 3rd Edition* you can see how the prices of all four colors continue to increase each year. Charm is performing better than the stock market!

Platters, dinner plates, and bowls are the most difficult pieces to find in any color, but Azurite anything sells! As slow as Forest Green and Royal Ruby cups and saucers are to sell, Azurite cups and saucers disappear! The same statement can be made for creamers and sugars.

Fire-King is extremely popular in Japan and Azurite Charm is among the favorites.

Be aware of the fact that Charm pieces are often unmarked. If you are looking for pieces with a Fire-King or Anchor Hocking mark you may look for a long time.

Forest green. *Back:* 9.25" dinner plate; *front row:* 6" soup bowl, creamer, sugar, cup & saucer.

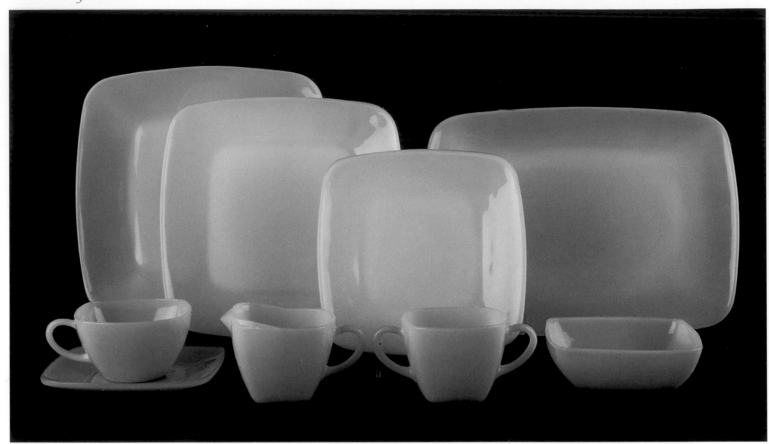

Above: Jade-ite. *Back row:* 9.25" dinner plate, 8.25" luncheon plate, 6.5" salad plate, platter; *front row:* cup & saucer, creamer, sugar, 4.75" dessert bowl.

Right & below: Azurite cup & saucer, 9.25" dinner plate, 8.5" luncheon plate, creamer, sugar.

FIRE-KING CHARM	Jade-ite White & Ivory	Azurite	Forest Green	Royal Ruby	Qty
Bowl, 4.75" dessert	24	10	6	8	____
Bowl, 6" soup	80	25	20		____
Bowl, 7.25" salad	80	35	18	25	____
Creamer	25	12	6		____
Cup	12	5	5	5	____
Plate, 6.5" salad	45	12	10		____
Plate, 8.25" luncheon	25	10	8	12	____
Plate, 9.25" dinner	65	20	30		____
Platter, 11" x 8"	80	25	25		____
Saucer	8	2	1	3	____
Sugar	25	12	6		____

Note: Pink saucer, $25. Azurite chili bowl marked "Fire-King Ovenware 4," $40.

FIRE-KING JANE RAY

(1946-1965 Anchor Hocking Glass Corporation)

Although Jane Ray prices have been creeping up through the years, it is still one of the most affordable ways to accumulate a pattern in jade-ite. So much Jane Ray was made for so many years that there seems to be a plethora of this highly recognizable glassware. Even with the attention paid to Fire-King and to jade-ite unused pieces with original stickers are still available.

The 6" plate is the same as a saucer but with no cup ring. The price has come down even though the availability has not increased. Simply put, the value is down because of the low demand. It seems as though collectors will simply pass on this plate rather than spend a great deal of money on one, or perhaps even eight, ten, or twelve depending on their needs. Creamers and sugars (especially sugar lids) have experienced the most dramatic change in price.

Very few collectors are looking for Ivory or Vitrock and for this reason few dealers carry these colors. If a greater interest in them develops one would surmise that a greater quantity of these pieces would find their way to the marketplace.

One of the problems of writing a book is that the actual writing occurs eight months before the book is available. Keeping this in mind the following information may or may not be accurate, but it should be shared, just in case it is true. By the time this goes to press we will know, and by the time this is an actual book you collectors and dealers may know. We have been told that Anchor Hocking is going to re-issue Jane Ray using the original molds. It will be a special 2000 edition and we were told that all pieces will be so marked. We've heard the marks will be molded on the bottom, and we've heard the marks will simply be paper labels. Be aware of this just in case.

FIRE-KING JANE RAY	Jade-ite	Qty
Bowl, 4.75" dessert	18	____
Bowl, 5.75" oatmeal	30	____
Bowl, 7.5" soup	28	____
Bowl, 8.25" vegetable	40	____
Bowl, 9" soup plate	trtp*	____
Creamer	15	____
Cup	7	____
Cup, demitasse	75	____
Plate, 6"	100	____
Plate, 7.75" salad	17	____
Plate, 9" dinner	15	____
Platter, 12"	35	____
Saucer	3	____
Saucer, demitasse	25	____
Sugar base	12	____
Sugar lid	30	____

*trtp = too rare to price

Note: Ivory & Vitrock items twice prices of Jade-ite.

Above: *Back row: 7.5" soup bowl, 12" platter, 9" dinner plate, 7.25" salad plate; front row: sugar w/ lid, creamer, cup & saucer, demitasse cup & saucer, 5.75" oatmeal bowl, 4.75" dessert bowl.*

Right: Jane Ray Starter Set in original box.

11" serving plate, 4.75" dessert bowl, 9.25" dinner plate.

Above: 1954 advertisement featuring Gray Laurel, Peach Lustre Laurel, and Jane Ray.

Right: Cup & saucer, 9.25" dinner plate, 4.75" dessert bowl, sugar, creamer.

FIRE-KING LAUREL
(1951-1965   Anchor Hocking Glass Corporation)

Of the Laurel color choices available, gray is the most popular with the other colors having a minimal following. Gray Laurel has a tendency to lose its shine showing wear to the color, particularly on the 9.25" dinner plates. However, it is not an impossibility to put together a service in good condition.

Peach Lustre is easily found, but at this time few are buying it. Some dealers don't keep Peach Lustre Laurel in stock as it is such a slow moving commodity. The Peach Luster color is also found on colonial rim mixing bowls, batter bowls, swirl mixing bowls, chili bowls, and mugs. It is also used in Fire-King Shell, a pattern presented in this book. The lighter color seen on ovenware is the equally overlooked "Copper Luster."

FIRE-KING LAUREL	Gray	Peach Lustre	Ivory, White, & Ivory white	Qty
Bowl, 4.75" dessert	10	4	12	____
Bowl, 7.5" soup plate	20	10	25	____
Bowl, 8.25" vegetable	30	10	40	____
Creamer	10	4	10	____
Cup	8	4	8	____
Plate, 7.25" salad	15	8	15	____
Plate, 9.25" dinner	12	8	15	____
Plate, 11" serving	30	15	40	____
Saucer	5	1	5	____
Sugar	10	4	10	____

Note: Jade-ite cup, too rare to price.

Reproduction Information: Jade-ite is made new in a totally wrong color with a bottom stamped "402," a diamond, and a "4."

FIRE-KING MISCELLANEOUS JADE-ITE

(Anchor Hocking Glass Corporation)

Fire-King jade-ite is such a popular area of collecting that it became necessary to cover the "odd ball" items that aren't part of the dinnerware lines. This listing is a direct result of requests by readers and users of the Mauzy Depression Glass books. We hope that it meets your needs, and if there are items we neglected please let us know so they can be included in the future.

Condition is very important when dealing with these pieces. Items listed that were kitchen glass received daily use. Collectors want their jade-ite to look as if it has never been used, with no wear or scratching and a shiny gleam.

The groupings should help to distinguish one item from another, but here are a few more insights. The clear lid on the butter dish may or may not say Fire-King. Add $15 if it does. Five-inch Swirl mixing bowls seem to be disappearing. For a while there was always one available on eBay, but this is changing. The Maple Leaf is actually a spoon rest albeit a really poorly designed one! It will, however, make a nice serving bowl, but if you try to use it for its intended purpose any large spoon will fall out. The Deco Vase is available in fired-on colors. These are also popular, but jade-ite is still the overall favorite.

And now a piece of Anchor Hocking trivia for you glass fanatics: Anchor Hocking numbered all boxes of glass. Cartons with jade-ite were prefixed with a "G" for "green."

One of the problems of writing a book is that the actual writing occurs eight months before the book is available. Keeping this in mind the following information may or may not be accurate, but it should be shared, just in case it is true. By the time this goes to press we will know, and by the time this is an actual book you collectors and dealers may know. We have been told that Anchor Hocking is going to re-issue various jade-ite pieces using the original molds. It will be a special 2000 edition and we were told that all pieces will be so marked. We've heard the marks will be molded on the bottom, and we've heard the marks will simply be paper labels. Be aware of this just in case.

Back row: Splash proof bowl, Swirl bowl, Beaded Rim bowl, Colonial rim bowl; *front row:* Swedish Modern (Teardrop) bowl, custard, Chili bowl.

The shaving mug is on the left. Note the flat bottom.

Milk pitcher from Breakfast Set next to Bead and Bar pitcher.

Batter bowl & Maple leaf both w/original stickers.

FIRE-KING MISCELLANEOUS JADE-ITE	Jade-ite	Qty
Bowl, batter .75" rim	45	____
Bowl, batter 1" rim	60	____
Bowl, Beaded Rim 4.75"	35	____
Bowl, Beaded Rim 6"	25	____
Bowl, Beaded Rim 7"	35	____
Bowl, Beaded Rim 8.5"	trtp*	____
Bowl, Chili, 5" diam., 2.25" deep	18	____
Bowl, Colonial Rim 6"	150	____
Bowl, Colonial Rim 7.25"	100	____
Bowl, Colonial Rim 8.75"	125	____
Bowl, Splash proof 6.75"	500	____
Bowl, Splash proof 7.5"	100	____
Bowl, Splash proof 8.5"	135	____
Bowl, Splash proof 9.5"	125	____
Bowl, Straight-sided 5"	30	____
Bowl, Swedish Modern, 1 pt., 6.5"	85	____
Bowl, Swedish Modern, 1 qt., 8"	200	____
Bowl, Swedish Modern, 2 qt., 9.5"	150	____
Bowl, Swedish Modern, 3 qt., 11"	150	____
Bowl, Swirl 5"	225	____
Bowl, Swirl 6"	35	____
Bowl, Swirl 7"	35	____
Bowl, Swirl 8"	30	____
Bowl, Swirl 9"	30	____
Butter dish base	125	____
Butter dish lid (clear)	40	____
Butter complete	165	____
Candy dish w/cover	110	____
Custard	80	____
Leaf & blossom set	40	____
leaf plate	17	____
blossom bowl	23	____
Maple leaf	30	____
Mug, thin 3.25" diam.	12	____

	Jade-ite	Qty
Pitcher, Bead & Bar	325	____
Range Set (grease & 2 shakers)	120	____
Grease Jar w/tulip lid	50	____
Shaker w/tulip lids ea.	35	____
Refrigerator dish w/clear lid 4" x 4"	45	____
Refrigerator dish w/clear lid 4" x 8"	75	____
Refrigerator dish w/lid, Philbe 4.5" x 5"	65	____
Refrigerator dish w/lid, Philbe 5.25" x 9.5"	85	____
Sea shell	35	____
Skillet, 1 spout	125	____
Skillet, 2 spout	175	____
Vase, Deco 5.25"	30	____

*trtp = too rare to price

Opposite page:
Center: *Back row:* 9.5" 3-compartment plate/grill, 9.5" 5-compartment plate, 9" dinner plate; *front row:* 5.5" bread & butter plate, 8" luncheon plate, 6.75" pie plate.

Bottom left: *Back row:* 7 oz. extra heavy coffee mug slightly different from one in front row, 7 oz. extra heavy cup & saucer; *front row:* 6 oz. slim hot chocolate mug, 7 oz. extra heavy coffee mug, 6 oz. straight cup & saucer.

FIRE-KING RESTAURANTWARE

(1948-1967 Anchor Hocking Glass Corporation)

Fire-King Restaurantware is the king of jade-ite dinnerware. It is the most popular line and offers the most options. Five years ago Restaurantware prices had a sudden and dramatic increase, but now are much more stable. Despite a huge increase in collectors, most pieces are still readily available. Typically, price is an indication of availability; commonly found pieces cost less and elusive pieces command a higher price.

There has been some confusion between Restaurantware bowls and chili bowls. Chili bowls are 2.25" deep with a diameter of 5" and have no rim unlike the G305 & G309 bowls, which are rimmed.

The price of the ball jug is for one in perfect condition. We do not recommend that you use a ball jug as it has a tendency to crack at the handle. Likewise before buying a ball jug be sure to hold it up to the light and examine the areas at the top and bottom of the handle as there are often "spiders" or cracks that are easy to miss with cursory examination.

9.5" 3-compartment grill plates are available with or without a tab. The tab is an extra area of glass designed to balance

Back row: 9.25" flat soup bowl, 8 oz. cereal bowl w/ flanged rim; *front row:* 15 oz. beaded rim bowl (deep), 4.75" fruit bowl.

these plates when they are stacked. If consistency is important to you take note as to whether or not your plates have these tabs. If you are just starting to accumulate grill plates those without tabs are usually easier to find and may actually cost a bit less although we assigned the same price to both. If you place a paper plate between "tab-less" grill plates they will stack as securely as plates having a tab.

We use Restaurantware as our "everyday" dishes. They look great with orange Bakelite in the fall, red and green Bakelite at Christmas, and any other color imaginable throughout the year. As there are no serving bowls we recommend using any of the Fire-King mixing bowls. If you check the listing "Fire-King Miscellaneous Jade-ite" you will see some of the great options that are available.

Back row: 9.75" oval "football" platter, 8.75" oval partitioned plate/indent platter, 11.5" oval platter; *front row:* 10 oz. bowl w/ beaded rim (sits on oval partitioned plate), 9.5" oval platter.

Demitasse cup & saucer.

Back row: two 9.5" 3-compartment grill plates, 11.5" platter; *middle row:* 7 oz. extra heavy coffee mug, 5" teardrop bowl ($20), 9.5" oval platter, 5.5" bread & butter plate; *front row:* 8 oz. cereal bowl w/ flanged rim, 4.75" fruit bowl, saucer, 6.75" pie plate. *Courtesy of Jesse Speicher.*

FIRE-KING REST. WARE	Jade-ite	White	Qty
Bowl, 4.75" fruit (G294)	18	8	____
Bowl, 5", handled	trtp*		____
Bowl, cereal w/flanged rim, 8 oz. (G305)	35	20	____
Bowl, 10 oz. (G309) w/beaded rim	50	25	____
Bowl, deep, 15 oz. (G300) w/beaded rim	40	20	____
Bowl, 9.25" flat soup (G298)	140	80	____
Cup, 6 oz. straight (G215) (resembles a mug)	14	8	____
Cup, 7 oz. extra heavy (G299) (resembles a coffee cup)	16	8	____
Cup, demitasse	75		____
Cup, handled soup	trtp*		____
Gravy/sauce boat	trtp*	35	____
Mug, coffee, 7 oz. (G212) (extra heavy and heavy)	25	7	____
Mug, slim hot chocolate, 6 oz.	30		____
Pitcher, ball jug (G787)	900		____
Plate, 5.5" bread & butter (G315)	20		____
Plate, 6.75" pie (G297)	15	7	____
Plate, 8" luncheon (G316)	80	25	____
Plate, 8.75" oval partitioned/ indent platter (G211)	110		____
Plate, 8.75" oval, no indent (G310)	150		____
Plate, 9" dinner (G306)	28	15	____
Plate, 9.5" 3-compartment/ grill w/or w/out a tab for stacking (G292)	35	12	____
Plate, 9.5" 5-compartment (G311)	55		____
Plate, 10.25" (G317)	trtp^x		____
Platter, 9.5" oval (G307)	60	25	____
Platter, 9.75" oval "football"	90	____	
Platter, 11.5" oval (G308)	50	30	____
Saucer, 6" (G295)	4	2	____
Saucer, demitasse	40		____
Saucer for soup mug	trtp*		____

Note: Azurite G294 Fruit bowl, $40. Roseite G299 Cup, $50.

*trtp = too rare to price

FIRE-KING SAPPHIRE BLUE

(1941-1956 Anchor Hocking Glass Corporation)

FIRE-KING SAPPHIRE BLUE	Blue	Qty
Baker, 1 pt., 4.5" x 5"	10	____
Baker, 1 pt., 5.5" round	8	____
Baker, 1 qt., 7.25" round	10	____
Baker, 1.5 qt., 8.25" round	12	____
Baker, 2 qt., 8.75" round	14	____
Bowl, 4.25" individual pie	25	____
Bowl, 5.25" cereal	24	____
Bowl, 5.75", 2.75" deep	trtp*	____
Bowl, 16 oz., w/measures	30	____
Cake pan, 8.75"	40	____
Casserole, 4.75" individual w/lid	12	____
Casserole, 1 pt., 5.5" knob-handled lid	20	____
Casserole, 1 qt., 7.25" knob-handled lid	25	____
Casserole, 1 qt., pie plate lid	20	____
Casserole, 1.5 qt., 8.25" knob-handled lid	30	____
Casserole, 1.5 qt., pie plate lid	25	____
Casserole, 2 qt., 8.75" knob-handled lid	30	____
Casserole, 2 qt., pie plate lid	25	____
Cup, 1 spout 8 oz. liquid measure	30	____
Cup, no spout 8 oz. dry measure	trtp*	____
Cup, 3 spouts, 8 oz. liquid measure	40	____
Custard cup, 2.75" deep	8	____
Custard cup, 3 shallower styles	6	____
Loaf pan	10	____
Mug, 2 styles	35	____
Nipple cover, "Binky's Nip-cap"	250	____
Nursing bottle, 4 oz.	20	____
Nursing bottle, 8 oz.	35	____
Nursing bottle, 8 oz., Fyrock	30	____
Nursing bottle, 8 oz., "Tuffy"	30	____
Percolator top, 2.25"	5	____
Pie plate, 8.25"	6	____
Pie plate, 9"	6	____
Pie plate, 9.5"	6	____
Pie plate, 10.25", juice saver	150	____
Popcorn popper**	40	____
Refrigerator dish w/lid, 4.5" x 5"	25	____
Refrigerator dish w/lid, 5.25" x 9.25"	20	____
Roaster, 8.75"	75	____
Roaster, 10.25"	60	____
Skillet, 7" w/4.5" handle	trtp*	____
Silex 2-cup dripolator	45	____
Silex 6-cup dripolator	200	____
Trivet w/2 tab handles	20	____
Utility bowl, 1 qt., 6.75"	30	____
Utility bowl, 1.5 qt., 8.25"	20	____
Utility bowl, 2 qt., 10.25"	20	____
Utility pan, 8.25" x 12.5"	35	____
Utility pan, 10.5" x 2" deep	35	____

*trtp = too rare to price

**Note: insert for popcorn popper to hold oil and corn, $25.

Anchor Hocking created Sapphire Blue as a practical and expansive line of ovenware. There is a vast array of cooking, baking, and storing pieces that still continue to be very useful.

Much is being said in regard to storing food in plastic. If you are going back to the "olden days" of storing leftovers in glass the casseroles and refrigerator dishes provide sizes for virtually all of your needs. We even have a few customers who are using pie plates as dinner plates!

The five-ounce custard cup is the most popular of all the sizes and styles. Shown are three variations with three different manufacturer marks. Note that the one in the middle does not have the Philbe design.

We have received some e-mail regarding the Sapphire Blue cake pan. Here is some clarification. The cake pan is Anchor Hocking item #B3450. It is 8.75" with two tab handles. The tab handles **do** have lines of glass that bump up from the tabs. Sound familiar? That is because the "Deep Cake Pan" as it was officially named, is actually one half of the small roaster.

As for the roasters, the tops and bottoms are identical. Both halves have tab handles with lines of extra glass that make it impossible to line up the handles. The handles of the lid will not fit correctly on top of the handles of the base. These pieces were designed to place the lid at a ninety-degree angle from the base. In other words, you will have handles at twelve o'clock, three o'clock, six o'clock, and nine o'clock.

Listed are a few numbers gleaned from original boxes:

Anchor Hocking marking	Listed as
B3407 1½-Quart Casserole	Casserole, 1.5 qt.
B3450 8 ¾" Cake Pan	Cake pan, 8.75"
B3461 9 5/8" Pie Plate	Pie Plate, 9.5"

Here is a hint if you find a piece of ovenware with baked-in dirt that fills the Philbe design: spray the glass with oven cleaner, let is stand for at least twenty minutes, and then scrub it with a stiff brush such as a discarded toothbrush. The dirt will break free from the glass and the item will be restored to its original beauty.

Back: 10.25" juice saver pie plate; *front row:* 4.75" individual casserole w/ lid, 1.5 quart casserole w/ knob-handled lid on trivet w/ 2 tab handles, 1.5 quart casserole w/ pie plate lid. *Courtesy of Charlie Diefenderfer.*

8 oz. nursing bottle, mug, 9.5" pie plate, 5 oz. custard, 4.5" x 5" refrigerator dish w/ lid on 5.25" x 9.25" refrigerator dish w/ lid. *Courtesy of Charlie Diefenderfer.*

Three variations of the five ounce custard cup.

FIRE-KING 1700 LINE
(1946-1958 Anchor Hocking Glass Corporation)

Three items in the 1700 Line are also part of the Breakfast Set: the St. Denis cup, the St. Denis saucer, and the 9.25" dinner plate. These will be the easiest pieces to find. Everything else in any color will be difficult. Many general collectors aren't even familiar with the 1700 Line. Ask them what a "Ransom cup" is and they might not have any idea, but serious Fire-King collectors might be able to tell you where they found their first one! The 5.75" cereal bowl is a 5.75" Jane Ray oatmeal bowl without the ribs.

It is very important to note that there is a line of "jade" glass from China being sold in gift shops that is meant to look the 1700 Line and Breakfast Set. These pieces are the wrong color, shape, and weight. We know for a fact that unscrupulous sellers have been placing Fire-King stickers and prices on these pieces that sell for only a few dollar apiece. You need to be an informed and educated consumer. A picture of these reproductions is shown with the information on "Fire-King Breakfast Set."

Back row: 9.25" dinner plate, 5.75" cereal bowl; *front row:* Ransom cup, St. Denis saucer, St. Denis cup & saucer.

FIRE-KING 1700 LINE	Jade-ite	Ivory	Milk white	Qty
Bowl, 5.75" cereal	15	25	8	____
Bowl, 7.5" flat soup	25	35	12	____
Bowl, 8.5" vegetable	35			____
Cup, 8 oz. Coffee	10		6	____
Cup, 9 oz. St. Denis w/round handle	8	10	5	____
Cup, 9 oz. Ransom w/pointy handle	15	30	6	____
Plate, 7.75" salad			8	____
Plate, 9.25" dinner	30	7	5	____
Platter, 9" x 12" oval	30		15	____
Saucer, 7.5"	5	5	2	____

Reproduction Information: Cup, too heavy, unmarked, 2.75" tall. Saucer, too heavy, unmarked, 5.25" diameter; base is almost a .25" pedestal. Dinner plate, too heavy, unmarked, has a double rim on the underside, 10"; original plate is 9.25". Flat soup, too heavy, unmarked, 8.25" diameter. Note: this glass is made in China. The color is a bit light and on the yellow side. The glass has minute ripples or lines that resemble sedimentary rock.

Back row: 9" x 12" platter, 9.25" dinner plate; *front row:* St. Denis cup & 5.75" cereal bowl.

FIRE-KING SHEAVES OF WHEAT
(1957-1959 Anchor Hocking Glass Corporation)

Only Alice offers fewer pieces than Sheaves of Wheat. Jade-ite pieces of this seldom-seen pattern are like trophies to hardcore Fire-King collectors as jade-ite Sheaves of wheat is rarely seen, anywhere. Crystal (clear) Sheaves of Wheat is getting little attention at this time, but it does offer tumblers, something not available in any jade-ite Fire-King. Crystal Sheaves of Wheat is also unmarked so may be overlooked by less experienced buyers.

FIRE-KING SHEAVES OF WHEAT	Jade-ite	Crystal	Qty
Bowl, 4.5" dessert	100	6	_____
Cup	60	4	_____
Plate, 9" dinner	125	15	_____
Saucer	25	2	_____
Tumbler, juice		12	_____
Tumbler, water		15	_____

FIRE-KING SHELL

(1965-1976 Anchor Hocking
Glass Corporation)

Shell has always been much harder to find than Jane Ray, and it has always commanded a higher price. The dinner plates are larger, but overall these two Anchor Hocking lines are similar. They have almost the same assortment of pieces, except for Shell having one more platter than Jane Ray. Jade-ite is the most popular color for both.

Shell is not as popular as Jane Ray or Restaurantware probably because many collectors have not been exposed to this less common pattern. Once collectors complete either a grouping of Jane Ray or Restaurantware they may move into another pattern and Shell is often selected. Many prefer the Shell 10" dinner plate to the 9" Jane Ray dinner plate. Because Shell is more difficult to find it also becomes the kind of challenge that many collectors find extremely rewarding. The cups and saucers are the easiest pieces to find; the oval vegetable bowl is almost impossible to find.

Demitasse Shell cups and saucers are the most common of all Fire-King demitasse sets. For this reason they continue to be inexpensive. They are readily available in Peach Lustre and white.

The gold trim on white dinnerware is real gold so do not microwave these pieces.

FIRE-KING SHELL	Jade-ite	"Mother of Pearl"	Other colors	Qty
Bowl, 4.75" dessert	18		4	____
Bowl, 6.25" cereal	35	15	10	____
Bowl, 7.75" soup	50	24	10	____
Bowl, 8.5" oval vegetable	trtp*			____
Bowl, 8.5" round vegetable	40	25	10	____
Creamer	30		3	____
Cup	12	8	3	____
Cup, demitasse		15	10	____
Plate, 7.25" salad	30	10	4	____
Plate, 10" dinner	25	15	4	____
Platter, 9" oval		20		____
Platter, 9.5" x 13" oval	110		10	____
Platter, 11.5" x 15.5" oval			20	____
Saucer	5	5	1	____
Saucer, demitasse		15	10	____
Sugar base	25	10	4	____
Sugar lid	100	15	8	____

*trtp = too rare to price

Top right: *Back row:* 8.5" round vegetable bowl, 7.75" soup bowl; *front row:* 6.25" cereal bowl, 4.75" dessert bowl.

Below: *Back row:* 7.25" salad plate, 10" dinner plate, 9.5" x 13" platter; *front row:* cup & saucer, sugar w/ lid, creamer.

FIRE-KING SWIRL
(1949-1962 Anchor Hocking Glass Corporation)

The listing for Swirl was expanded from "Sunrise" to all Fire-King Swirl patterns at our readers' request. Again, let us know how to provide the best book possible and we will try to comply.

About the only Swirl color not being collected at this time is white. Jade-ite is very difficult to find. Serious Fire-King collectors make sure they have at least a piece or two just to satisfy a need to own it all! Inexperienced collectors and dealers sometimes confuse Swirl and Shell or use the names interchangeably as they both have a swirling design at the rim. Jade-ite Swirl is much harder to find, much more valuable, and available in far fewer pieces than Jade-ite Shell. The design of Swirl is very subtle and shallow; Jade-ite Shell has very dominant swirls large enough to place fingers in.

Azurite Swirl, like Azurite Charm, has become very popular in both America and in Japan. Although not particularly common, if you are diligent eventually your search will be rewarded with a pile of Azurite. The color is a gray-blue not to be confused with Turquoise Blue Fire-King, which is the very next listing in the book. Sugar lids are getting scarce so perhaps they will go the way of the jade-ite Shell lid and realize a bold price increase. Our suspicion is that there is a lot of Azurite Swirl yet to make it to the marketplace. As collectors continue to request it, eventually more inventory will appear in shops and shows. The lesson here is: if you don't see it, ask for it!

Sunrise and Pink Swirl are also extremely popular. Sunrise is pictured; it has a bold red edge. Condition of this trim is paramount as this is an applied color that will be negatively affected if cleaned in a dishwasher. It can fade, chip, or scratch. Most collectors want pieces with a true red tone that has maintained its integrity. Cups and saucers are the easiest Pink Swirl items to find although none of the pieces poses an overwhelming challenge. The pink color has a tendency to fade and some pieces have become so pale they almost look white. Color is the key to Pink Swirl; the pink must be a deep, even color.

A note regarding Pink Swirl versus Rose-ite: when you turn over pieces of Pink Swirl there will be white in the very center where there is the Fire-King mark. If you turn a piece over and see pink throughout you have probably found a rare piece of Rose-ite. Rose-ite is pink glass, not glass with pink color on top. If you break a piece of Pink Swirl there will be white in the center of the shard; if you break a piece of Rose-ite it will be solid pink inside and out. Rose-ite is very uncommon and considered a real trophy to Fire-King collectors.

FIRE-KING SWIRL	Ivory w/red rim (Sunrise) & Azurite	Jade-ite	Pink	White (un-trimmed looks almost Ivory)	Qty
Bowl, 4.75" dessert	12		15	8	____
Bowl, 5.75" cereal	25			20	____
Bowl. 7.75" soup	25		35	15	____
Bowl, 8.25" vegetable	30		35	20	____
Creamer	12		20	10	____
Cup	8	75	12	8	____
Plate, 7.25" salad	12		17	10	____
Plate, 9.25" dinner	12	110	14	10	____
Plate, 11"			25		____
Platter	25	trtp*		20	____
Saucer	4	25	6	4	____
Sugar base	12		20	10	____
Sugar lid	24		24	20	____

*trtp = too rare to price

Note: White trimmed in 22K gold worth half of untrimmed white. Rose-ite: 4.75" dessert bowl and 7.75" soup bowl, $75; 8.5" oval vegetable bowl, $100; footed creamer and footed sugar, $50 each; cup, $50; 9.25" dinner plate, $75; platter, $125; footed sherbet, $75.

Back row: platter, 9.25" dinner plate, 7.25" salad plate; *front row:* cup & saucer, creamer.

FIRE-KING TURQUOISE BLUE
(1956-1958 Anchor Hocking Glass Corporation)

Back row: 10" dinner plate, 9" dinner plate, 7.25" salad plate; *front row:* mug, cup & saucer, cup trimmed in gold.

Turquoise Blue Fire-King is extremely popular and still quite plentiful. Much like Fire-King jade-ite, Anchor Hocking manufactured more than dinnerware in Turquoise Blue. There are a variety of bowls, ashtrays, relish plates, and even a handled batter bowl, which is the most difficult piece of all to find.

Prices are slowly escalating, as there is increased competition for Turquoise Blue Fire-King both in America and in Japan. Cups are common, saucers are harder to find as many more cups were produced to accompany the 9" plate with a cup indent. Creamers and sugars are still abundant but the 6.25" bread and butter plate is hard to locate and the 10" dinner plate is downright difficult to find.

When buying Swedish Modern (Teardrop) bowls, take extra care to examine the spout. These do have a tendency to have nicks and chips. What a clever design this was; one could stir and then effortlessly pour!

Remember, pieces with a gold rim are trimmed in real gold. These items should never go into a microwave oven.

Back row: hard boiled egg plate, three-part relish, both w/ gold trim; *front:* creamer & sugar.

Original 12-piece "Starter Set" of Turquoise Blue Dinnerware.

FIRE-KING TURQUOISE BLUE	Turquoise blue	Qty
Ash tray, 3.5"	15	
Ash tray, 4.0"	15	____
Ash tray, 5.75"	20	____
Batter bowl, w/spout & 1 handle	400	____
Bowl, 4.5" dessert	15	____
Bowl, 5" cereal, 2" tall	15	____
Bowl, 5" chili, 2.25" tall	20	____
Bowl, 6.5" soup	30	____
Bowl, 8" vegetable	22	____
Bowl, Swedish Modern, 1 pt., 6.5"	45	____
Bowl, Swedish Modern, 1 qt., 8"	55	____
Bowl, Swedish Modern, 2 qt., 9.5"	55	____
Bowl, Swedish Modern, 3 qt., 11"	60	____
Bowl, Splash Proof, 1 qt., 6.75"	40	____
Bowl, Splash Proof, 2 qt., 7.5"	35	____
Bowl, Splash Proof, 3 qt., 8.5"	30	____
Creamer	14	____
Cup	5	____
Mug	16	____
Plate, 6.25" bread & butter	22	____
Plate, 7.25" salad	20	____
Plate, 9" dinner	15	____
Plate, 9" w/indent for cup	6	____
Plate, 10" dinner	45	____
Plate, hard boiled egg w/ gold rim	25	____
Relish, 3-part w/gold rim	15	____
Saucer	5	____
Sugar	14	____

Three Splash Proof bowls.

Four Swedish Modern (Teardrop) bowls.

Back row: 13.5" tray w/ center indent, 13.5" tray; *front row:* butter, shaker, sherbet, candy dish w/ 1 handle. *Courtesy of Marie Talone.*

Sugar w/ lid, 10 oz. tumbler, cup & saucer, creamer, 4.5" square berry bowl. *Courtesy of Marie Talone.*

FLORAGOLD
(1950s   Jeannette Glass Company)

Iridescent Floragold is sometimes mistaken as Carnival Glass. This error is often made with a number of iridescent Depression Glass patterns when first discovered. The years of production make it much newer than Carnival Glass and among one of the newest patterns featured in this book.

There are many Floragold pieces from which to choose with a broad range of prices. The 5.5" ruffled fruit bowl and 5.25" oval candy are extremely common and can often be found on tray lots at auctions. On the other end of the spectrum is the vase/celery. This item is quite rare and we are pleased to have one pictured. We would love to have comports in the next book. Let us know if you can help!

The white plastic tops on the salt and pepper shakers are authentic. In fact half of the value of the shakers is in these tops. They must be in excellent condition so take note as they do crack.

Boxed sets of Depression Glass continually find their way to the marketplace after all these years. Thank goodness our grandmothers saved everything! Found in Floragold was a "Goldtone One Egg Nog Set Made in USA" consisting of "One Large Bowl and Six Cups;" the 9" deep salad bowl and six cups. These sets were given away at a Cedar Rapids, Iowa gas station in the late 1950s.

A question was raised by one of our readers regarding the tidbit. If you have any information please let us know. She has a tidbit that has a metal post and knows of another one that also has a metal post. Is there anyone who can confirm what is truly accurate, metal or wood? Also, she informed us that a tidbit sold at a Tennessee auction and realized $110. We would appreciate additional pricing input here, too, so the values we present are accurate. And finally, one more call for comports!

Vase/celery. *Courtesy of Paul Reichwein.*

Back row: 8.25" square dinner, 11.25" platter; *front row:* 9.5" deep salad bowl, 5.5" cereal bowl, 4" ashtray/coaster, crystal ashtray/coaster w/ only 1 indent for cigarette. *Courtesy of Marie Talone.*

FLORAGOLD	Iridescent	Qty
Ash tray/coaster, 4"	7	____
Bowl, 4.5" square berry	8	____
Bowl, 5.5" cereal	65	____
Bowl, 5.5" ruffled fruit	8	____
Bowl, 8.5" square	20	____
Bowl, 9.5" deep salad	50	____
Bowl, 9.5" ruffled	8	____
Bowl, 12" ruffled fruit	8	____
Butter dish base (1/4 lb.)	35	____
Butter dish lid (1/4 lb.)	15	____
Butter complete (1/4 lb.)	50	____
Butter dish base (6.25" square base)	20	____
Butter dish lid (round to fit 6.25" base)	40	____
Butter dish complete (square base, round lid)	60	____
Butter dish, 5.5" complete (square base, rd. lid)	trtp*	____
Candlestick, ea.	35	____
Candy dish, 1 handle	12	____
Candy/Cheese dish w/lid	60	____
Candy, 5.25" oval scalloped w/4 feet	8	____
Comport, 5.25" smooth rim	trtp*	____
Comport, 5.25" ruffled rim	trtp*	____
Creamer	12	____
Cup	5	____
Pitcher, 8.25"	45	____
Plate, 5.25" sherbet/saucer	12	____
Plate, 8.25" square dinner	45	____
Platter, 11.25"	25	____
Salt & pepper	70	____
Sherbet	14	____
Sugar base	10	____
Sugar lid	14	____
Tid-bit, 2-tier, 9.5" ruffled bowl above 12" ruffled bowl	40	____
Tray, 13.5"	25	____
Tray, 13.5" w/center indent	75	____
Tumbler, 10 or 11 oz., 5" tall	20	____
Tumbler, 15 oz.	125	____
Vase/celery	500	____

Note: Shell Pink 5.25" scalloped candy, $25.
Crystal ashtray/coaster with indent for only
one cigarette, $15

*trtp = too rare to price

Above: *Back:* candy/cheese dish w/ lid; *front row:* candlestick, 1/4 lb. butter, 5.25" scalloped oval candy w/ 4 feet. *Courtesy of Diefenderfer's Collectibles & Antiques.*

Right: Salt & pepper. *Courtesy of Michael Rothenberger/Mike's Collectibles.*

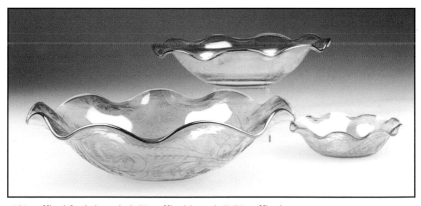

12" ruffled fruit bowl, 9.5" ruffled bowl, 5.5" ruffled fruit bowl. *Courtesy of Marie Talone.*

Two variations of the 5" tumbler. On the left there is a band of plain glass, but the tumbler on the right has the Floragold motif to the rim.

10.25" footed lemonade pitcher, 5.25" lemonade tumbler, 8" footed pitcher. *Courtesy of Donna L. Cehlarik.*

FLORAL
Reproduced
(1931-1935 Jeannette Glass Company)

Floral (also known as Poinsettia) is a Depression Glass pattern that is equally collected in pink and green. Delphite is quite difficult to find and the treasures pictured in our first edition are truly one of a kind.

The options available to collectors are many, as Floral has an abundance of dinnerware plus additional pieces such as a lamp, refrigerator dish, flower frog, and vases. Prices are moderate and go up from there with $12 saucers as the least expensive piece. This is a pattern that has performed well through the years and one could expect it to continue to do so.

Interesting and newly found Floral items have been discovered in England. Fortunately for collectors, dealers and auctioneers in the States have networked with sources abroad to have Depression Glass sent to America. Apparently higher prices can be obtained in the American market than in Europe and England, but we benefit by having the opportunity to add wonderful new discoveries to our collections. Several of these British additions are shown, including a 4" flat tumbler, the 9" dinner plate with a rim, and the butter dish in a slightly bluer tint. Sherbets with a design on the foot also come from England. One sold on eBay in September 2000 for $45.

Back row: 8" salad plate, 10.75" platter, 9" dinner; *front row:* cup & saucer, 8" vegetable bowl w/ cover. *Courtesy of Diefenderfer's Collectibles & Antiques.*

Back row: 4" footed salt & pepper, 2-part relish, candy jar w/ lid, sugar w/ lid;
front row: butter, creamer, 4" candlesticks. *Courtesy of Donna L. Cehlarik.*

11″ faceted rim platter.

6" flat salt &
pepper. *Courtesy
of Maria
McDaniel.*

4" footed salt & pepper shakers
in 2 colors. *Courtesy of Michael
Rothenberger/Mike's Col-
lectibles.*

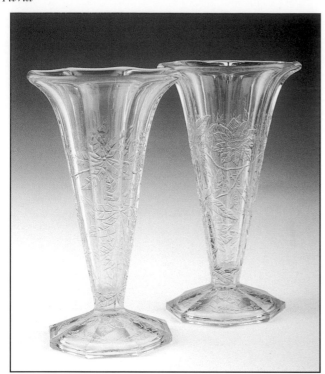

6.75" 8-sided vases. *Courtesy of Diefenderfer's Collectibles & Antiques.*

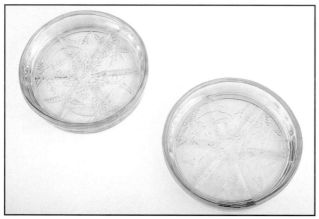

Two 3.25" coasters. *Courtesy of Charlie Diefenderfer.*

FLORAL	Pink	Green	Delphite	Qty
Bowl, 4" berry, smooth rim	25	30	100	____
Bowl, 4" berry, ruffled rim	175	175		____
Bowl, 5.5" cream soup	850	850		____
Bowl, 7.5" salad, smooth rim	35	35	75	____
Bowl, 7.5" salad, ruffled rim	400	400		____
Bowl, 8" vegetable	30	40	85	____
Bowl, 9" oval vegetable	30	30		____
Butter dish base	40	35		____
Butter dish lid	85	75		____
Butter complete	125	110		____
Candlestick, 4" each	40	45		____
Candy jar w/lid	50	50		____
Coaster, 3.25"	18	14		____
Comport, 9"	1000	1200		____
Cover for 8" vegetable bowl	30	30		____
Creamer	18	18	100	____
Cup	15	15		____
Dresser set		1800		____
powder jar w/lid, ea. (set has 2 powder jars)		400		____
rouge box w/lid (1 per set)		600		____
tray		400		____
Frog, for vase		825		____
Ice tub, 3.5" tall, oval	1000	1000		____
Lamp	325	325		____
Pitcher, 5.5" flat		575		____
Pitcher, 8" with foot	50	45		____
Pitcher, 10.25" with foot (lemonade pitcher)	375	375		____
Plate, 6" sherbet	10	10		____
Plate, 8" salad	15	15		____
Plate, 9" dinner	20	20	300	____
Plate, 9" grill		300		____
Platter, 10.75"	25	25	250	____
Platter, 11", facetted rim	150	trtp*	trtp*	____
Refrigerator dish w/lid (inside of lid embossed w/Floral motif)		65	65	____
Relish, 2-part	25	25	200	____
Salt & pepper, 4" footed *R*	60	60		____
Salt & pepper, 6" flat	65			____

Back: 9" oval vegetable bowl; *front row:* 2-part relish, 4.5" flat water tumbler, cup & saucer. *Courtesy of Diefenderfer's Collectibles & Antiques.*

Saucer	12	12		____
Sherbet	20	22	100	____
Sugar base	18	18	100	____
Sugar lid (same lid on candy jar)	30	30		____
Tray, 6" square w/ tab handles	30	40		____
Tray, 9.25" oval for dresser set		400		____
Tumbler, 3.5" w/foot		225		____
Tumbler, 4" juice w/foot	20	25		____
Tumbler, 4.5" flat		200		____
Tumbler, 4.75" water w/foot	25	30	250	____
Tumbler, 5.25" lemonade w/foot	60	65		____
Vase, rose bowl w/3 feet		850		____
with frog		1650		____
Vase, flared w/3 feet		700		____
Vase, 7" w/8 sides		600		____

Reproduction information: Shakers: red, cobalt, & dark green were never originally produced. Pink shakers: the color is wrong & the threads to screw on the lid **should have** two parallel threads; new shakers have one continuous thread winding around the top. New shakers missing Floral pattern on feet or pressed on top of feet; old - pattern on underside of feet.

Note: Jade-ite: Canisters (cereal, coffee, sugar, tea), 5.25" tall, square with Floral motif inside lid, $225 each. Jade-ite refrigerator dish, 5" square with Floral design inside lid, $65. Transparent green refrigerator dish, $50. Cremax 7.5" bowl, creamer, & sugar, $200 each. Crystal: 3-footed flared vase, $500; with frog, $950; 6.75" 8-sided vase, $450.

*trtp = too rare to price

Above: Butter dish from England. *Courtesy of Charlie Diefenderfer.*

Above: Two 4.5" flat water tumblers; the one on the right is from England and only has the pattern at the top. *Courtesy of Charlie Diefenderfer.*

Left: Close-up of the English 9" dinner plate w/ a rim. *Courtesy of Charlie Diefenderfer.*

Candlesticks.

Delphite Floral creamer & sugar. *Courtesy of Vic & Jean Laermans.*

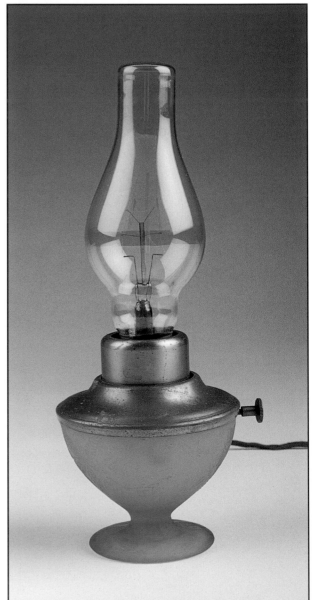

Lamp.

FLORAL AND DIAMOND BAND

(1927-1931 U.S. Glass Company)

This is a pattern that has rough molds created during production. As you examine a piece of Floral and Diamond Band you may feel and see lots of roughness and extra glass. This may not necessarily be damage, but the result of careless manufacturing. For this reason, the short list of glassware, and the difficulty many have finding more than sherbets, Floral and Diamond Band is not a particularly popular pattern.

While traveling in the Midwest we found sherbets everywhere at all kinds of prices. These were obviously distributed to the Midwest back in the late 1920s and early 1930s probably as some kind of premium. Once the sherbets are purchased, a collector has a bit of a challenge ahead.

The butter dish base is the same, plain base used in other U.S. Glass Company patterns like Aunt Polly, Cherryberry, and Strawberry. The only detail in this base is a starburst centered in the bottom.

Above: 8" luncheon plate & butter. *Courtesy of Diefenderfer's Collectibles & Antiques.*

Left: *Back row:* 5.25" sugar w/ lid & 4.75" creamer; *front row:* 2.5" sugar & 2.5" creamer. *Courtesy of Vic & Jean Laermans.*

Floral and Diamond Band pieces are heavier than many other Depression Glass patterns. This pattern has an older look and feel to it as if mimicking earlier pressed glass patterns, and its production dates show that it is one of the first Depression Glass patterns made.

Back row: 4.75" creamer, 8" pitcher; *front row:* sugar, butter dish, sherbet.

4" water tumbler & 5" iced tea tumbler. *Courtesy of Diefenderfer's Collectibles & Antiques.*

FLORAL AND DIAMOND BAND	Pink & green	Qty
Bowl, 4.5" berry	12	____
Bowl, 5.75" w/handles	15	____
Bowl, 8" berry	18	____
Butter dish base (no design of any kind)	75	____
Butter dish lid	75	____
Butter complete	150	____
Compote, 5.5"	25	____
Creamer, small, 2.5"	12	____
Creamer, 4.75"	20	____
Pitcher, 8"	120	____
Plate, 8" luncheon	55	____
Sherbet	10	____
Sugar, small, 2.5"	12	____
Sugar base, 5.25"	20	____
Sugar lid	70	____
Tumbler, 4" water	30	____
Tumbler, 5" iced tea	65	____

Note: Iridescent butter & pitcher, $300 each. Crystal items ½ of pink & green.

Back row: 10" grill plate, 10" dinner plate, 8.5" salad plate; *front row:* 5.5" ashtray, 6" sherbet plate, cup & saucer, sherbet, salt & pepper. *Courtesy of Lorraine Penrod.*

FLORENTINE NO. 1
Reproduced
(1932-1934 Hazel-Atlas Glass Company)

Florentine No. 1 has a decorative edge, Florentine No. 2 has a smooth edge. Hopefully this will end all confusion!

Due to the delicate nature of the Florentine No. 1 rim it is very difficult to find pieces in perfect condition. Collectors are so desperate to own enough Florentine No. 1 dinner plates, they are starting to buy them with minor inner rim damage (like Royal Lace) as long as the outer edge is perfect. We are not advocating that one compromises any standards of perfection, but merely reporting what is happening in the marketplace. If one intends to use a set of Depression Glass there is nothing more basic than dinner plates.

Overall, green is the most common color, with yellow and pink more difficult to find. Cobalt blue pieces are not often seen, and crystal (clear) seems to be overlooked by collectors at this time.

Pictured is a crystal tumbler that has been cast in copper. It was found on the Internet and the seller indicated he recently owned a creamer and sugar also cast in copper. If you are the lucky owner please let us know.

We are indebted to Lorraine Penrod for shipping her Florentine No. 1 and Florentine No. 2 collections from Louisiana to Pennsylvania. We all get to benefit from her generosity!

Back row: sugar w/ruffled rim, 11.5" platter, sugar; *front row:* creamer w/ruffled rim, butter dish, creamer. *Courtesy of Lorraine Penrod.*

FLORENTINE NO. 1	Green	Yellow	Pink	Cobalt	Qty
Ash tray, 5.5"	25	30	30		____
Bowl, 5" berry	20	20	20	35	____
Bowl, 5.25" ruffled nut/ cream soup	25		25	65	____
Bowl, 6" cereal	40	40	50		____
Bowl, 8.5" berry	45	45	45		____
Bowl, 9.5" oval vegetable	50	60	65		____
Butter dish base	40	60	60		____
Butter dish lid	100	120	120		____
Butter complete	140	180	180		____
Coaster/ash tray. 3.75"	20	20	25		____
Comport, 3.5" w/ruffled rim	50		25	75	____
Cover for 9.5" oval vegetable	40	45	45		____
Creamer, 3"	10	20	20		____
Creamer w/ruffled rim	50		40	75	____
Cup	10	10	10	100	____
Pitcher, 6.5" w/foot	50	50	50	trtp*	____
Pitcher, 7.5" flat with or without ice lip	85	200	150		____
Plate, 6" sherbet	10	10	10		____
Plate, 8.5" salad	15	15	15		____
Plate, 10" dinner	30	32	35		____
Plate, 10" grill	20	22	25		____
Platter, 11.5"	30	35	35		____
Salt & pepper *R*	50	60	70		____
Saucer	10	10	10	25	____
Sherbet	15	15	15		____
Sugar base	10	20	20		____
Sugar lid, glass	25	35	35		____
Sugar lid, metal	15				____
Sugar w/ruffled rim	50		40	75	____
Tumbler, 3.25" juice w/foot	20				____
Tumbler, 3.75" juice w/foot	20	25	30		____
Tumbler, 4" w/ribs	25		30		____
Tumbler, 4.75" water w/foot	25	30	30		____
Tumbler, 5.25", 9 oz. lemonade			150		____
Tumbler, 5.25", 12 oz. iced tea w/foot	35	40	40		____

Reproduction information: Shakers: Cobalt & red never originally produced. Pink: new poppy resembles a cauliflower, missing 7 distinct circles around blossom.

*trtp = too rare to price

Note: Crystal comport, $10; ruffled nut, $13; salt & pepper, $30; cup, $5; sherbet, $5; 8.5" salad plate, $7; saucer, $3. Ruffled nut, $13. Crystal may be trimmed in gold.

Above: 3.5" comport w/ ruffled rim & creamer w/ ruffled rim. *Courtesy of Don & Terry Yusko.*

Left: 5" berry bowl. *Courtesy of Charlie Diefenderfer.*

Below: 3.25" juice tumbler w/foot, 3.75" juice tumbler w/ foot, 4" tumbler w/ribs, 4.75" water tumbler w/foot. *Courtesy of Lorraine Penrod.*

Back row: 5" berry bowl, 6" cereal bowl, 8.5" berry bowl; *front row:* 9.5" oval vegetable bowl w/cover, 5.25" ruffled nut/cream soup. *Courtesy of Lorraine Penrod.*

Footed crystal tumbler that has been cast in copper. *Courtesy of Mark Fors / Marwig Glass Store.*

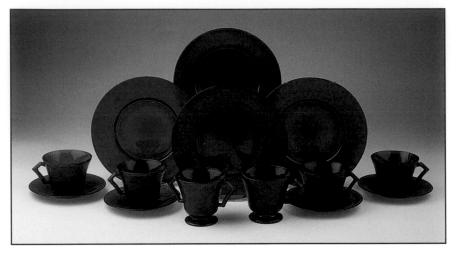

FLORENTINE NO. 2
Reproduced
(1932-1935 Hazel-Atlas Glass Company)

Florentine No. 2 has a smooth edge, Florentine No. 1 has a decorative edge. Hopefully this will end all confusion!

Few patterns are more popular in yellow than any other color, but Florentine No. 2 is one of them. The shade is a pure, bright yellow that is clean and cheerful. Many people react positively to yellow Florentine No. 2.

However, the most interesting find in this pattern since the first book isn't yellow, but blue. Shown is a blue fired-on luncheon set that Jo Timko found in a chicken coop in southern New Jersey! The glassware was wrapped in newspaper dated 1987, so for thirteen years it sat forgotten, and thankfully protected. The set consists of four 8.5" luncheon plates, four cups, four saucers, a creamer, and a sugar. Now the mystery is, what other colors are really out there!?

Found in Canada are variations of the same (?) pitcher. The pink pitcher has a pulled ice lip that is .5" across at the tip; the green one has a plain ice lip that is .25" at the tip. The pink pitcher measures 6.75" from the base to the top of the handle, while the green pitcher is 6.5" from the base to the top of the handle. The pink pitcher has one inch of glass with no Florentine motif at the top, the green pitcher has .25" of glass without a design. At first glance these seem to be the same pitcher, but they have some interesting differences.

A sign of popularity is when an item has been reproduced. Be sure to read the reproduction information on this pattern. Reproduction pitchers and tumblers are appearing in greater numbers in antique malls.

Top: Blue fired-on luncheon set consisting of four 8.5" plates, four cups & saucers, creamer and sugar. *Courtesy of Jo Timko / Snowflake58 Collectibles.*

Center top: *Back row:* 3.25" ruffled comport, 4" tumbler; *middle row:* sugar w/ruffled rim, 5" berry bowl (this is Florentine No. 1); *front row:* creamer w/ruffled rim, 5.25" ruffled nut/cream soup. *Courtesy of Lorraine Penrod.*

Center bottom: 6" footed parfait/vase, 5" blown tumbler, 5" flat iced tea tumbler, 4.5" footed water tumbler, 3.5" blown tumbler, 3.25" flat juice tumbler, 3.25" flat juice tumbler, 3.25" footed juice tumbler. *Courtesy of Lorraine Penrod.*

Bottom: Candy jar w/lid, butter dish, candlesticks. *Courtesy of Donna L. Cehlarik.*

FLORENTINE NO. 2	Green	Yellow	Pink	Qty
Bowl, 4.5" berry	20	25	20	____
Bowl, cream soup, 4.75"	18	25	18	____
Bowl, 5", ruffled nut/cream soup	25		25	____
Bowl, 5.5"	40	45		____
Bowl, 6" cereal	40	50		____
Bowl, 7.5"		100		____
Bowl, 8" berry	30	40	40	____
Bowl, 9" oval vegetable	40	50		____
Bowl, 9" round	35			____
Butter dish base	40	60		____
Butter dish lid	100	120		____
Butter complete	140	180		____
Candlestick, ea.	30	40		____
Candy jar w/lid	150	200	165	____
Coaster/ash tray, 3.75"	18	25	18	____
Coaster/ash tray, 5.5"	20	35		____
Comport, 3.25" tall, 2.25" diam., w/ruffled rim	50		30	____
Cover for 9" oval vegetable	40	45		____
Creamer	10	10	12	____
Cup	10	10	10	____
Custard/jello, 3.75" diam., 2" deep	75	100		____
Gravy boat		75		____
Pitcher, 6.25" w/foot		200		____
Pitcher, 7.5", 28 oz. w/foot *R*	40	40		____
Pitcher, 7.5", 48 oz.	85	225	150	____
Pitcher, 8.25"	120	500	250	____
Plate, 5.75" sherbet	8	8		____
Plate, 6.25" w/indent	25	40		____
Plate, 8.25" salad	10	10	10	____
Plate, 10" dinner	20	20		____
Plate, 10.25" grill	15	15		____
Plate, 10.25" grill w/cream soup ring	45			____
Platter, 11"	25	25	30	____
Platter, 11.5" to elevate gravy boat		60		____
Relish, 10", 3 part	25	35	35	____
Salt & pepper	50	60		____
Saucer	8	8		____
Sherbet	12	12		____
Sugar base	12	12		____
Sugar lid	25	25		____
Tray, 8.75", round with indents for salt, pepper, cream, sugar		100		____
Tumbler, 3.25" flat juice, 2 styles	18	25	18	____
Tumbler, 3.25" footed juice	15	22	20	____
Tumbler, 3.5" flat (blown)	22			____
Tumbler, 4" footed juice *R*	15	18		____
Tumbler, 4" flat water	15	22	18	____
Tumbler, 4.5" footed water	30	40		____
Tumbler, 5" flat (blown)	25			____
Tumbler, 5" flat iced tea	45	60	50	____
Vase/parfait 6" footed	40	70		____

Note: Crystal items ½ of Yellow EXCEPT for the crystal covered candy, $150. Cobalt comport & 4" tumbler, $75 each. Ice blue pitcher, $750. Amber: tumbler & cup, $75 each; saucer, $20; sherbet, $50. Blue fired-on: 8.5" plate, $25; cup, $12; saucer, $6; creamer, $20; and sugar, $20.

Reproduction information: Tumblers and pitchers are being made in colors not originally produced. Measurements for these items are a "tad" smaller than the old ones. Old tumblers measure 4" tall with a base of almost 4". New tumblers are about 1/8 inch smaller in both of these measurements and are missing pattern in center on underside of foot. New pitchers are 1/4" shorter with handles 1/8" wider than the 3/4" width of the old pitchers' handles. New pitchers and tumblers are heavier and may have bubbles in glass.

Top: Gravy boat & 11.5" platter. *Courtesy of Donna L. Cehlarik.*

Center: 3.25" ruffled comport. *Courtesy of Neil McCurdy-Hoosier Kubboard Glass.*

Bottom: Two pitchers, although similar they have differences. Note the pulled spout on the pink pitcher where the Florentine motif ends in respect to the rim. *Walter Lemiski / Waltz Time Antiques.*

FLOWER GARDEN WITH BUTTERFLIES

(Late 1920s U.S. Glass Company)

This pattern is a tribute to wonderful design. Look carefully at the close-up of the pattern, you should be able to see a butterfly fluttering among the flowers, hence this name.

Finding absolutely anything in Flower Garden with Butterflies is difficult. This is a high quality pattern with relatively expensive pieces. One's best bet for finding this pattern is attending Depression Glass shows where dealers often display their very best.

Most collectors of Flower Garden with Butterflies buy any color they find. There are some who specialize in one color, as is the norm for the majority of collectors of other patterns, but individuals hunting for this pattern are usually delighted to find and purchase anything they don't own, regardless of color.

We would love to have your collection fly into the studio. If you can help, do let us know!

Above: Close-up of pattern.

Right: Two 8.25" plates. *Courtesy of Charlie Diefenderfer.*

Below: *Back row:* 4.75" tall/10.25" wide comport, 7.25" plate; *front row:* 8.25" plate, candy jar base. *Courtesy of Neil McCurdy - Hoosier Kubboard Glass.*

Opposite page
Top: Candlestick w/6.5" candle. *Courtesy of Neil McCurdy-Hoosier Kubboard Glass.*

Center: 7.75" x 11.75" rectangular tray. *Courtesy of Marie Talone and Paul Reichwein.*

Bottom: Cup & saucer.

FLOWER GARDEN sWITH BUTTERFLIES	Black	Blue & Blue-Canary yellow	Pink & green, & Green	Amber & Crystal	Qty
Ashtray		200	200	175	____
Bon bon w/cover, 6.5" across	300				____
Bottle, cologne w/stopper, 7.5"		250	350		____
Bowl, 7.25" w/lid	400				____
Bowl, 8.5" console w/base	200				____
Bowl, 9" rolled edge w/base	250				____
Bowl, 11" orange w/foot	300				____
Bowl, 12" console w/rolled edge	250				____
Candlestick, 4" each	50	75	75	45	____
Candlestick, 6" each	250				____
Candlestick, 8" each	200	85	85	45	____
Candlestick, w/candle, 12" (candle is 6.5" tall and .75" square)	500				____
Candy w/lid, 6", no foot			175	150	____
Candy w/lid, 7.5"		150	200	100	____
Candy w/lid, heart-shaped		trtp*	trtp*		____
Cheese & cracker, 10" base, 5.25" tall	400				____
Cigarette box w/lid, 4.25" long	200				____
Comport w/lid, 2.75" tall for 10" indented plate	250				____
Comport, 2.75" tall		50	50		____
Comport, 4.25" tall, 4.75" wide			50		____
Comport, 4.25" tall, 10" wide; tureen	300				____
Comport, 4.75" tall, 10.25" wide		80	100	65	____
Comport w/foot, 5.5" tall, 10" wide	250				____
Comport, 5.75" tall, 11" wide			120	75	____
Comport w/foot, 7" tall	200				____
Comport, 7.25" tall, 8.25" wide		100		85	____
Creamer		100			____
Cup		70			____
Mayonnaise, 3-piece set		150	175	100	____
Mayo. comport		75	85	50	____
Mayo. ladle		20	25	20	____
Mayo. under plate		55	65	30	____
Plate, 7.25"		35	50	25	____
Plate, 8.25", 2 styles		35	45		____
Plate, 10"		65	75		____
Plate, 10" w/indent for 3" comport	150	65	70	45	____
Powder jar, 3.5", no foot		120			____
Powder jar, 6.25" w/foot		150	225	100	____
Powder jar, 7.5" w/foot		150	120	100	____
Sandwich server w/center handle	150	70	100	55	____
Saucer		35			____
Sugar		100			____
Tray, 5.5" x 10" oval		65		65	____
Tray, 7.75" x 11.75" rectangular		75		65	____
Tumbler, 7.5 oz.				200	____
Vase, 6.25" Dahlia, cupped	150	120	175	80	____
Vase, 8" Dahlia, cupped	200				____
Vase, 9", wall	350				____
Vase, 10" w/2 handles	250				____
Vase, 10.5" Dahlia, cupped	300	150	250		____

*trtp = too rare to price

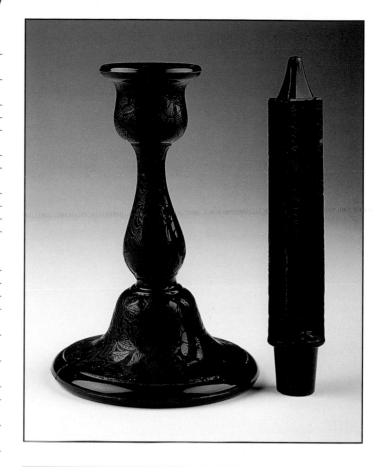

FOREST GREEN
(1950-1967 Anchor Hocking Glass Company)

Many users of *Mauzy's Depression Glass* requested the addition of Forest Green and Royal Ruby, so here is our start. We have attempted to give you a complete listing of the pieces and prices in this edition and will increase the photographic offerings in our third edition. Be sure to cross reference Bubble, Fire-King Charm, and Sandwich (Anchor Hocking) as these patterns are available in Forest Green.

Remember, Forest Green is a color, not a pattern, so the format of this list is a bit different than the others in this book. We hope this presentation will be useful. Again, let us know what you think as this book is designed to be helpful to YOU!

Forest Green tumblers are as prolific as blades of grass. There are few collectors buying them and more and more dealers choosing not to keep them in stock. However, dinnerware is another story. Forest Green dinnerware was produced for a short period of time because it was unsuccessful. Consumers simply did not like the way food looked on dark green glass and when there was no demand for Forest Green dinnerware, Anchor Hocking terminated its production. Years later many collectors feel differently and love green glassware, particularly in the Christmas season. You can't serve a meal without plates, and plates are becoming the most sought-after pieces in Forest Green. Vases, ashtrays, and other occasional pieces may end up in a collection but rarely in any quantity. People are looking for the glass they need to set a table and serve a meal. Forest Green offers little for serving a meal, but one can set a complete table.

Back row: 4.5" square ashtray & 5.75" square ashtray; *front row:* 7" shell bowl & maple leaf (spoon rest).

Inspiration footed tumblers: 6.75" iced tea tumbler, 5.75" water goblet, 4.5" juice tumbler, 3.75" cocktail, 3.5" sherbet.

MAPCO vase (not Anchor Hocking); plain 6.25" vase w/foot, wide middle, pinched near top; 4.75" plain bud vase.

Forest Green		Qty
Ashtrays		
3.5" square	8	____
4.5" square	8	____
5.75" square	10	____
Hexagonal, 5.75"	12	____
Swedish Modern, 5" x 5.75"	20	____
Bottle w/lid (ribbed)	50	____
Bowls		
Batter, 7.5" w/tab handle & spout	25	____
Bon-bon, triangular 6.25"	10	____
Bubble		
Dessert, 4.5"	10	____
Cereal, 5.25"	16	____
Vegetable, 8.25"	25	____
Burple (vertical rows of balls & lines)		
Dessert, 4.5"	6	____
Berry, 8"	18	____
Charm (square)		
Dessert, 4.75"	6	____
Soup. 6"	20	____
Salad, 7.5"	18	____
Mixing (add $5 for decorations)		
4.75" round w/ beaded rim	10	____
5.5" Splash-Proof	12	____
6" round w/ beaded rim	12	____
7.25" round w/ beaded rim	18	____
7.5" batter w/ tab handle & spout	25	____
Scalloped, ruffled & flared, 6.5"	8	____
Scalloped, ruffled, flared, swirled, 7.5"	8	____
Shell, 7"	10	____
Swedish Modern		
Candy, 2.25" tall, 6.5" diam.	25	____

Candy, 3.5" tall, 6.5" diam.	25	____
Whirly Twirly (series of horizontal bulges), 3.75"	14	____
Other Bowls		
4.75"	8	____
5.25" popcorn	18	____
6.25" w/3 feet, textured	8	____
8.25" oval vegetable	35	____
10" punch	30	____
Creamers		
Bubble	14	____
Flat, Charm (squarish)	6	____
Cups		
Bubble	8	____
Charm (square)	5	____
Punch	3	____
Lamps, various styles	45	____
Leaf & Blossom Sets	30	____
Bowl, 4.5"	12	____
Plate. 8.25"	18	____
Maple Leaf (spoon rest)	10	____
Moskeeto-lites, ea.	25	____
Pitchers		
Milano (all-over bumpy texture)	40	____
Plain or decorated w/ice lip 36 oz., 10"	30	____
Plain w/ice lip 86 oz.,	35	____
Decorated 86 oz. w/ice lip, various styles	35	____
Roly Poly (flat bottom, smooth sides curve inward at base)	35	____
Whirly Twirly (series of horizontal bulges)	85	____
Plates		
Sherbet, (round) 6.5"	8	____
Salad, Charm (square), 6.5"	10	____
Salad, Bubble, 6.75"	18	____
Luncheon, Charm (square), 8.25"	8	____
Dinner, Bubble, 9.25"	30	____
Dinner, Charm (square), 9.25"	30	____
Dinner, Bubble, 9.75"	40	____
Platter, Charm, 11" x 8" (rectangular)	25	____
Punch bowl, 10"	30	____
Punch bowl base	50	____
Refrigerator Dishes (round ribbed "bowls" w/lids)		
5" base	30	____
5" lid (green)	35	____
6.25" base	30	____
6.25" lid (crystal)	15	____
7" base	30	____
7" lid (green)	40	____
Relish Tray, 8.25" x 4"	18	____
Saucer		
Bubble	5	____
Charm (square)	1	____
Sherbets		
Baltic (rounded foot/base), 2.25" tall, 2.5" diam.,	7	____
Inspiration (twisted vertical rows of balls & plain glass), 3.75"	14	____
Spoon rest (Maple Leaf)	10	____
Sugars		
Bubble	14	____
Flat, Charm (squarish)	6	____
Tray, relish, 8.25" x 4"	18	____
Tumblers		
Baltic (rounded foot/base)		
Juice, 3.5"	8	____
Goblet, 4.5"	8	____
Belmont (slight bulge in center), 5"	8	____
Blown (Flared with 3 center rings)		
Juice, 3.75"	7	____
Tall, 4.5"	7	____
Iced Tea, 5.25"	8	____

Clear "bubble" foot		
Early American (rows of "balls" w/largest ones at outer edge)		
Cocktail, 3.5"	16	____
Sherbet, 4.25"	12	____
Juice, 4.5"	14	____
Goblet, 5.25"	14	____
Goblet, 6"	20	____
Inspiration (twisted vertical rows of balls & plain glass)		
Sherbet, 3.75"	14	____
Cocktail, 3.75"	16	____
Juice, 4.5"	16	____
Goblet, 5.75"	16	____
Iced Tea, 6.75"	20	____
Georgian (honeycomb-like bottoms), 4.25"	8	____
Milano (all-over bumpy texture)		
5.5" (12 oz.)	10	____
15 oz.	12	____
Roly Poly (flat bottom, smooth sides curve inward at base)		
Juice, 3.25"	5	____
Water, 4.25"	6	____
Iced Tea, 5"	8	____
Straight sided		
4.75"	5	____
6"	5	____
6.25"	5	____
6.5" (Large Iced Tea) plain or decorated	5	____
7" (Giant Iced Tea w/foot)	8	____
Whirly Twirly (series of horizontal bulges w/foot)		
3.5"	10	____
4.25"	10	____
5"	10	____
6.5"	10	____
Windsor (small cube-like design at bottom), 4"	7	____
Others		
Bulbous base w/foot, 4"	6	____
Bulbous base w/foot, 5"	6	____
Bulbous base w/foot, 5.75"	6	____
Juice, 3.75" (similar to Whirly Twirly, less bumps)	6	____
Decorated, various styles 4.75"	5	____
Decorated 4.75" Davy Crockett	20	____
Gay Nineties, 6.5"	5	____
Square Dance Set, 6.5" & 5.25"	5	____
Other decorated 6.5" glasses	5	____
Vases		
Bud, 3.75" various styles w/or w/out gold overlay	5	____
Bud, plain, 4.75"	5	____
Bud, decorated, 4.75"	10	____
Bud, crimped, 6.5"	8	____
Plain, ball at bottom, 3 ridges in middle, 6.25"	5	____
Plain, foot, wide middle, pinched near top, 6.25"	5	____
Plain, foot, wide middle, pinched near top, 6.25," decorated,	10	____
Wide mouth, 7"	12	____
Crimped w/horizontal bulges, 7"	10	____
Crimped, 8"	8	____
Bud, (one bulge in middle) 9"	10	____
Paneled "Rocket," 9"	35	____
Plain, ruffled opening, 9"	20	____
Square textured bottom, flared top, 9"	20	____

Note: Unused tumblers found in paper carriers, add $20 for carrier in good condition.

FORTUNE

(1936-1937 Hocking Glass Company)

There are just enough pieces in Fortune to serve a luncheon or dessert with a variety of bowls and even two tumblers, but no dinner plate. Fortune is a true pink color, not an orange-pink like some Depression Glass, in a weight that is not as heavy as some patterns. Add to this a very pleasant geometric design and you have glassware that is not usually overlooked. Someone simply looking for a present or wanting a piece of pink glass often buys the bowls.

FORTUNE	Pink	Qty
Bowl, 4" berry	10	----
Bowl, 4.5" dessert	10	----
Bowl, 4.5" w/tab handles	10	----
Bowl, 5" w/ one handle	10	----
Bowl, 5.25" w/flared top	18	----
Bowl, 7.75" salad	25	----
Candy dish w/lid	35	----
Candy dish w/ Ruby lid	50	----
Cup	10	----
Plate, 6" sherbet	8	----
Plate, 8" luncheon	25	----
Saucer	5	----
Tumbler, 3.5" juice	15	----
Tumbler, 4.25" water	18	----

Note: Crystal items ½ of pink

Back row: 4.5" bowl w/ 2 tab handles, saucer, 4.25" water tumbler, 3.5" juice tumbler; *front row:* 5" bowl w/ 1 handle, 4.5" dessert bowl, 4" berry bowl. *Courtesy of Neil McCurdy - Hoosier Kubboard Glass and Staci & Jeff Shuck/Gray Goose Antiques.*

Candy dish w/lid. *Courtesy of Mike Rothenberger / Mike's Collectibles.*

FRUITS

(1931-1953 Hazel-Atlas Glass Company & others)

Although made for more than 20 years, this is a pattern that has few pieces and most of them are difficult to find. Sherbets and luncheon plates are prolific, but beyond these items Fruits begins to pose a challenge to collectors. Bowls seem to have disappeared along with the smallest and largest tumblers and the pitcher.

Fruits is primarily collected in green. Pink pieces are much harder to find than green, but a low demand suppresses these values.

Collectors need to be aware of the variations of the Fruits motifs if seeking consistency within a collection.

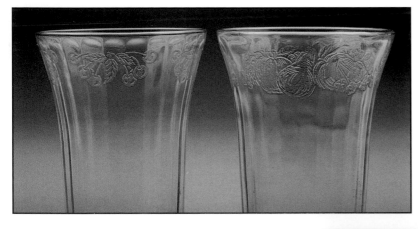

Above: Close-up of a pattern variations on 4" tumblers. *Courtesy of Neil McCurdy - Hoosier Kubboard Glass and Staci & Jeff Shuck/Gray Goose Antiques.*

Right: Cup, saucer, sherbet.

FRUITS	Green	Pink	Qty
Bowl, 5" cereal	40	30	____
Bowl, 8" berry	90	60	____
Cup	10	12	____
Pitcher	120		____
Plate, 8" luncheon	10	12	____
Saucer	6	8	____
Sherbet	10	10	____
Tumbler, 3.5" juice	60	50	____
Tumbler, 4" multiple fruits	25	25	____
Tumbler, 4.25" single			
fruit shown	20	18	____
Tumbler, 5"	150		____

Note: Crystal & iridescent ½ of green items.

8" luncheon plates, two 4" tumblers. *Courtesy of Neil McCurdy - Hoosier Kubboard Glass and Staci & Jeff Shuck/Gray Goose Antiques.*

Pitcher.

GEORGIAN LOVEBIRDS
(1931-1935 Federal Glass Company)

One of the most popular patterns of green Depression Glass is Georgian Lovebirds so named as most pieces have groupings of lovebirds between cascading garlands. Georgian Lovebirds is sometime confused with Cameo, Rose Cameo, and Sylvan (Parrot). Look for birds on round pieces and you have Georgian Lovebirds.

This is a complete pattern from bowls to tumblers. With a little legwork most pieces can be found and those that pose a challenge won't affect one's ability to serve a meal. The 6.5" deep bowl has gotten very difficult to find. Demand for these bowls has caused a noticeable price increase. Hot plates, 4" sugar lids, and 5.25" tumblers continue to allude most collectors, and the Cold Cut Server is rare indeed. But plates of all sizes, cups and saucers, sherbets, and berry bowls are available and moderately priced. Remember to make note of which size creamer or sugar you have so when buying the mate you have a matched set. We recommend that you carry *Mauzy's Comprehensive Handbook of Depression Glass Prices* and inventory your collection using the quantity column to avoid mistakes.

Back row: 7.5" berry bowl, 9.25" dinner plate; *front row:* 4.5" berry bowl, 5.75" cereal bowl, 6.5" deep bowl. *Courtesy of Ardell & George Conn.*

Top: Butter, 11.25" platter w/ tab handles, 3" creamer, 3" sugar w/ lid. *Courtesy of Ardell & George Conn.*

Center: 4" tumbler, 5.25" tumbler, 9.25" dinner plate, cup & saucer, sherbet. *Courtesy of Ardell & George Conn.*

Bottom: *Back row:* 9" oval vegetable bowl, 8" luncheon plate, 5" hot plate dish; *front:* 6" sherbet plate. *Courtesy of Ardell & George Conn.*

GEORGIAN LOVEBIRDS	Green	Qty
Bowl, 4.5" berry	12	____
Bowl, 5.75" cereal	25	____
Bowl, 6.5", deep	100	____
Bowl, 7.5" berry	70	____
Bowl, 9" oval vegetable	60	____
Butter dish base	30	____
Butter dish lid	55	____
Butter complete	85	____
Cold Cut Server (18.5" wooden lazy Susan w/7 indentations for 5" hot plate dishes)	trtp*	____
Creamer, 3"	14	____
Creamer, 4"	18	____
Cup	12	____
Hot plate dish, 5"	100	____
Plate, 6" sherbet	10	____
Plate, 8" luncheon	12	____
Plate, 9.25" dinner	40	____
Plate, 9.25" dinner, center design only	25	____
Platter, 11.25" w/tab handles	70	____
Saucer	8	____
Sherbet	15	____
Sugar base, 3"	14	____
Sugar lid for 3" base	50	____
Sugar base, 4"	18	____
Sugar lid for 4" base	300	____
Tumbler, 4"	80	____
Tumbler, 5.25"	150	____

Note: Crystal hot plate, $35. Amber sherbet, $40.

*trtp = too rare to price

HARP

(1954-1957 Jeannette Glass Company)

Harp isn't really a Depression Glass pattern as it was manufactured in the 1950s. However, it has a large following and needs to be included.

There are only a few pieces of Harp. Pedestal cake stands are the most important of these as they continue to be a very popular accessory. Many people stack pedestal cake stands creating a dramatic arrangement. Harp cake stands are available in a variety of colors including crystal (clear), ice blue, shell pink, and transparent pink.

Crystal Harp normally has a gold trim that collectors expect to be in good, unworn condition.

The 7" plate is the only plate available making Harp appropriate for desserts, luncheons, and given its time of production, Bridge Parties. This plate is found in two styles: the edge may be flat or the edge may be slightly rolled up. Do make note of the style you have if you want your collection consistent.

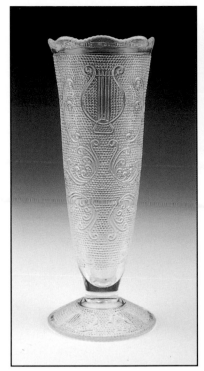

Above: Tray w/open handles in shell pink. *Courtesy of Scott & Rhonda Hackenburg / Blue Jay Antiques & Collectibles.*

Left: 7.5" vase.

Below: *Back:* tray w/ open handles; *front:* 9" cake stand, cup & saucer, ashtray/coaster, 7" plate. *Courtesy of Bettye S. James.*

HARP	Crystal	Qty
Ashtray/coaster	10	____
Coaster	8	____
Cup	35	____
Cake stand, 9"	25	____
Plate, 7", 2 styles	25	____
Saucer	15	____
Tray w/2 open handles	40	____
Vase, 7.5"	35	____

Note: Colored cake stands, $100 each; pink cake stands, $200. Ice blue cake stand found with more than one surface motif. Look for Harp design on pedestal. Shell Pink tray, $70.

Jeannette Glass Company Sticker found on Harp glassware. *Courtesy of Scott & Rhonda Hackenburg / Blue Jay Antiques & Collectibles.*

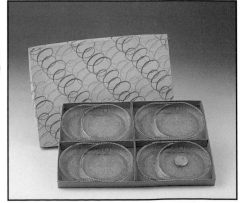

Boxed set of ashtrays/coasters. *Courtesy of Scott & Rhonda Hackenburg / Blue Jay Antiques & Collectibles.*

Creamer & sugar.

HERITAGE
Reproduced
(1940-1955 Federal Glass Company)

When Heritage was introduced in 1940 pink was no longer the fashionable color that it had been in previous years. Thus, Federal Glass Company issued this pattern primarily in crystal (clear). There are only ten items in this pattern with the 8.5" berry bowl and 10.5" fruit bowl being the most difficult to find. There are not many collectors of this pattern, so the competition among potential owners to have these bowls is not as great as the demand for many other Depression Glass patterns and pieces.

Take note of the reproduction information prior to making a purchase. The reproduction green color is more like the avocado seen in the 1960s and 1970s. Indiana Glass Company used this shade of green in newer releases of Daisy. The older green bowls are produced in the transparent green color seen in other Depression Glass patterns.

Back row: 9.25" dinner plate, 8" luncheon plate; *front row:* 10.5" fruit bowl, 5" berry bowl, cup & saucer.

HERITAGE	Crystal	Pink	Blue & Green	Qty
Bowl, 5" berry *R*	8	50	60	____
Bowl, 8.5" berry *R*	45	125	200	____
Bowl, 10.5" fruit	15			____
Creamer, 3"	30			____
Cup	8			____
Plate, 8" luncheon	10			____
Plate, 9.25" dinner	14			____
Plate, 12" sandwich	15			____
Saucer	5			____
Sugar, 3"	28			____

Reproduction information: All berry bowls marked "MC" or "N" connected to a horizontal bar are new. All amber pieces are new. Green pieces that are too dark are new.

HEX OPTIC
(1928-1932 Jeannette Glass Company)

Hex Optic is sometimes confused with Pebble Optic (Raindrops) and Thumbprint. If you are having doubts about a piece you may want to check the listings of these patterns as well.

Jeannette Glass Company manufactured Hex Optic with some "signature" characteristics. The creamer has a triangular handle that is found on some Jeannette Glass measuring cups. Jeannette is known for their wonderful ultramarine color. We are including the ultramarine tumbler for your consideration. One can see that although there is a honeycomb-type of design, it is larger than the genuine Hex Optic texture. Even the shape is a bit different, however, the color is undeniably Jeannette.

Iridescent pitchers and tumblers seem to be everywhere and it appears as though no one is buying them. But pieces in pink and green are difficult to find, particularly ruffled edged mixing bowls. These normally have some kind of damage somewhere along the rim, as do the refrigerator dishes. When dealing with kitchen glass one sometimes needs to be a bit forgiving and consider the difference between use and abuse. It is much harder to find perfect kitchen glass than it is to find perfect dinnerware.

9" footed pitcher, 5.75" footed tumbler. *Courtesy of Michael Rothenberger/Mike's Collectibles.*

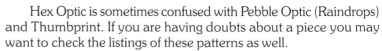

Ice bucket w/ metal handle, 5" pitcher w/ sunflower base.

HEX OPTIC	Pink & green	Qty
Bowl, 4.25" berry, ruffled edge	10	____
Bowl, 7.5" berry	15	____
Bowl, 7.25" mixing, ruffled edge	20	____
Bowl, 8.25" mixing, ruffled edge	22	____
Bowl, 9" mixing, ruffled edge	25	____
Bowl, 10" mixing, ruffled edge	28	____
Bucket reamer	65	____
Butter dish base (rectangular)	50	____
Butter dish lid (rectangular)	50	____
Butter complete (rectangular to hold 1 lb. of butter)	100	____
Creamer, 2 handle designs	10	____
Cup, 2 handle designs	10	____
Ice bucket w/ metal handle	40	____
Pitcher, 5" w/ sunflower base	28	____
Pitcher, 8" flat	240	____
Pitcher, 9" w/foot	65	____
Plate, 6" sherbet	8	____
Plate, 8" luncheon	10	____
Platter, 11" round	25	____
Refrigerator dish, 4" x 4"	30	____
Refrigerator dishes, 3 round containers stacked w/ 1 lid	120	____
Salt & pepper	50	____
Saucer	8	____
Sherbet	12	____
Sugar, 2 handle designs	10	____
Tumbler, 2" whiskey	12	____
Tumbler, 3" flat	8	____
Tumbler, 4.75" w/foot	10	____
Tumbler, 5" flat	8	____
Tumbler, 5.75" w/foot	12	____
Tumbler, 7" w/foot	15	____

5" flat tumbler, 4.75" ultramarine tumbler, 3.75" flat tumbler.

Salt & pepper shakers in 2 colors. *Courtesy of Michael Rothenberger/Mike's Collectibles.*

Creamer.

Cup & saucer.

Note: Iridescent items worth ½ of those in pink & green, except tumbers and pitcher worth 1/4 of those in pink and green. Tumblers may be found in thick & thin styles. Ultramarine 4.75" flat tumbler, $20.

7.25" ruffled edge mixing bowl, 5.75" footed tumbler, 5" flat tumbler.

HIAWATHA
(Late 1930s-1940s Dominion Glass Company Limited)

Dominion Glass Company Limited produced the Hiawatha pattern primarily in crystal (clear). Also pictured is a fired-on red sherbet, so perhaps additional pieces will be found. This is another wonderful Canadian pattern that we also discovered in Oregon. It is natural to expect some Canadian glassware would have drifted south, but after seeing the great pieces and patterns that Canadians have enjoyed we suspect many Americans will broaden their collections and actively seek this glassware.

On cursory inspection, Hiawatha appears similar to Saguenay, another Canadian pattern featured in this book. Hiawatha and Saguenay were produced by the same company and have the same bottoms. The Hiawatha design is that of a series of squared-off diamond shapes while the Saguenay design has fine ribs that resemble Jeannette Glass Company's Homespun pattern. Saguenay was produced in a broader palette of colors, which are also presented in this book.

HIAWATHA	Crystal	Qty
Butter dish base	8	____
Butter dish lid	8	____
Butter complete	16	____
Creamer	6	____
Plate, 6" sherbet	4	____
Sherbet	4	____
Sugar	6	____

Note: Red fired-on sherbet $8.

Back row: 6" sherbet plate, creamer; *front row:* butter dish, sherbet, fired-on sherbet, sugar. *Courtesy of Ian Warner & Mike Posegay.*

HOBNAIL

(1934-1936 Hocking Glass Company)

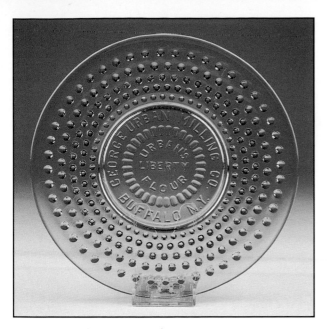

8.5" luncheon plate w/ advertisement ($35).

Hobnail is equally available in pink and in crystal (clear). One tends to find the same pieces of pink again and again and the same pieces of crystal over and over again. It is the pieces with the red trim that are the most difficult to find. With many collectors opting to use red as the basic color of their kitchen it is possible that this red-trimmed Hobnail will become popular. Some Hobnail items aren't particularly common, such as the decanter. However, there is not a great demand for this pattern so the prices have not risen. Because Hobnail has a distinct look it is not often mixed with other patterns, either.

The pink luncheon plate with the advertisement was issued in 1934 as a centennial celebration for Liberty Flour, George Urban Milling Co. in Buffalo, New York. This was the first year of production for Hobnail.

If you find glassware that looks like Hobnail but is opalescent you may have found Moonstone or some Fenton Glassware.

4.75" water tumbler, 3.75" juice tumbler, 2.5" whiskey tumbler w/red trim.

Above: 8.5" luncheon plate, 3 oz. footed tumbler w/ red trim, sherbet.

Left:as Sherbet. *Courtesy Of Neil McCurdy-Hoosier Kubboard Glass.*

HOBNAIL	Pink & crystal	Qty
Bowl, 5.5" cereal	10	____
Bowl, 7" salad	10	____
Creamer	10	____
Cup	8	____
Decanter w/stopper	45	____
Goblet, 10 oz. water	10	____
Goblet, 13 oz. iced tea	10	____
Pitcher, 18 oz. milk	35	____
Pitcher, 67 oz.	45	____
Plate, 6" sherbet	8	____
Plate, 8.5" luncheon *R*	10	____
Saucer, same as 6" sherbet plate	8	____
Sherbet *R*	10	____
Sugar	10	____
Tumbler, 1.5 oz. flat whiskey, 2.5"	10	____
Tumbler, 3 oz. ftd. juice, 4"	10	____
Tumbler, 5 oz. flat juice, 4"	10	____
Tumbler, 5 oz. ftd. cordial, 3.75"	10	____
Tumbler, 9 or 10 oz. flat water, 4.5"	10	____
Tumbler, 15 oz. flat iced tea	12	____

Note: Items with red trim worth 50% more.

Reproduction information: 8.5" luncheon plates and sherbets are currently being made in blue, green, and a deeper shade of pink.

HOLIDAY
(1947-1949 Jeannette Glass Company)

Holiday is a pattern that is primarily collected in pink, however Dave and Jamie Moriarty found an interesting iridescent piece and brought it to our attention. They have a 10.25" serving plate with open handles. It looks similar to the common Windsor plate of the same size also with open handles. The point that shouldn't be missed is that Jeannette Glass Company used the Windsor molds from 1932 to create the Holiday line. However, we know of no other Holiday iridescent 10.25" plates so we don't know if this was a result of a worker in the factory having a little fun or if this is a piece that has just gone undocumented. Because we don't know if any others exist it is currently listed as too rare to price. If you have

one of these, or any other unlisted pieces do let us know!

Glass fanatics often like some trivia so here are a few numbers to throw around as we have had the good fortune to use information from original boxes:

Jeannette marking	listed as
#2809 dinner plate pink	Plate, 9" dinner
#2812 sherbet pink	Sherbet
#2813 sherbet plate pink	Plate, 6" sherbet
#2842 tumbler pink	Tumbler, 4" flat
#2865 cake plate pink	Plate, 10.25" cake w/3 feet

Holiday is not a difficult pattern to collect in pink. As with most Depression Glass patterns, there are a few pieces that will require more effort to find. These include the 10.75" console bowl, 10.25" cake plate, 13.75" chop plate, and 6" footed tumbler. As there are dozens and dozens of edges on each piece be sure to examine a piece carefully before making a purchase. If you are using eBay as a source you will do best to search under "buttons and bows."

10.5" sandwich tray, 10.25" cake plate, 13.75" chop plate, 9" dinner plate. *Courtesy of Donna L. Cehlarik.*

10.25" plate with open handles. *Courtesy of Dave & Jamie Moriarty.*

Back row: 11.25" platter, 6.75" pitcher; *front row:* sugar w/ lid, 4.75" milk pitcher, creamer. *Courtesy of Donna L. Cehlarik.*

HOLIDAY	Pink	Qty
Bowl, 5.25" berry	15	____
Bowl, 7.75" soup	60	____
Bowl, 8.5" berry	40	____
Bowl, 9.5" oval vegetable	30	____
Bowl, 10.75" console	150	____
Butter dish base	25	____
Butter dish lid	50	____
Butter complete	75	____
Candlestick, ea.	75	____
Creamer	12	____
Cup, 2 styles	10	____
Pitcher, 4.75" milk	85	____
Pitcher, 6.75"	50	____
Plate, 6" sherbet	10	____
Plate, 9" dinner	20	____
Plate, 10.25" cake w/3 feet	125	____
Plate, 13.75" chop	125	____
Platter, 11.25"	35	____
Saucer	8	____
Sherbet	10	____
Sugar base	12	____
Sugar lid	38	____
Tray, 10.5" sandwich	25	____
Tumbler, 4" flat	25	____
Tumbler, 4" footed	50	____
Tumbler, 6" footed	175	____

Note: Iridescent pieces ½ the value of pink, except 10.25" with two open handles, too rare to price.

Top: *Back row:* butter, 9.5" oval vegetable bowl, sherbet on 6" sherbet plate; *front row:* 5.25" berry bowl, candlesticks, cup & saucer. *Courtesy of Donna L. Cehlarik.*

Center: *Back:* 7.75" soup bowl; *front row:* 8.5" berry bowl, 10.75" console bowl. *Courtesy of Donna L. Cehlarik.*

Bottom: 6" footed tumbler, 4" flat tumbler, 4" footed tumbler. *Courtesy of Donna L. Cehlarik.*

HOMESPUN
(1938-1940 Jeannette Glass Company)

As Homespun was only produced for two years, you may experience some frustration during your hunt. The 4" footed juice tumbler and 6" sherbet plate are quite common. Beyond these two items, the search gets increasingly difficult, culminating with the butter dish and child's tea set. Actually the single most prized piece in this pattern is the cover for the child's tea pot.

Hazel-Atlas manufactured several finely ribbed items that blend nicely with Homespun, but these are not Jeannette pieces. If you enjoy enhancing a collection with additional treasures, you may appreciate knowing about them. The tumblers pose the greatest concern, so if you are a purist, consult the Homespun listing for measurements prior to making a purchase. Both 9 ounce Hazel-Atlas water tumblers are not straight-sided; rather they curve outwardly in the middle and are rimmed at the top with a smooth band of glass. One style is completely ribbed while the other has bands of ribs separated by panels of plain glass. Smaller juice glasses in both of these designs are also available. Hazel-Atlas pitchers that resemble Homespun include an 80 ounce tilt pitcher that is fairly common and a 70 ounce water pitcher whose ribs are in an inverted "U" design. This second pitcher is not easily found. Two additional pitchers include an 80 ounce blown pitcher with an ice lip with clusters of fine ribs in between panels of smooth glass and a ribbed diminutive 20 ounce milk pitcher.

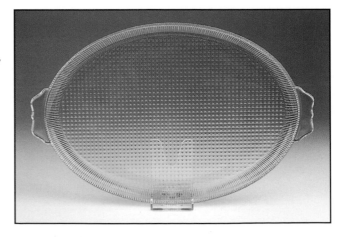

Top: *Back:* 9.25" dinner plate; *front row:* 4" footed juice tumbler w/ ribs extending to the top rim, 4" footed juice tumbler w/ smooth glass at rim, sherbet. *Courtesy of Diefenderfer's Collectibles & Antiques.*

Center: Sugar w/ Jeannette Glass Company lid (there is no Homespun sugar lid), butter, creamer. *Courtesy of Vic & Jean Laermans.*

Bottom: 13" platter/tray w/ tab handles. *Courtesy of Charlie Diefenderfer.*

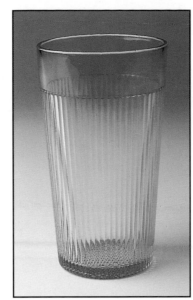

Right: 5.25" flat iced tea tumbler. *Courtesy of Charlie Diefenderfer.*

Below: 6.5" footed tumbler & 5.75" flat iced tea tumbler, Hazel-Atlas tumbler. *Courtesy of Vic & Jean Laermans.*

HOMESPUN	Pink	Qty
Bowl, 4.5" berry w/tab handles	20	____
Bowl, 5" cereal w/tab handles	35	____
Bowl, 8.25" berry	40	____
Butter dish base	40	____
Butter dish lid	80	____
Butter complete	120	____
Coaster	12	____
Creamer	15	____
Cup	20	____
Plate, 6" sherbet	10	____
Plate, 9.25" dinner	20	____
Platter/tray, 13" w/tab handles	20	____
Saucer	10	____
Sherbet	25	____
Sugar	15	____
Tumbler, 3.75", 5 oz. ftd. juice	10	____
Tumbler, 3.75", 7 oz.	25	____
Tumbler, 4", 8 oz. flat water w/flare	25	____
Tumbler, 4.25", 9 oz. flat	25	____
Tumbler, 4.75", 9 oz. flat	25	____
Tumbler, 5.25", 12.5 oz. flat iced tea	35	____
Tumbler, 5.75", 13.5 oz. flat iced tea	35	____
Tumbler, 6.25", 15 oz. w/foot	40	____
Tumbler, 6.5", 15 oz. w/foot	40	____

Note: Crystal items worth ½ value of pink.

HOMESPUN CHILD'S TEA SET	Pink	Crystal	Qty
Cup	40	20	____
Plate	20	10	____
Saucer	25	10	____
Tea pot	60		____
Tea pot cover	150		____
Complete set			
Pink 14 items	550		____
Crystal 12 items		160	____

Complete Homespun Child's Tea Set.

HORSESHOE

(1930-1933 Indiana Glass Company)

The majority of collectors ask for this pattern by name rather than number, so to simplify matters we have elected to list this pattern by its nickname rather than by the accurate name of "Number 612."

In our first book we indicated that green collectors outnumbered yellow collectors. Although that is still true, there has been a shift and an increasingly larger number of people are now looking for yellow. Yellow Horseshoe has a bright, truly yellow color that is pleasing and cheerful and deserves to be finally noticed.

The butter dish continues to be the most difficult piece to find, and pitcher will also be a challenge as well as three of the tumblers while the 11.5" sandwich plate is extremely common. Here's another eBay hint: "Indiana Horseshoe" will give the most successful search results.

Horseshoe is particularly susceptible to two types of damage. The first of these is scratching. It is difficult to find any plate that has not suffered knife damage. It behooves you to hold up to the light any Horseshoe plate that you may be considering for purchase. Finding a perfectly unscathed piece will be next to impossible, but you may want to pass on a plate that has a myriad of criss-crossed scratches. The second damage to consider involves the actual manufacture of these pieces. Horseshoe was molded with a minute rim of extra glass along the outer edge of many pieces. When running a fingernail along this rim, one should expect to find some nicking here as it was unavoidable. The dings to this extra glass do not represent the same kind of damage and chipping that would negatively impact the value of other Depression Glass patterns.

Back row: 9.5" luncheon plate, 10.5" grill plate, 9.5" bowl; *front row:* 9 oz. footed tumbler, cup & saucer, sugar, creamer. *Courtesy of Diefenderfer's Collectibles & Antiques.*

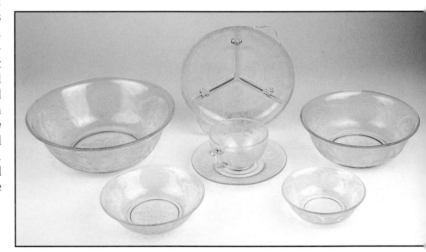

Back: 3-part relish; *middle row:* 8.5" vegetable bowl, cup & saucer, 7.5" salad bowl; *front row:* 6.5" cereal bowl, 4.5" berry bowl. *Courtesy of Vic & Jean Laermans.*

HORSESHOE	Green	Yellow	Qty
Bowl, 4.5" berry	30	30	----
Bowl, 6" cereal	35	35	----
Bowl, 7.5" salad	30	30	----
Bowl, 8.5" vegetable	40	40	----
Bowl, 9.5"	50	50	----
Bowl, 10.5" oval vegetable	40	40	----
Butter dish base	trtp*		----
Butter dish lid	trtp*		----
Butter complete	trtp*		----
Candy dish, lid has design, 3-part base is plain (may be in metal holder)	300		----
Creamer	20	25	----
Cup	12	15	----
Pitcher	400	500	----
Plate, 6" sherbet	10	10	----
Plate, 8.25" salad	15	15	----
Plate, 9.5" luncheon	15	15	----
Plate, 10.5" grill	125	175	----
Plate, 11.5" sandwich	25	35	----
Platter, 10.75"	30	40	----
Relish, 3-part	30	45	----
Saucer	10	10	----
Sherbet	18	18	----
Sugar	20	25	----
Tumbler, 4.25" flat	200		----
Tumbler, 4.75" flat	200		----
Tumbler, 9 oz. w/foot, 4.75"	30	40	----
Tumbler, 12 oz. w/foot	200	200	----

Note: Pink candy dish, $200

*trtp = too rare to price

9 oz. footed tumbler, 12 oz. footed tumbler, pitcher. *Courtesy of Vic & Jean Laermans.*

Butter. *Courtesy of Debora & Paul Torsiello, Debzie's Glass.*

INDIANA CUSTARD
(1933-1935 Indiana Glass company)

Herbert Moller submitted the patent for Indiana Custard in 1933. It was manufactured only in ivory for two short years. In 1957, Indiana Glass Company slightly altered Moller's design and manufactured a line of milk (white) glass named Orange Blossom.

Indiana Custard is a substantial glass that is nicely finished with no rough seams and molds. The ivory color is rich and blends well with virtually any décor. For a period of time it looked as though this pattern was becoming increasingly popular, but it seems as though that has not happened.

All of the pieces are available to set the table and eat the meal except for tumblers and shakers. The most important serving pieces are also a part of this pattern so it is truly usable. It does appear that most collectors prefer transparent glassware. If you are considering starting a collection of Depression Glass this is a pattern worth considering.

Creamer & sugar w/ lid. *Courtesy of Vic & Jean Laermans.*

12" x 9" platter, 9.5" oval vegetable bowl. *Courtesy of Staci & Jeff Shuck/Gray Goose Antiques.*

INDIANA CUSTARD	Ivory	Qty
Bowl, 5.5" berry	20	____
Bowl, 6.5" cereal	30	____
Bowl, 7.5" soup	40	____
Bowl, 9" berry	50	____
Bowl, 9.5" oval vegetable	40	____
Butter dish base	20	____
Butter dish lid	40	____
Butter complete	60	____
Creamer, 3.5"	20	____
Cup	40	____
Plate, 6" sherbet	12	____
Plate, 7.5" salad	25	____
Plate, 8.75" luncheon	25	____
Plate, 9.75" dinner	45	____
Platter, 12" x 9"	60	____
Saucer	10	____
Sherbet	125	____
Sugar base, 3.5"	20	____
Sugar lid	30	____

IRIS

(1928-1932, iridescent in 1950 & 1969,
white in 1970 Jeannette Glass Company)

The big news in Iris is that reproductions still continue to be made. New glass is coming from Asia. First let's address the dinner plate. Where the "herringbone" design ends near the rim of the new Iris dinner plate this design is connected in an exacting zigzag kind of arrangement. The "herringbone" in old dinner plates is not connected and ends in a feather-like design with increasingly smaller lines. The 6.5" tumbler with a foot is also reproduced and, in South Carolina, Pennsylvania, and points in between, we have seen them in Depression Glass dealers' booths marked as if old. Please educate yourself and buy with care. The new 6.5" tumblers are missing a stem of smooth glass that extends up and toward a mold line. There are two mold seams and both should have a stem coming up and pointing to the left. Old tumblers have two, but new ones are missing one. (Be sure to examine the picture showing the new and old tumbler next to each other). However, if this is confusing to you there is another way to tell these apart. Turn the 6.5" tumbler upside down. New tumblers have a pointy zigzag of glass circling near the outer edge. This is significantly rounder and smoother on old tumblers.

Production of Iris in America continued into the 1970s with red and gold Iris being made in 1946. There is no way of determining the age of most Jeannette pieces. However, the footed base of the oldest candy jars have lines or rays and newer ones do not. Keep in mind these "newer" candy jars are already over thirty years old.

Included in this presentation are two interesting pieces. First is a 11.5" fired-on ruffled fruit bowl with a chrome base and hand painted flowers. This sold on eBay for about $170. Second is a nine-ounce flat tumbler that is listed as a Jeannette Glass #318 tumbler, worth $35. This is Chrysanthemum and Herringbone and shares the same "herringbone" background as Iris. We understand that a matching pitcher may exist and now the mystery to be solved is whether or not there is dinnerware.

Worth noting is that a pink Iris vase sold on eBay in August 2000 for more that $150. If you are looking for this pattern on eBay you will find the most success by searching for "iris herringbone."

Glass fanatics often like some trivia so here are a few numbers to throw around as we have had the good fortune to use information from original boxes:

Center: *Back row:* pitcher, candlesticks; *front row:* 4.25" wine goblet, sherbet on 5.5" sherbet plate, 6" tumbler w/ foot. *Courtesy of Carol L. Ellis.*

Right: 9" dinner plate, 8" luncheon plate, 5.5" sherbet plate, 11.75" sandwich plate. *Courtesy of Lucille & Joseph Palmieri.*

Jeannette marking	listed as
#309 tumbler	Tumbler, 6" w/foot
#390 plate	Plate, 11.75" sandwich

All Iris pieces are three digit numbers that start with the number 3. It is interesting to note that the Chrysanthemum and Herringbone tumbler also begins with the number 3.

Finally, we are asking for some information on frosted Iris. A collector with 8" and 11.75" plates that are frosted contacted us. If you know the dates of production and have information regarding the pieces that were made with this finish we would appreciate hearing from you.

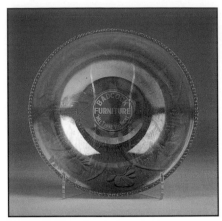

8" beaded rim berry bowl advertising Babcock Furniture, $150. *Courtesy of Walter Lemiski / Waltz Time Antiques.*

Back row: 7.5" coupe soup, 9" vase; *front:* candlestick, cup & saucer, 4" flat tumbler, demitasse cup & saucer. *Courtesy of Lucille & Joseph Palmieri.*

Back row: butter, sherbet, 9.5" pitcher; *front row:* sugar w/ lid, creamer, candy jar w/ lid, coaster. *Courtesy of Lucille & Joseph Palmieri.*

Back: 11.5" nut bowl; *front:* 9.5" nut bowl, 11.5" fruit bowl. (Note: fruit bowls have 4 slots for knives; nut bowls have holes for a nut cracker and 6 picks.) *Courtesy of Lucille & Joseph Palmieri.*

IRIS	Crystal	Iridescent	Qty
Bowl, 4.5" berry w/beaded rim *R*	60	30	____
Bowl, 5" sauce w/ruffled edge	15	30	____
Bowl, 5" cereal w/straight side	145		____
Bowl, 7.5" coupe soup	185	75	____
Bowl, 8" berry w/ beaded rim	100	40	____
Bowl, 9.5" salad w/ ruffled edge	15	10	____
Bowl, 9.5" nut w/ metal foot and center	125		____
Bowl, 11" fruit w/ flat rim	75		____
Bowl, 11.5" fruit w/ruffled edge	15	10	____
Bowl, 11.5" nut w/ metal foot and center	145	150	____
Bowl, 11.5" fruit w/ metal foot and center	125		____
Butter dish base	15	15	____
Butter dish lid	35	35	____
Butter complete	50	50	____
Candlesticks, ea.	25	25	____
Candy jar w/lid *R*	225		____
Coaster	140		____
Creamer	15	15	____
Cup, coffee	20	18	____
Cup, demitasse	50	200	____
Goblet, 4" wine		35	____
Goblet, 4.25" wine, 3 oz. 2" diameter	20		____
Goblet, 4.25" cocktail, 4 oz. 2.75" diameter	30		____
Goblet, 5.75", 4 oz. wine 2.25" diameter	30	225	____
Goblet, 5.75", 8 oz. water 3" diameter	30	225	____
Lamp shade, 11.5"	75		____
Pitcher, 9.5"	40	50	____
Pitcher, 9.5" w/iris on foot	trtp*		____
Plate, 5.5" sherbet	20	15	____
Plate, 8" luncheon	130		____
Plate, 9" dinner *R*	65	50	____
Plate, 11.75" sandwich	35	35	____
Saucer, coffee	12	12	____
Saucer, demitasse	150	250	____
Sherbet, 2.5" w/foot	30	18	____
Sherbet, 4" w/stem 3.5" diameter	30	250	____
Sugar base	15	15	____
Sugar lid	20	25	____
Tumbler, 4" flat	160		____
Tumbler, 6" w/foot	25	25	____
Tumbler, 6.5" w/foot *R*	40		____
Tumbler, 6.5" w/iris on foot	200		____
Vase, 9"	30	20	____

Note: Items in green or pink, $125 each. Lamp shade frosted in pink, blue, or white, $65. Demitasse cups & saucers in other colors too rare to price. White vase, $10.

Reproduction Information: Crystal 9" dinner plate: new- herringbone texture ends with an exacting zigzag .25" (1/4") from inner rim, old- herringbone texture ends in a "blur." The Iris design on new dinners looks "puffy" and the outer rim tilts down and may end with an fine but extra ridge of glass before dipping down to the eating surface. Crystal tumblers: new- herringbone texture is not crisp & rays on underside of the feet are pointy, old- herringbone background is crisp and even with smooth rays on the underside of the feet. Crystal 4.5" beaded rim bowl: new- irises have texture unlike the smooth, transparent old flowers. Candy jar: new- foot is missing rays found on foot of old jar.

8" berry bowl w/ beaded rim, 4.5" berry bowl w/ beaded rim, 5" cereal bowl. *Courtesy of Lucille & Joseph Palmieri.*

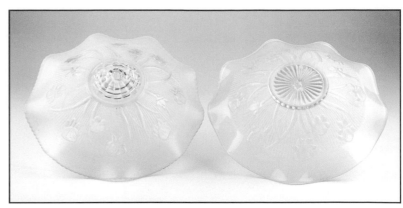

11.5" lamp shade w/ scalloped edge & 11.5" lampshade w/ smooth edge. *Courtesy of Lucille & Joseph Palmieri.*

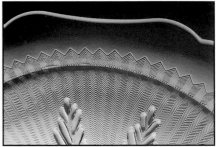

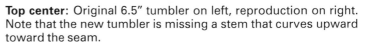

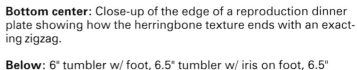

Water goblet with diameter of 3"/height of 5.75", wine goblet with diameter of 2.25"/height of 5.75", wine goblet with diameter of 2"/height of 4.25", cocktail goblet with diameter of 2.75"/height of 4.25", sherbet with diameter of 3.5"/height of 4". *Courtesy of Lucille & Joseph Palmieri.*

Top center: Original 6.5" tumbler on left, reproduction on right. Note that the new tumbler is missing a stem that curves upward toward the seam.

Bottom center: Close-up of the edge of a reproduction dinner plate showing how the herringbone texture ends with an exacting zigzag.

Below: 6" tumbler w/ foot, 6.5" tumbler w/ iris on foot, 6.5" tumbler w/ foot. *Courtesy of Lucille & Joseph Palmieri.*

11.5" fired-on ruffled fruit bowl w/ chrome base & hand painted flowers.

This Jeannette Glass Company tumbler has the same "herringbone" design. *Courtesy of Janice Johnston / Behind The Green Door.*

JUBILEE
(1930 Lancaster Glass Company)

There are many etched patterns of Depression glass. Jubilee is easy to identify because the flowers have twelve petals. The only exceptions are the candy jar and sherbet: both have eleven petals. Lancaster Glass Company made a variety of lovely pieces, many in yellow. Without the flowers it is not Jubilee.

Pieces that make up a luncheon set, 8.75" luncheon plates, cups, saucers, creamers, and sugars are the most common items in yellow Jubilee. Absolutely nothing is common in pink.

If you have a collection of pink or yellow Jubilee it would make us jubilant to get it into the studio for our third edition.

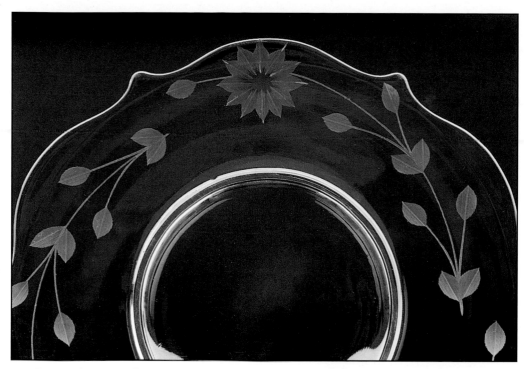

Detail of pattern. *Courtesy of Connie & Bill Hartzell.*

Back row: 11" sandwich plate, 8.75" luncheon plate; *front:* cup & saucer. *Courtesy of Deborah D. Albright.*

6" footed water tumbler. *Courtesy of Deborah D. Albright.*

Creamer & sugar on go-along tray. *Courtesy of Vic & Jean Laermans.*

JUBILEE	Yellow	Pink	Qty
Bowl, 8" w/3 feet	250	350	____
Bowl, 9" fruit w/handles	150		____
Bowl, 11.5" fruit (flat)	175	225	____
Bowl, 11.5" w/3 feet	300	300	____
Bowl, 11.5" w/3 feet (curves inward)	250		____
Bowl, 13" w/3 feet	250	300	____
Candlestick, ea.	125	125	____
Candy jar w/lid (only 11 petals on this piece)	400	500	____
Cheese & cracker set	300	350	____
Creamer, 3.25"	25	35	____
Cup	15	45	____
Goblet, 4", 1 oz. cordial	300		____
Goblet, 4.75", 4 oz. oyster cocktail	100		____
Goblet, 4.75", 3 oz. cocktail	200		____
Goblet, 5.5", 7 oz. champagne or sherbet	125		____
Goblet, 7.5", 11 oz. water	200		____
Mayonnaise, under plate & spoon	300	400	____
Plate, 7" salad	15	30	____
Plate, 8.75" luncheon	15	40	____
Plate, 11" sandwich w/2 handles	50	70	____
Saucer, 2 styles	5	15	____
Sherbet (only 11 petals on this piece)	100		____
Sugar, 3.25"	25	35	____
Tumbler, 5" ftd. juice	120		____
Tumbler, 6" ftd. water	40	80	____
Tumbler, 6.25" ftd. iced tea	175		____
Tray, 11" sandwich w/center handle	225	225	____
Tray, 13.5" salad w/3 feet	250	250	____
Vase, 12"	450	650	____

Note: Crystal items worth ½ yellow prices.

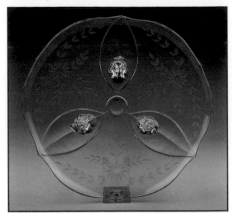

Left: 13.5" salad tray w/ 3 feet. *Courtesy of Diefenderfer's Collectibles & Antiques.*

Center top: 11" sandwich tray w/ center handle. *Courtesy of Diefenderfer's Collectibles & Antiques.*

Center bottom: Mayonnaise & under plate. *Courtesy of Connie & Bill Hartzell.*

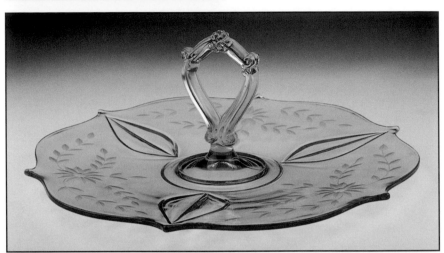

Below: Mayonnaise w/ under plate & spoon, sugar, 11" sandwich tray w/ center handle. *Courtesy of Debora & Paul Torsiello, Debzie's Glass.*

Back: 9" vegetable bowl; *front:* candlesticks, cup, 4.5" sauce bowl, 4" tumbler.

Above: *Back:* 8.5" salad plate; *front row:* 3.5" mayonnaise compote, 5" cereal bowl, sugar, creamer. *Courtesy of Vic & Jean Laermans.*

Right: Sugar, cup & saucer, creamer. *Courtesy of Vic & Jean Laermans.*

KATY
(1930s Imperial Glass Company)

Imperial Glass Company created a number of pieces that resemble Katy. Similar geometric textured, lacy-edged opalescent glass was produced as "Sugar Cane Line" and "Tradition Pattern." There were also numerous Imperial console sets with the same general look as Katy. Many Katy collectors are content to add these to their displays.

Although this is a relatively short pattern, everything is available to set a table and serve a meal. This is one pattern that seems to look even better with every piece added, and a table full of Katy is magnificent!

We have done a fair amount of traveling since the release of the first edition of *Mauzy's Depression Glass*. We've been to Canada, Florida, Maine, Oregon and points in between. We are finding no Katy whatsoever! It doesn't seem to be on the Internet either. Collectors who are trying to complete a set must be very frustrated.

KATY	All opalescent colors	Qty
Bowl, basket	250	____
Bowl, +/- 4.5" sauce	40	____
Bowl, 5" cereal	50	____
Bowl, 5.5"	40	____
Bowl, 5.75"	40	____
Bowl, 7" soup	100	____
Bowl, 9" vegetable	120	____
Bowl, 11" 2-part oval	120	____
Bowl, 11" oval	165	____
Candlestick, ea.	100	____
Creamer	40	____
Cup	50	____
Mayonnaise complete w/under plate & spoon	160	____
Plate, 6.5" bread & butter	20	____
Plate, 8.5" salad	35	____
Plate, 10" dinner	100	____
Plate, 12" cake plate	80	____
Platter, 13"	200	____
Saucer	20	____
Sugar	50	____
Tidbit, 8" & 10" plates	150	____
Tumbler, 4"	75	____

LA FURISTE
(1920s-1930s Lotus Glass Company)

Ohio-based Lotus Glass Company produced La Furiste in the 1920s and 1930s. Lotus made no glass, instead they embellished it. Overlays, etchings, and colors were added to blanks received from glass manufacturers. The gold was often 24 Karat and the silver was Sterling.

La Furiste, etching No. 0907, was available in amber, crystal (clear), green, and rose (pink). The border may have included a 22 Karat embellishment. Items listed came from Lotus catalog pages. We have received no input from collectors or dealers as to the pricing provided.

This is a pattern not normally found on Internet auction sites, however it can be found on websites devoted to Depression Glass.

Back: 12.5" x 10" platter w/ 2 open handles; *front row:* 5.5" candlesticks, sugar, creamer, 10.5" muffin plate w/ 2 handles that turn up. *Courtesy of Bob & Cindy Bentley.*

LA FURISTE	Rose, Green, Amber, Crystal	Qty
Bowl, 7.75" x 5.5" rose bowl w/3 feet	65	____
Bowl, 8.5" x 11" oval	75	____
Bowl, 8.75" x 5.5" rose bowl	65	____
Bowl, 9" bell w/ handles (8-sided)	75	____
Bowl, 10" nut w/center handle (8-sided)	85	____
Bowl, 10" w/rolled edge	75	____
Bowl, 10.5" x 4.5" celery(boat shaped)	80	____
Bowl, 11.25" w/rolled edge w/3 feet	85	____
Bowl, 12" crimped w/3 feet	75	____
Bowl, 12" flared rim w/3 feet	75	____
Bowl, 12" x 3.5" w/rolled edge	85	____
Bowl, 12.25" x 4.5" celery w/2 handles	75	____
Bowl, 12.5" x 3" w/flared rim	75	____
Bowl, 13" w/flared rim	80	____
Candlestick, ea. 3.5"	50	____
Candlestick, ea. 5.5"	55	____
Cheese & Cracker	85	____
Comport, 7"	60	____
Creamer	40	____
Cup	30	____
Decanter w/stopper	175	____
Fruit Salad w/foot (similar to a sherbet in other patterns)	40	____
Goblet, 9 oz.	45	____
Ice tub, 4" w/2 handles	65	____

	Rose, Green, Amber, Crystal	Qty
Pitcher	150	____
Plate, 6" bread & butter	20	____
Plate, 7.5" salad	25	____
Plate, 8" salad	25	____
Plate, 9" dinner	25	____
Plate, 10" cake w/center handle	35	____
Plate, 10.5" muffin w/2 handles that turn up	35	____
Plate, 11" sandwich w/2 open handles	35	____
Plate, 12" service (8-sided)	50	____
Plate, 12" pastry w/2 handles	45	____
Platter, 12.5" x 10" w/2 open handles (8-sided)	50	____
Relish, 6" w/3 sections & lid	45	____
Saucer	15	____
Sherbet, 6.5 oz. high (tall stem)	40	____
Sherbet, 6.5 oz. low (short stem)	40	____
Stem, 1.5 oz. cordial	45	____
Stem, 2.75 oz. wine	45	____
Stem, 3.5 oz. cocktail	45	____
Sugar	40	____
Tumbler, 2.5 oz. whiskey w/foot	40	____
Tumbler, 6 oz. w/foot	40	____
Tumbler, 10 oz. w/foot	40	____
Tumbler, 12 oz. iced tea w/foot	45	____
Whipped cream, 3 pieces (comport, under plate, & spoon)	85	____

LAKE COMO
(1935-1937 Anchor Hocking Glass Company)

Lake Como is a blending of Anchor Hocking molds and materials. Glassware used for Lake Como is plain white Vitrock with blue embellishments. The St. Denis cup and saucer is the same mold used in the Fire-King Breakfast Set and the Fire-King 1700 Line.

This is a pattern that is not easy to find, particularly with bright, unworn colors. Although not in high demand dealers find that whatever they have is usually fairly easy to sell.

Like many of the Fire-King lines there are few pieces of Lake Como from which to select. However, everything you need to set a table (except for tumblers) is available with the added benefit of a few serving pieces.

Salt & pepper. *Courtesy of Michael Rothenberger/Mike's Collectibles.*

Back: 7.25" salad plate; *front row:* St. Denis cup & saucer, sugar.

11" platter. *Courtesy of Charlie Diefenderfer.*

LAKE COMO	White w/ decorations	Qty
Bowl, 6" cereal	35	____
Bowl, 9.75" vegetable	80	____
Bowl, flat soup	120	____
Creamer	35	____
Cup	35	____
Cup, St. Denis	35	____
Plate, 7.25" salad	25	____
Plate, 9.25" dinner	40	____
Platter, 11"	85	____
Salt & pepper	55	____
Saucer	15	____
Saucer, St. Denis	15	____
Sugar	35	____

LAUREL

(1930s   McKee Glass Company)

Glass companies often copied from each other as they competed for consumers' dollars. Anchor Hocking produced Fire-King and McKee produced Laurel. Although Fire-King jade-ite has dominated the marketplace for the past five years since the jade-ite craze began, Laurel is quite popular and performs particularly well on Internet auctions.

Laurel offers a nice variety of pieces some having no Fire-King counterparts such as shakers, tumblers, and candlesticks. Jade Laurel is a more yellow, light green color than Anchor Hocking jade-ite and is marked with the McK in a circle found on most McKee glassware.

However, Laurel has more to offer than Jade glass; there is Poudre Blue. It is hard to assess the value of Poudre Blue as there doesn't appear to be a great quantity of collectors competing for these pieces and prices seem to go all over the place. Consider the following: a sugar sold on eBay for $127.50 in September 2000, yet the rare commemorative plate we have pictured sold for $104.27 in June of 2000.

Regardless of the color of Laurel you select be aware of the fact that plates are made with round (smooth) edges and scalloped edges. Scalloped edges tend to have damage to the delicate points and therefore these pieces are worth more than those with round edges.

6" bowl showing 3 feet on bottom, shaker, 6" sherbet plate, creamer, sugar. *Courtesy of Connie & Bill Hartzell.*

Back: 10.75" platter; *front row:* cheese dish w/ lid, candlestick, cup & saucer. *Courtesy of Connie & Bill Hartzell.*

9.25" grill plate, 9.25" dinner plate, 9.25" dinner plate w/ smooth rim, 7.5" salad plate. *Courtesy of Connie & Bill Hartzell.*

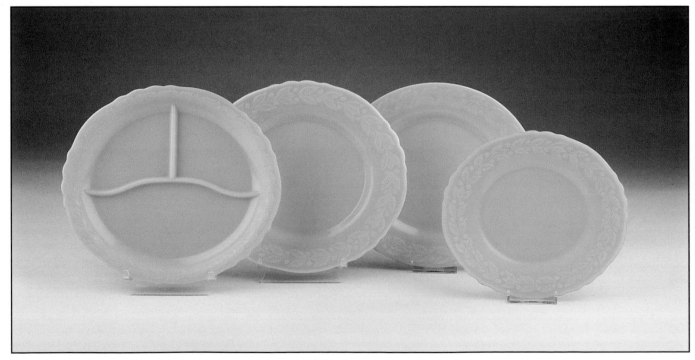

Back row: 4" creamer & sugar; front row: 3" creamer & sugar. Courtesy of Vic & Jean Laermans.

Child's Tea Set with decorated rim. Courtesy of Walter Lemiski / Waltz Time Antiques.

Three different Child's Tea Set creamers & sugars. Courtesy of Vic & Jean Laermans.

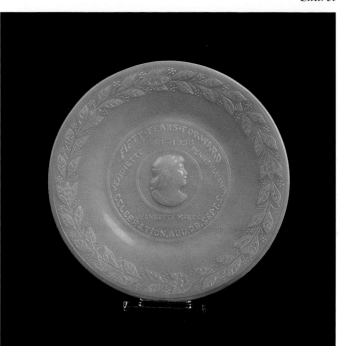

Poudre Blue commemorative 6" plate, which reads, "FIFTY YEARS FORWARD, JEANNETTE PENNSYLVANIA 1888-1938 JEANNETTE MCKEE CELEBRATION AUG. 28. SEPT. 5." *Courtesy of Samantha Parish.*

LAUREL	Jade & Poudre blue	Other colors	Qty
Bowl, 4.75" berry	15	10	____
Bowl, 6" cereal	25	15	____
Bowl, 6" w/3 feet	30	20	____
Bowl, 7.75" soup	85	40	____
Bowl, 9" berry	65	30	____
Bowl, 9.75" oval vegetable	65	30	____
Bowl, 10.5" w/3 feet	90	65	____
Bowl, 11"	70	40	____
Candlestick, ea.	40	20	____
Cheese dish w/lid	375	45	____
Creamer, 3" & 4"	35	15	____
Cup	20	10	____
Plate, 6" sherbet	18	8	____
Plate, 7.5" salad/cheese base	20	25	____
Plate, 9.25" dinner	25	15	____
Plate, 9.25" grill	25	15	____
Platter, 10.75"	95	30	____
Salt & pepper	300	75	____
Saucer	8	5	____
Sherbet	20	12	____
Sugar, 3" & 4"	35	15	____
Tumbler, 4.5", 9 oz.	90	50	____
Tumbler, 5", 12 oz.		90	____
Wine, 3.75"	110	75	____

Note: Round edges are 75% of scalloped edges as priced above.

LAUREL CHILD'S TEA SET	Ivory	Decorated rim	Scotty on Jade	Scotty on Ivory	Qty
Creamer	35	50	150	120	____
Cup	30	40	125	75	____
Plate	20	25	125	75	____
Saucer	12	15	100	50	____
Sugar	35	50	150	120	____
Complete 14-piece set	318	370	1700	1040	____

Back row: 9.25" dinner plate, creamer; front row: candlesticks, 4.75" berry bowl, cup & saucer, shaker.

LINCOLN INN

(1928-1929 Fenton Art Glass Company)

In its one short year of production Lincoln Inn was made in a rainbow of colors: pink, green, ruby, Royal Blue, jade-ite, and crystal (clear), with a list of pieces equally as impressive. Several new finds have even been added: the 5" ruffled bowl with handles, a 4" goblet, and a 3.75" stemmed sherbet. All of these additions are shown and all measurements were carefully confirmed when the pieces were photographed.

Thanks to Kathy McCarney and Doris McMullen for graciously bringing "inn" their wonderful Lincoln Inn collections!

4.25" sherbet w/stem, cup & saucer, 9.75" vase, 5.75" water goblet, 4.5" cone sherbet. *Courtesy of Kathy McCarney.*

6.75" bread & butter plate & 6" water goblet. *Courtesy of Kathy McCarney.*

4.25" sherbets in four colors. *Courtesy of Kathy McCarney.*

LINCOLN INN	All Colors	Qty
Ashtray	25	_____
Bonbon, handles square or oval	20	_____
Bowl, finger	20	_____
Bowl, 5" fruit	15	_____
Bowl, 5" ruffled w/ handles	20	_____
Bowl, 6" cereal	18	_____
Bowl, 6" crimped	18	_____
Bowl, 9"	30	_____
Bowl, 9.25" footed	75	_____
Bowl, 10.5" footed	65	_____
Bowl, 1-handled olive	30	_____
Comport plate	35	_____
Comport, shallow	40	_____
Creamer	30	_____
Cup	20	_____
Goblet, 4"	30	_____
Goblet, cocktail/wine, 5.5"	40	_____
Goblet, water, 6"	40	_____
Mint, flat	30	_____
Mint, oval	30	_____
Nut	30	_____
Pitcher, 7.25"	1000	_____
Plate to line finger bowl	10	_____
Plate, 6.75" bread & butter	10	_____
Plate, 8" salad	15	_____
Plate, 10" dinner	45	_____
Plate, 11.75"	40	_____
Salt & pepper	350	_____
Sandwich server w/ center handle	200	_____
Saucer	8	_____
Sherbet, 3.75" w/stem	25	_____
Sherbet, 4.25" w/stem	25	_____
Sherbet, 4.5" cone	20	_____
Sugar	30	_____
Tumbler, 4 oz. ftd. juice	30	_____
Tumbler, 7 oz. ftd. water, 5.75"	30	_____
Tumbler, 9 oz. flat water	30	_____
Tumbler, 12 oz. ftd. ice tea, 6"	50	_____
Tumbler, 12 oz. flat Shigh ball	30	_____
Vase, 9.75"	150	_____
Vase, 12"	175	_____

Note: Black & Jade-ite salt & pepper, $500 each pair. Add 30% for items with fruit design pressed into center.

4" goblet (green), 4.25" sherbet w/stem (ice blue), 4.5" cone sherbet (red), 5.75" footed water tumbler (crystal), 6" water goblet (cobalt blue), 6" footed iced tea tumbler (crystal). *Courtesy of Kathy McCarney.*

Back row: 11.5" platter, 9.75" oval vegetable bowl, 8" 4-part relish; *front:* cup & saucer, sherbet on 5.5" sherbet plate. *Courtesy of Brad & Tammy James.*

LORAIN
Reproduced

(1929-1932 Indiana Glass Company)

Often when Depression Glass patterns were made in more than one color the listing for the different colors is not the same as certain pieces seemed to have been made in one color and other pieces made in another. This is not true of Lorain as the list of pieces in green is identical to the list of pieces in yellow. Green is much more popular than yellow, much more available than yellow, and much more reasonably priced than yellow.

Both colors suffer with the same problem: plates were manufactured with a line of extra glass along the top surface near the outer edge. Naturally, this glass received bumps and became nicked simply because it extends away from the plate. Many collectors have learned to ignore this as an idiosyncrasy of the pattern.

The 5.75" Lorain goblet is a new addition to the listing. The Avocado green sherbet is from the 1960s.

Back row: 8.25" luncheon plate, 10.25" dinner plate; *front row:* 5.75" goblet, 6" cereal bowl, cup & saucer, 8" deep berry bowl.

LORAIN	Green	Yellow	Qty
Bowl, 6" cereal	60	75	____
Bowl, 7.25" salad	50	60	____
Bowl, 8" deep berry	120	175	____
Bowl, 9.75" oval vegetable	50	60	____
Creamer	20	30	____
Cup	15	20	____
Goblet, 5.75"	40		____
Plate, 5.5" sherbet	10	14	____
Plate, 7.75" salad	15	20	____
Plate, 8.25" luncheon	20	35	____
Plate, 10.25" dinner	75	100	____
Platter, 11.5"	35	55	____
Relish, 8", 4-part	25	40	____
Saucer	7	8	____
Sherbet *R*	28	35	____
Sugar	20	30	____
Tumbler, 4.75"	25	35	____

Note: Crystal prices ½ of yellow, except for Snack Tray with colored trim, $50.

Reproduction Information: Sherbets made in avocado green and milk white are from the 1960s.

Avocado green sherbet from the 1960s. *Courtesy of Marie Talone.*

MADRID
Reproduced
(1932-1938 Federal Glass Company)

Let's begin with the Madrid "Hot Dish Coaster." The price provided is higher than other guides and is still probably too conservative. Several collectors have been forwarding the end of auction reports on eBay whenever one was offered. Consider this: in April 2000 an amber hot dish coaster with indent sold for $495.13. This was the most expensive one we saw, but none were cheap and all were well above our new price of $175.

Since we are on the subject of eBay…in May 2000 a "rare Madrid lamp shade" was offered with a starting bid of $29.95. The description read, "I can find no mention of this shade in any of my books. The shade is 9 ½ inches across and aprox. (sic) 3 inches deep." Have you figured this out? Fortunately all Madrid buyers did as the auction ended with no bids. This was a deep salad bowl that had been made into a "lamp shade" when someone drilled a hole through it. It is imperative that we all be educated consumers.

Now for a new find: a paneled cup in amber. This cup has sixteen distinct facets or panels in the inside and the photograph shows some of them. The panels circle completely around the cup and are evenly spaced. Let us know if this variation is available in other colors.

Shown is the extremely elusive Lazy Susan. The revolving base is wood with indents for hot dish coasters. Other hard-to-find items include the gravy boat and its platter, the ashtray, and even perfect dinner plates! Damaged dinners aren't hard to find, but where are the perfect ones? It's really hard to use your dinnerware if you don't have dinner plates.

Green Madrid is harder to find than amber. The cups, saucers, and sherbets are abundant, but additional items become increasingly challenging to locate. Pink is seen less than green. The 11" flared out console bowl is common and very popular with general collectors of pink Depression Glass who are often drawn to its unique, low shape.

Other pieces of pink are more difficult to find. Blue Madrid is the most elusive color of all, which is reflected in the value of these items.

There are two Madrid sherbets. The 2.75" cone-shaped sherbet made with the Sylvan (Parrot) mold is extremely common. The 2.25" squatty sherbet is much harder to find. One could easily stumble upon fifty cone-shaped sherbets for each squatty sherbet.

This brings us to another interesting point regarding Madrid. As with several other Depression Glass patterns, Madrid came from previously used molds. Federal Glass Company manufactured Sylvan (Parrot) in 1931 and 1932. Although Sylvan is an extremely popular pattern today, Federal executives were dissatisfied with it, believing Sylvan had too much undecorated glass. Plain glass would show any of the inevitable scratching that occurred from use and these decision makers were concerned that homemakers would be unhappy with the long-term performance of the pattern. So, the directive came for the designers to develop a busier design that would fill the plate, thereby providing camouflage for potential scratching. Madrid resulted, and there are few patterns busier than Madrid.

Amber Madrid was reproduced in 1976. New collectors sometimes express concern over this, but there is no mystery to identifying reproduction pieces. Look for a "76" worked into the design near the outer edge of reproduced amber Madrid items. The photograph showing old and new Madrid side by side demonstrates the apparent differences: both in the "76" and the color variance. There is an R after any listed item that has been reproduced, and you can check the reproduction information provided to easily recognize new Madrid.

Back row: 11.5" platter, 10.5" dinner plate; *front row:* 7" soup bowl, 6" sherbet plate, cup, 5.5" flat iced tea tumbler, 5.5" juice pitcher. *Courtesy of Corky & Becky Evans.*

Footed salt & pepper shakers. *Courtesy of Mike Rothenberger / Mike's Collectibles.*

Top: *Back row:* 6" sherbet plate, 8" salad bowl, 10.5" grill plate; *middle row:* cup & saucer, 7" soup bowl, sugar w/lid, creamer; *front row:* footed shaker, flat shaker. *Courtesy of Charlie Diefenderfer.*

Bottom: *Back row:* 8.75" luncheon plate, 10.5" dinner plate, 11.5" platter; *middle row:* 10" oval vegetable bowl, 2.75" cone sherbet, 5.5" footed tumbler, 5.5" flat tumbler; *front row:* hot dish coaster, 5" dessert bowl, 4.25" flat tumbler. *Courtesy of Charlie Diefenderfer.*

Gravy boat on tray/under platter. *Courtesy of Corky & Becky Evans.*

Lazy Susan.
Courtesy of Charles & Theresa Converse.

Facetted cup. *Courtesy of Charles & Theresa Converse.*

MADRID	Amber	Green	Pink	Blue	Qty
Ashtray	225	225			____
Bowl, 4.75" cream soup	25				____
Bowl, 5" dessert	10	10	10	35	____
Bowl, 7" soup *R*	25	25		75	____
Bowl, 8" salad	20	22			____
Bowl, 9.25" berry	25		30		____
Bowl, 9.5" deep salad	40				____
Bowl, 10" oval vegetable	30	30	30	55	____
Bowl, 11" flared out console	25		22		____
Butter dish base *R*	30	40			____
Butter dish lid *R*	55	65			____
Butter complete *R*	85	105			____
Candlestick, ea. *R*	15		15		____
Cookie jar/lid	55		50		____
Creamer *R*	20	20		35	____
Cup *R*	8	10	12	20	____
Cup, paneled	16				____
Gravy boat w/ 6" x 8.25" tray	3000				____
Hot dish coaster, 5"	175	175			____
Hot dish coaster w/indent	175	175			____
Jam dish, 7"	30	40		50	___
Jello mold, 2" high	18				____
Lazy Susan, wooden w/glass hot dish coasters	trtp*				____
Pitcher, 5.5", 36 oz., juice	50				____
Pitcher, 8", 60 oz., square w/applied handle		200		250	____
Pitcher, 8", 60 oz., square w/molded handle	50	150	50	200	____
Pitcher, 8", 80 oz., no ice lip	85	250			____
Pitcher, 8.5", 80 oz., with ice lip	85	250			____
Plate, 6" sherbet	7	7	5	15	____
Plate, 7.5" salad	15	15	12	25	____
Plate, 8.75" luncheon	10	15	12	25	____
Plate, 10.25" relish	25	25	18		____
Plate, 10.5" dinner *R*	60	60		100	____
Plate, 10.5" grill *R*	10	20			____
Plate, 11.25" cake	40		30		____
Platter for under gravy boat	800				____
Platter, 11.5"	25	25	25	40	____
Salt & pepper, footed	140	145		175	____
Salt & pepper, flat *R*	50	75			____
Saucer *R*	5	7	7	12	____
Sherbet, 2.75" cone (Similar to Sylvan sherbet)	5	12		18	____
Sherbet, 2.25", squatty	30				____
Sugar base *R*	20	20		35	____
Sugar lid	65	65		200	____
Tumbler, 4", 5 oz., juice, flat	18	35		45	____
Tumbler, 4", 5 oz., footed	30	45			____
Tumbler, 4.25", 9 oz., water, flat	18	25	20	40	____
Tumbler, 5.5", 12 oz., iced tea, 2 styles, flat	25	35		45	____
Tumbler, 5.5", 10 oz., footed	35	50			____

*trtp = too rare to price

Reproduction information: New colors: AMBER may be too dark and may have a "76" worked into the design, BLUE may be too dark and appear to be glowing, PINK: may be too pale or too bright and the design may be less distinct, CRYSTAL: difficult to discern. The following items **were never originally** produced: 9.5" footed bowl, footed (pedestal) cake stand, footed goblet, 2-part grill plate, preserve stand, short salt & pepper shakers, 10.25" snack tray with 2" cup indent, 11 oz. tumbler with design different from vintage tumblers, and vase. 7" soup bowl: old- design on rim is compact, new-design seems to have 4 layers. Butter: new made in amber & pink and is too dark, knob on lid has vertical mold seam rather than old having horizontal mold seam. Candlestick: new made in amber & crystal with glass ridges to grasp a candle, old are smooth inside. Creamer: new made in amber, crystal, pink, and perhaps blue: new- spouts are formed by applying extra glass, old spouts are formed below top rim. The old handles form pointed pear shape where they meet the sides. New handles form a rounder shape. New has a cup-like appearance and the color may be wrong, particularly amber which may be considerably darker. Saucer: new made in amber, crystal, & pink. New amber & pink have colors that just look wrong, crystal is difficult to discern but the saucer will have less quality. 10.5" dinner plate: new made in amber, blue, crystal, and pink. New- diamond in Madrid motif found in center of dinner plate is surrounded by filled in glass resembling a fat blade of grass with a hook, old- diamond is surrounded by glass that resembles a curved sewing needle with an eye, and then there is the same hook. Points in corners of old dinners are more pronounced than those on new ones. Shakers: new shakers made in crystal & blue are shorter & heavier than old and were issued with plastic lids. Sugar: new made in amber, blue, & crystal. The old handles form pointed pear shape where they meet the sides. New handles form a rounder shape and the color may be wrong.

Note: Crystal hot dish coaster, $40, 8" pitcher, $175. Iridescent items same price as Amber.

Above: *Back:* gravy boat on 6" x 8.25" tray/under platter, 8.5" pitcher w/ no ice lip; *front:* salt & pepper, 5" dessert bowl, creamer, sugar w/ lid. *Courtesy of Corky & Becky Evans.*

Right: Reproduction and original issue 10" oval vegetable bowls. (Note: reproduction is darker and has "76" worked into the design at the top of the item near the rim.)

MANHATTAN
Reproduced
(1939-1941 Anchor Hocking Glass Company)

The popularity of Manhattan continues to grow as new, and often young, collectors come to appreciate the Deco look that is as stylish in an urban setting as it is comfortable in a retro kitchen. Paired with black Bakelite utensils, crystal Manhattan makes a strong statement of one's sense of style and good taste.

Crystal (clear) Manhattan and crystal Iris and are the two most popular clear Depression Glass patterns. As is often the case, once a pattern is in demand reproductions follow. We are aware of reproduction dinner plates in crystal Manhattan that were sold in Canada and a variety of light green items that seem to have infiltrated the Shenandoah Valley of Virginia. Do take the time to read the reproduction information that is provided following the price list, as it is very specific. We would appreciate any additional information if other items are being reproduced.

The 14" relish tray that has no sections is designed to take five inserts along the outer ring with a circular insert in the center. These outer inserts are available in crystal, pink, and Royal Ruby. By collecting five of each color one can create a variety of looks that change with the season. The center insert is always crystal and does not have a bubble foot. Occasionally sellers try to squeeze in a sherbet as the center insert. Seen on the Internet was a Manhattan Lazy Susan, which was a seven-piece relish set on a ball-baring base that allowed the entire unit to revolve.

Companion pieces include a water bottle and cookie jar, which are pictured. There are also go-along cocktail and wine goblets that work well with Manhattan. As there are no goblets with the original line, and only one tumbler, these companion pieces extend the use of the pattern. The water bottle would work nicely as a wine decanter, and the go-along stems finish the look.

5.75" comport, 8" vase, 24 oz. tilted pitcher.
Courtesy of Michael & Kathleen Jones.

Pink is much harder to find than crystal and we still have never had a pink dinner plate. The creamer, sugar, and open candy with three feet are quite common, but beyond these pieces, pink Manhattan becomes a challenge.

There are many edges to each piece of Manhattan. Careful scrutiny of all of them is essential if seeking pristine condition. Additional attention must be paid to bowls for if they have been stacked chances are good that some rim damage has occurred. Before buying a pitcher it should be held up to the light with extra energy spent examining where the handle was applied. This is an area that is often cracked and the Manhattan design tends to conceal it with only cursory inspection.

The jade-ite Manhattan pitcher that was discussed in our first book did find its way to eBay in March 2000 where it reached $11,000 and still failed to meet its reserve.

Sugar, 10.25" dinner plate, tumbler. *Courtesy of Michael & Kathleen Jones.*

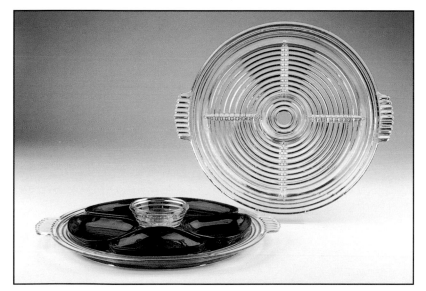

14" relish tray (no sections) w/ 5 outer ruby inserts and center insert having straight-sided base, 14" relish w/ 5 sections. *Courtesy of Michael & Kathleen Jones.*

MANHATTAN	Crystal	Pink	Ruby	Qty
Ashtray, sherbet style	35			
Ashtray, 4" round	15			____
Ashtray, 4.5" square	18			____
Bowl, 4.5" sauce w/handles	10			____
Bowl, 5.25" berry w/handles	20	25		
				____
Bowl, 5.25" cereal	65	125		
Bowl, 7.25" berry w/handles	15			____
Bowl, 8" w/handles	20	25		____
Bowl, 9" salad	25			____
Bowl, 9.5" fruit, w/foot & 2 open handles	45	45		
Candlestick, 4.5" square, ea.	8			____
Candy dish, open w/3 feet		15		____

Coaster	20			____
Comport, 5.75"	42	50		____
Creamer	18	18		____
Cup	20	200		____
Insert for relish tray, outer	8	8	6	____
Insert for relish tray, center	10			____
Pitcher, 24 oz., tilted	35			____
Pitcher, 80 oz., tilted	45	75	450	____
Plate, 6" sherbet/saucer	12	75		____
Plate, 8.5" salad *R*	20			____
Plate, 10.25" dinner *R*	25	275		____
Plate, 14" sandwich	35			____
Salt & pepper, square	40	75		____
Sherbet, bubble foot	12	25		____
Sugar	15	18		____
Tray, 14" relish, 5 sections	20	35		____
Tray, 14" relish, no sections	20			____
Tumbler, bubble foot *R*	20	24		____
Vase, 8", bubble foot *R*	30			____

Note: Companion pieces by Anchor Hocking: Candy dish w/ lid, $45; Cocktail & Wine, 3.5", $12; Decanter w/stopper, $25. Water bottle: clear, $18; Ruby, $250; Forest Green, $150. Go-along cookie jar, $50.

Note: Ashtray w/advertisement, $15. Ruby 24 oz. Pitcher, $500. Green tumblers, $25 each. Iridized tumblers, $15 each. Jade-ite pitcher, too rare to price.

Reproduction Information: 8.5" salad plate new measures 8". Tumblers new made without bubble feet. Vase new is 9.75" rather than 8". Many new pieces in light green are being found. Items include: tumblers, large bowls, and various sizes of plates. This listing may not be complete. 10.25" dinner in crystal: Target Stores were selling new crystal Manhattan dinners. Edges on old are smooth, new have *slight* bead. Old dinners have rounded rings and center circle is 3/8". New dinners have crisp, almost pointy rings, and center circle is 1/4".

Comport, 80oz. tilted pitcher, creamer, sugar.

Ashtray w/ advertisement. *Courtesy of Michael & Kathleen Jones.*

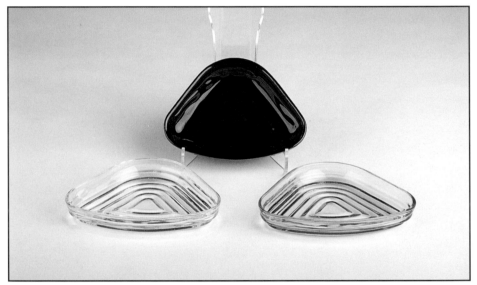

Inserts for the 14" relish are available in crystal, Royal Ruby, & pink.

"Go-along" wine goblet in another style.

"Go-along items" include this wine goblet, water bottle, & cookie jar. *Courtesy of Mike Rothenberger / Mike's Collectibles.*

MAYFAIR "FEDERAL"
(1934 Federal Glass Company)

The look of Mayfair is reminiscent of the facets of gemstones, which were probably the inspiration for the designer who was also a jeweler. Federal Glass Company had advertised Mayfair prior to receiving patent rights. The patent was rejected because Hocking Glass Company already had claimed the name with their own Mayfair pattern. Federal redesigned the molds and changed the name to Rosemary. Shown are some transitional pieces which are a cross between the more decorative Mayfair produced briefly in 1934 and the more simple Rosemary manufactured in 1935 and 1936.

Mayfair "Federal" was only produced for one year. It is usually found in amber although it was made in three colors. There are only thirteen pieces available in this pattern, but all the items necessary to set the table were produced. Some items are quite difficult to find as this is a pattern that few collect, and dealers are often reluctant to keep slow-moving merchandise in their inventory. The supply is low, but the demand continues to be low so the prices are not increasing at this time.

Top: *Back row:* 5" sauce bowl, 6" cereal bowl, 12" platter; *front row:* 10" oval vegetable bowl. *Courtesy of Ardell & George Conn.*

Center: 4.5" tumbler, 9.5" grill plate, cup & saucer, cream soup bowl. *Courtesy of Ardell & George Conn.*

Right: 6.75" salad plate, 9.5" dinner, sugar, creamer. *Courtesy of Ardell & George Conn.*

MAYFAIR "FEDERAL"	Green	Amber	Crystal	Qty
Bowl, 5" sauce	15	10	5	____
Bowl, cream soup	24	20	10	____
Bowl, 6" cereal	10	15	5	____
Bowl, 10" oval vegetable	30	25	15	____
Creamer	20	15	5	____
Cup	15	10	5	____
Plate, 6.75" salad	12	10	5	____
Plate, 9.5" dinner	25	15	10	____
Plate, 9.5" grill	20	12	10	____
Platter, 12"	35	30	15	____
Saucer	8	5	4	____
Sugar, no handles	20	15	5	____
Tumbler, 4.5"	45	30	15	____

Back row: creamer & cream soup bowl in true Mayfair; *front row:* creamer & cream soup bowl in "transitional Mayfair." (Note: transitional has simpler pattern without lattice inside arches.) *Courtesy of Ardell & George Conn.*

MAYFAIR "OPEN ROSE"
Reproduced
(1931-1936 Hocking Glass Company)

Mayfair "Open Rose" is one of the most popular Depression Glass patterns of all. Pink is the most commonly sought-after color and it is not only more abundant, it is more affordable than blue, green, and yellow. Pink Mayfair is available today because it was so popular at its time of manufacture, Hocking Glass Company produced it in large quantities. Many pieces of pink are readily found, such as the 10" vegetable bowl with handles and the 5.75" plate. Others are quite rare. Only about ten pink sugar lids are known to exist, so most collectors will need to resolve themselves to owning an open sugar.

The most common piece of green Mayfair is the sandwich server with center handle. Except for this server, green and yellow Mayfair is much harder to find than blue.

It takes a good deal of time and a great deal of money to assemble a collection of Mayfair in blue, green, or yellow. Pieces in these colors are often looked upon as among the paramount of Depression Glass possibilities.

Of the least interest to collectors, but definitely gaining in popularity is satinized or frosted pink Mayfair which may or may not be found with hand painted embellishments. If pieces do have hand painted decorations collectors expect this to have survived in excellent condition with no chips or wear to the paint.

We were told of a yellow goblet with a square foot. If you have any information regarding this piece please let us know.

A final question for you readers is a report of a pink Mayfair 10" vegetable cover with an inner lip that apparently had a nice, secure fit to the bowl. It was seen in Canada for $150 (American dollars). Again, if you have any information on this or other undocumented Mayfair your help is appreciated.

Do be aware of the Mayfair reproductions that are turning up everywhere. Originally available in catalogues, reproductions are in the secondary marketplace now.

Back row: 9.5" grill plate. 9.5" dinner plate; *front row:* 8.5" luncheon plate, 6.5" round sherbet plate, 5.75" plate. *Courtesy of Dottie & Doug Hevener/The Quacker Connection.*

Back: 12" platter w/ open handles; *front row:* salt & pepper, creamer, sugar base, cup & saucer. *Courtesy of Dottie & Doug Hevener/The Quacker Connection.*

5" cream soup bowl, vase, sandwich server w/ center handle. *Courtesy of Dottie & Doug Hevener/The Quacker Connection.*

12" scalloped fruit "hat" bowl, candy dish w/lid, 10" vegetable bowl w/lid. *Courtesy of Paul Reichwein.*

7.25" goblet, 6.5" footed iced tea tumbler, 5.25" footed iced tea tumbler, 4.75" sherbet. *Courtesy of Paul Reichwein.*

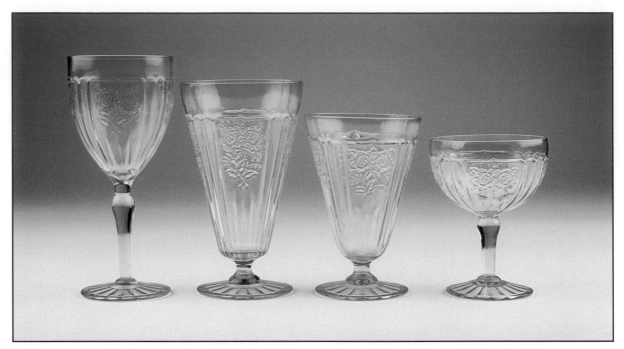

7.25" goblet, 4.75" sherbet w/foot, 4.5" wine, 3.25" sherbet w/foot, 4" goblet (cocktail). *Courtesy of Dottie & Doug Hevener/The Quacker Connection.*

5.25" flat iced tea tumbler, 4.75" flat water tumbler, 4.25" flat water tumbler, 3.5" flat juice tumbler. *Courtesy of Paul Reichwein.*

Decanter w/ stopper, 11.75" shallow fruit bowl. *Courtesy of Dottie & Doug Hevener/The Quacker Connection.*

10" vegetable bowl w/ 2 open handles (note the bowl does have a lid), 7.5" x 11" oval bowl w/ 2 open handles. *Courtesy of Dottie & Doug Hevener/The Quacker Connection.*

Above: Sugar w/ lid. *Courtesy of Vic & Jean Laermans.*

Left: 12" cake plate w/ handles, candy jar w/ lid, cookie jar w/ lid. *Courtesy of Dottie & Doug Hevener/The Quacker Connection.*

Back row: 12" cake plate w/handles, 5.75" plate; *front row:* salt & pepper, cup, butter dish. *Courtesy of Paul Reichwein.*

Back row: 11.75" shallow bowl, *front row:* cookie jar w/lid, sugar, creamer. *Courtesy of Paul Reichwein.*

MAYFAIR "OPEN ROSE"

	Pink	Blue	Green	Yellow	Qty
Bowl, 5" cream soup	65				____
Bowl, 5.5" cereal	30	65	100	125	____
Bowl, 7" vegetable w/tab handles	40	65	150	160	____
Bowl, 9" console w/3 legs	6000		6000		____
Bowl, 9.5" vegetable, oval	40	80	150	160	____
Bowl, 10" vegetable w/handles	35	85		165	____
Bowl, 10" vegetable w/cover	135	185		1000	____
Bowl, 11.75", shallow	85	100	85	250	____
Bowl, 12" scalloped fruit, "hat"	75	145	85	375	____
Butter dish base	40	100	300	400	____
Butter dish lid	60	250	1200	1300	____
Butter complete	100	350	1500	1600	____
Candy dish w/lid	75	350	700	600	____
Celery dish, 9", 2 sections			250	250	____
Celery dish, 10"	60	75	200	200	____
Celery dish, 10", 2 sections	275	75			____
Cookie jar/lid *R*	70	350	700	1000	____
Creamer	35	100	250	275	____
Cup, squarish	20	65	200	200	____
Cup, round	375				____
Decanter w/stopper	250				____
Goblet, 3.75" cordial	1300		1100		____
Goblet, 4" cocktail	100		450		____
Goblet, 4.25"	1100		1100		____
Goblet, 4.5" wine	120		500		____
Goblet, 5.25" claret	1300		1100		____
Goblet, 5.75" water	85		525		____
Goblet, 7.25"	300	250			____
Lid for 10" vegetable bowl	100	150	175	200	____
Pitcher, 6" *R*	70	175	600	625	____
Pitcher, 8", 60 oz.	85	200	600	600	____
Pitcher, 8.5" 80 oz.	130	330	800	800	____
Plate, 5.75"	15	30	100	100	____
Plate, 6.5" sherbet, round	20				____
Plate, 6.5" sherbet, round w/off center indent	50	60	150	150	____
Plate, 8.5" luncheon	30	65	150	150	____
Plate, 9.5" dinner	60	100	200	200	____
Plate, 9.5" grill	45	65	100	100	____
Plate, 10" cake w/feet & tab handles	50	85	200		____
Plate, 11.5" grill w/handles				150	____
Plate, 12" cake w/handles	70	100	100		____
Platter, 12" w/open handles, no feet	45	85	200	200	____
Platter, 12.5" w/closed handles			300	300	____
Relish, 8.5" w/4 sections	45	75	200	200	____
Relish, 8.5", not sectioned	300		375	375	____
Salt & pepper flat *R*	85	350	1300	1000	____
Salt & pepper, footed	trtp*				____
Sandwich server w/center handle	70	120	80	170	____
Saucer	50			150	____
Sherbet, 2.25" w/out stem or foot	300	300			____
Sherbet, 3.25" w/foot	25				____
Sherbet, 4.75" w/foot	100	100	200	200	____
Sugar base	35	100	250	275	____
Sugar lid	2000		2000	2000	____
Tumbler, 2.25" whiskey *R*	85				____
Tumbler, 3.25" juice, footed	100				____
Tumbler, 3.5" juice, flat *R*	60	150			____
Tumbler, 4.25" water, flat	55	150			____
Tumbler, 4.75" water, flat	225	150	250	250	____
Tumbler, 5.25" iced tea, footed	60	150		225	____
Tumbler, 5.25" iced tea, flat	80	300			____
Tumbler, 6.5" iced tea, footed	60	300	250		____
Vase	350	175	450		____

*trtp = too rare to price

Note: Satinized/frosted pink items worth the same as transparent pink pieces if the paint is in excellent condition. Crystal items 1/3 of pink prices.

Reproduction information: Whiskeys were only made in pink; new may be wrong shade. New have one stem for blossoms with veins molded in the leaves; old have branching stems and leaves have no veins. New bottoms have more glass than old ones. Cookie jar bottoms: new have indistinct design & bottom is totally smooth; old bottoms have pronounced 1.75" mold circle rim which is missing from the new ones. Cookie jar lids: new have curved edges of design, almost like a scallop, where design approaches outside edge of flat rim edge; old lids end the design in a straight line. Shakers: new are made in wrong colors and have opening smaller than the .75" opening of the old. New shakers have ridges on 4 corners that extend to the top of the shaker; old ones have ridges that only go about ½ way up. 6" pitchers: new have totally smooth bottoms missing the pronounced 2.25" mold circle rim found on the old. Handles misshapen, should be able to squeeze a dime between handle & shoulder of pitcher. Old spout does not extend beyond shoulder of pitcher, new spout is ½" beyond side of pitcher. 3.5" juice tumblers: reproduced in pink & blue. New are missing a smooth band near top of tumbler & have raised ridges around the blossoms. Old tumblers have blossoms inside the smooth band.

8.5" 80 oz. pitcher, 8"
60 oz. pitcher, 6"
pitcher. *Courtesy of
Paul Reichwein.*

6.5" round sherbet plate
w/ off center indent &
2.25" sherbet. *Courtesy
of Paul Reichwein.*

Vase, butter.
*Courtesy of Donna
L. Cehlarik.*

Back row: 9.5" dinner plate, 5.75" plate; front: creamer & sugar. Courtesy of Paul Reichwein.

Back row: 8.5" 4-sectioned relish, 9" divided celery; front: 10" celery. Courtesy of Paul Reichwein.

Reproduction whiskey tumblers. Courtesy of Charlie Diefenderfer.

Reproduction cookie jar. Courtesy of Jane O'Brien.

MISS AMERICA
Reproduced
(1933-1936 Hocking Glass Company)

Back row: 10.25" dinner plate, 5.75" sherbet plate, 10.25" grill plate; *front row:* sherbet, cup & saucer, 6.25" cereal bowl. *Courtesy of Diefenderfer's Collectibles & Antiques*.

Prices for pink Miss America have been zooming upward and some may still be conservative. We have seen the development of an intense interest in this pattern. Shopping via "brick and mortar" will prove that pink Miss America has gotten very difficult to find. There seems to be a few Internet favorites, with the cup, saucer, creamer, and sugar among these. We saw a pink cup with a huge chip in it (more like a bite out of the glass) sell for $40 on eBay. It has to make you stop and shake your head.

As with most popular patterns, Miss America has been reproduced; use the information provided after the pricing to avoid making an unfortunate mistake. Confusion between Miss America and English Hobnail may lead to you a bargain so be aware of the differences. For the most part the starburst in the center of English Hobnail pieces is neither circular nor even as it is in Miss America. The points on English Hobnail are rounder and a bit stretched while Miss America points are sharper and more distinct at the tips. English Hobnail plates often have indents while Miss America plates are smooth and level until the rim. If you are using eBay as a source, searching for English Hobnail will often reveal pieces of Miss America that have been incorrectly identified.

Crystal (clear) Miss America is not in great demand, but there are more collectors of crystal Miss America than many other patterns available in crystal. This may be due in part to the pleasing look of Miss America and also to the vast array of pieces that were made in crystal.

If you are finding pink difficult to find, consider green or Royal Ruby. Most dealers are pleased to have even a handful of green Miss America in stock, and few are ever fortunate enough to possess red. There was very little made in these colors but fortunately there are also few collectors competing for them.

Back row: 8.75" 4-sectioned relish, 8.5" salad plate; *front row:* 11.5" candy jar w/ lid, 10.5" oval celery. *Courtesy of Diefenderfer's Collectibles & Antiques*.

4" juice tumbler, 4.5" water tumbler, 5.75" iced tea tumbler, 5.5" water goblet,
3.75" wine goblet. *Courtesy of Diefenderfer's Collectibles & Antiques*.

12" footed cake plate, 8" bowl. *Courtesy of Diefenderfer's Collectibles & Antiques*.

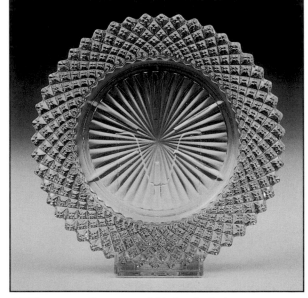

5.75" coaster. *Courtesy of Diefenderfer's Collectibles & Antiques*.

Far left: Butter. *Courtesy of Charlie Diefenderfer*.

Left: Salt & pepper. *Courtesy of Michael Rothenberger/ Mike's Collectibles*.

MISS AMERICA	Pink	Crystal	Green	Ruby	Qty
Bowl, 4.5" berry			15		____
Bowl, 6.25" cereal	50	15	25		____
Bowl, 8", curves inward	175	65		600	____
Bowl, 8.75", straight sides	100	50			____
Bowl, 10" oval vegetable	70	15			____
Bowl, 11"	trtp*			1000	____
Butter dish base (same as 6.25" cereal bowl)	50	15			____
Butter dish lid *R*	800	300			____
Butter dish complete	825	315			____
Candy jar w/lid, 11.5"	200	125			____
Coaster, 5.75"	50	20			____
Comport, 5"	50	20			____
Creamer	40	10		500	____
Cup	40	10	20	400	____
Goblet, 3.75" wine	125	25		400	____
Goblet, 4.75" juice	150	30		400	____
Goblet, 5.5" water	100	25		400	____
Pitcher, 8" w/no ice lip *R*	225	75			____
Pitcher 8.5" w/ice lip	300	85			____
Plate, 5.75" sherbet	30	8	12	65	____
Plate, 6.75"			10		____
Plate, 8.5" salad	60	10	12	225	____
Plate, 10.25" dinner	55	20			____
Plate, 10.25" grill	50	12			____
Plate, 10.5" oval celery	50	15			____
Plate, 12" footed cake	90	40			____
Platter, 12.25"	100	20			____
Relish, 8.75", 4 sections	75	15			____
Relish, 11.75", 5 sections	trtp*	50			____
Salt & pepper *R*	100	40	500		____
Saucer	20	6		80	____
Sherbet	35	10		225	____
Sugar	40	10		500	____
Tumbler, 4" juice *R*	100	25		400	____
Tumbler, 4.5" water *R*	80	20	35		____
Tumbler. 5.75" iced tea *R*	175	35			____

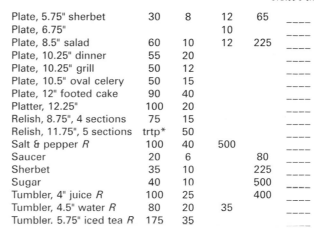

Note the hump of extra glass above where the handles are attached to these pitchers indicating these are not reproductions. *Courtesy of Diefenderfer's Collectibles & Antiques*.

Reproduction information: Anything in cobalt is new. Butter lids: pronounced curve near bottom, inside area where knob touches lid is filled with glass (old lid has hollow area where knob and lid meet). Look for a pronounced "star" with distinct points when looking from the underside of the lid through the knob as evident in only the old lids. Shakers: new measure 3.25" and old are actually a bit taller; old allow one to insert a finger inside and reach almost to the bottom with an absence of extra glass at the base that is found in new. New approx. 2" deep; old approx. 2.5" deep. Old shakers have neat ridges with which to screw & unscrew the lids; new have rounded off ridges that overlap. Points of the Miss America design are sharper and consistent in quality with other pieces on old; new are more rounded. Pitchers without ice lip: old have a hump of extra glass above where the handle is attached; new are perfectly even around the rim. Tumblers: new have 2 vertical mold marks, old have 4. New have approx. ½" glass on bottom; old have approx. 1/4".

*trtp = too rare to price

Note: Ice blue pieces 10 times the price of pink.

Cup & saucer, 10.25" dinner plate, 8.75" 4-sectioned relish, 3.75" wine goblet, 4.75" juice goblet.

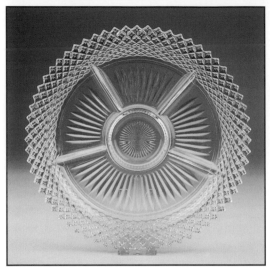

11.75" 5-section relish.

Sugar w/ metal lid & creamer. *Courtesy of Vic & Jean Laermans.*

Back row: 12.25" platter, 6.25" cereal bowl; *front row:* sugar, creamer, sherbet.

Reproduction shakers. (Don't be fooled by the legitimately old shaker tops.) *Courtesy of Charlie Diefenderfer.*

MODERNTONE

(1934-early 1950s Hazel-Atlas Glass Company)

Cobalt blue Moderntone is one of the most popular color/pattern combinations of all Depression Glass possibilities. Hazel-Atlas made so many of the basic dinnerware pieces, much of Moderntone continues to be readily available with a minimum investment. Once the basics are gathered the search and the investment get more serious.

The dinner plate is a mere 8.75" (actually a "tad" larger, but we are working in quarter-inch intervals). Some are finding the small size inadequate and have moved to the 10.5" sandwich plate for dining purposes. Granted, this will be more costly. Cereal and soup bowls are difficult to find. Collectors are so desperate to own them, many are overlooking minor rim chipping that would be unacceptable in other patterns where bowls are abundant.

Sugar w/ metal lid. *Courtesy of Charlie Diefenderfer.*

Added to the listing is the 4" tall Platonite mug, which was found in white with red trim. Three fingers of the average woman would fit in the handle.

Pictured is a set that was brought into a friend's shop. It consists of a circular chrome tray with the Moderntone creamer, sugar with a metal lid, shakers, and a bowl resembling American Pioneer that is covered with a chrome lid. The original owner stated that this is how he had originally purchased this grouping.

Amethyst, originally called "Burgundy," is harder to find than cobalt and gaining more favor with collectors. Prices for amethyst Moderntone have been rising as a direct result of this increased demand. Thanks to Steve Wasko & Jeaneen Heiskell for bringing their amethyst collection (and more) to the studio.

Readers requested that we provide the prices for the "Little Hostess Party Sets," so this information is now included. Sadly, dealers will make more money selling pieces

Back row: 12" platter, 11" platter; *front row:* salt & pepper, sugar, creamer. *Courtesy of David G. Baker.*

Back row: 10.5" sandwich plate, 8.75" dinner plate, 7.75" luncheon plate; *front row:* cup & saucer, sherbet on 5.75" sherbet plate. *Courtesy of David G. Baker.*

8.75" berry bowl, 4.75" cream soup bowl, 5" ruffled nut/cream soup bowl, custard. *Courtesy of David G. Baker.*

separately rather than keeping sets in tact. This is such a shame as these sets have survived for half a century and really deserve to remain as originally packaged. Here is where the Internet has negatively impacted glassware prices. There is a glut of these sets online causing the supply to outweigh the demand resulting in tumbling prices. There are collectors looking for an item or two to complete a set. Items sold separately are holding their value and teapot lids are in demand as naturally they got lost or broken. A black lid sold for $177 on eBay in November 2000.

Unusual set that includes Moderntone pieces, as found.

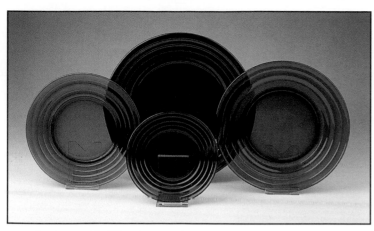

Back row: 7.5" luncheon plate, 10.5" sandwich plate, 8.75" dinner plate; *front row:* 5.75" sherbet plate. *Courtesy of Steve Wasko & Jeaneen Heiskell.*

Back row: 7.75" flat soup bowl, 9" berry bowl; *front row:* 5" berry bowl, 4.75" cream soup bowl. *Courtesy of Steve Wasko & Jeaneen Heiskell.*

MODERNTONE	Cobalt	Amethyst	Platonite-pastels	Platonite-others	Qty
Ashtray, 7.75"	175				____
Bowl, 4.75" cream soup	25	25	8	20	____
Bowl, 5" berry	35	30	8	15	____
Bowl, 5" deep cereal, w/white			8		
Bowl, 5" deep cereal, no white			12		____
Bowl, 5" ruffled nut/ cream soup	100	55			____
Bowl, 6.5" cereal	140	140			____
Bowl, 7.75" soup	220	220			____
Bowl, 8", rim			15	35	____
Bowl, 8", no rim			20		____
Bowl, 9" berry	65	50		35	____
Butter dish complete w/metal cover	150				____
Cheese dish complete w/metal cover	500				
Creamer	15	18	10	20	____
Cup	15	15	5	15	____
Custard	30	25			____
Mug, 4"				15	____
Plate, 5.75" sherbet	10	8	5	8	____
Plate, 6.75" salad	15	12			____
Plate, 7.75" luncheon	15	12			____
Plate 8.75" dinner	20	15	8	20	____
Plate, 10.5" sandwich	100	65	20		____
Platter, 11"	50	50		30	____
Platter, 12"	100	80	15	40	____
Salt & pepper	45	50	20		____
Saucer	5	5	3	4	____
Sherbet	15	15	6	12	____
Sugar base	15	18	10	20	____
Sugar lid (metal)	60				____
Tumbler, 2.25" whiskey	50				____
Tumbler, 3.75" juice	65	65			____
Tumbler, 4" water	50	45	12		____
Tumbler, 5.25" iced tea	160	150			____

Note: Items in pink and green ½ price of cobalt EXCEPT pink cup, $100, & pink saucer, $35. Crystal 25% of cobalt.

Back row: 12" platter; *front row:* creamer, sugar, salt & pepper, custard, sherbet, cup & saucer. *Courtesy of Steve Wasko & Jeaneen Heiskell.*

5.25" tumbler, 4" tumbler, 3.75" tumbler. *Courtesy of Steve Wasko & Jeaneen Heiskell.*

Cup & saucer. *Courtesy of Steve Wasko & Jeaneen Heiskell.*

"Little Hostess Party Set" in gold, gray, orange, & turquoise. *Courtesy of Steve Wasko & Jeaneen Heiskell.*

Decorated 10.5" sandwich plates, $30 each. *Courtesy of Steve Wasko & Jeaneen Heiskell.*

"Little Hostess Party Set" in aqua, pink, tan,& yellow. *Courtesy of Steve Wasko & Jeaneen Heiskell.*

Boxed set of "Pastelware." *Courtesy of Charlie Diefenderfer.*

Souvenir "Little Hostess Party Set" cup & saucer. *Walter Lemiski / Waltz Time Antiques.*

Decorated 5.75" sherbet plate, $15.

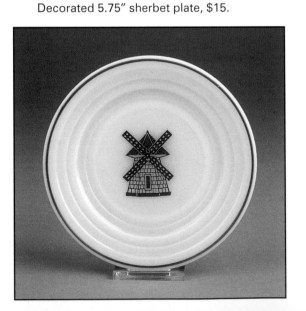

"Little Hostess Party Set"	gold, gray, orange, turquoise	aqua, pink, tan, yellow	blue, green, pink, yellow	back, pink, white	chartreuse, green, gray, maroon	Qty
Creamer	15	15	15	15	15	____
Cup	10	15	10	15	10	____
Plate, 5.25"	8	12	10	12	8	____
Saucer	5	10	5	10	5	____
Sugar	15	15	15	15	15	____
Teapot	45	50		50	40	____
Teapot lid	75	175		175	70	____

Add $20 for boxes in good condition, $35 for boxes in excellent condition.

MOONDROPS

(1932-1940s New Martinsville Glass Manufacturing Company)

Some of the most spectacular designs in Depression Glass came from New Martinsville Glass Manufacturing Company. Moondrops is a pattern that does a wonderful job of showcasing lovely pieces in an array of colors.

Moondrops glassware is quite unique in its design. There are handles, ruffles, feet, wings, and finials decorating almost everything. Even the tumbler has an intricate foot made of a series of ridges of glass. Nothing is simple, yet due to the lack of surface patterns and designs the clean, smooth glass is able to simply glow with colors that seem to be richer and deeper than those of other manufacturers.

New Martinsville Glass Manufacturing Company sold Moondrops as "No. 37 Line." It was produced for about ten years in amber, Ritz blue, crystal, evergreen, green, jade, rose, and ruby. Collectors may have their favorite color, but collecting Moondrops is a bit different than collecting most other patterns of Depression Glass. Many who are hunting for Moondrops are interested in all colors, not simply one. Presented are all of the colors except for jade and crystal.

Butter. *Courtesy of Debora & Paul Torsiello, Debzie's Glass.*

2.75" sugar, 4" compote, 2.75" creamer. *Courtesy of Debora & Paul Torsiello, Debzie's Glass.*

Two 8.25" 53 oz. pitchers, two 4.75" tumblers. *Courtesy of Michael Rothenberger/ Mike's Collectibles.*

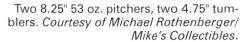

7.5" tray & 2.75" sugar. *Courtesy of Vic & Jean Laermans.*

Previously unlisted 9.25" etched bowl. *Courtesy of Michael Rothenberger/Mike's Collectibles.*

Creamer & sugar on 7.5" x 2.75" tray. *Courtesy of Vic & Jean Laermans.*

9.75" oval bowl w/ handles, 5" candle holders. *Courtesy of Debora & Paul Torsiello, Debzie's Glass.*

5.25" candle holder (holds 3 tapers), 5.25" tumbler. *Courtesy of Debora & Paul Torsiello, Debzie's Glass.*

Trays, creamers, & sugars in a variety of colors. *Courtesy of Vic & Jean Laermans.*

Back row: 8" pitcher w/ice lip, cocktail shaker w/ handle; *middle row:* 8.5" relish bowl w/3 feet, 4.75" tumbler, 9.5" ruffled bowl w/3 legs; *front row:* 4" candy dish, 2.75" whiskey tumbler w/handle. *Courtesy of Charlie Diefenderfer.*

2.75" creamer & 2.75" sugar on 7.5" tray, cocktail shaker w/ out metal lid, cup & saucer. *Courtesy of Vic & Jean Laermans.*

MOONDROPS	Red & Cobalt	Ice Blue	Other colors	Qty
Ashtray	40	35	20	____
Bottle, perfume ("rocket")	300	250	200	____
Bowl, cream soup	125	100	50	____
Bowl, 5.25" berry	25	20	15	____
Bowl, 5.25" mayonnaise	75	60	40	____
Bowl, 6.75" soup	125	100	50	____
Bowl, 7.5" pickle	35	25	20	____
Bowl, 8.25" concave top	65	50	35	____
Bowl, 8.5" relish, divided w/3 feet	50	35	20	____
Bowl, 9.25"			75	____
Bowl, 9.5" ruffled w/3 legs	80	75	45	____
Bowl, 9.75" casserole (base only)	100	75	50	____
Bowl, 9.75" oval vegetable	60	45	35	____
Bowl, 9.75" oval w/2 handles	75	60	45	____
Bowl, 11.5" celery, boat shape	45	35	25	____
Bowl, 12" casserole w/3 feet	100	85	45	____
Bowl, 13" console	150	135	85	____
Butter dish base	150	125	100	____
Butter dish lid	400	325	250	____
Butter dish complete	550	450	350	____
Candle holder, 2" ruffled, ea.	40	35	30	____
Candle holder, 4.5", ea.	35	30	25	____
Candle holder, 5" ruffled, ea.	35	30	25	____
Candle holder, 5", ea.	75	60	45	____
Candle holder, 5.25", holds 3, ea.	100	75	50	____
Candle holder, 8.5" metal stem, ea.	30	25	20	____
Candy dish, 4"	50			____
Candy dish, 8"	50	40	30	____
Cocktail shaker, may or may not have handle	80	70	50	____
Compote, 4"	35	30	25	____
Compote, 11.5"	75	65	45	____
Creamer, 2.75"	25	20	15	____
Creamer, 3.75"	20	18	12	____
Cup	20	18	12	____
Decanter w/stopper, 7.75"	80	70	50	____
Decanter w/stopper, 8.5"	90	75	60	____
Decanter w/stopper, 10.25" ("rocket")	500	450	400	____
Decanter w/stopper, 11.25"	150	125	75	____
Goblet, 2.75" liquor/cordial	50	40	30	____
Goblet, 4" wine	30	25	20	____
Goblet, 4.25" wine ("rocket")	70	60	40	____
Goblet, 4.75"	30	25	20	____
Goblet, 5.25" wine w/metal stem	25	20	15	____
Goblet, 5.5" wine w/metal stem	25	20	15	____
Goblet, 6.25" water w/metal stem	35	30	20	____
Gravy	150	125	100	____
Lid for 9.75" casserole	175	125	75	____
Mug	50	40	30	____
Pitcher, 6.75", 22 oz.	180	160	120	____
Pitcher, 8", 50 oz. (with ice lip)	200	175	130	____
Pitcher, 8.25", 32 oz.	190	170	135	____
Pitcher, 8.25", 53 oz. (no ice lip)	200	175	130	____
Plate, 5.75" bread & butter	15	12	10	____
Plate, 6" sherbet w/off- center indent	18	15	12	____
Plate, 6.25" sherbet	12	10	8	____
Plate, 7.25" salad	18	15	12	____
Plate, 8.5" luncheon	18	15	12	____
Plate, 9.5" dinner	35	30	20	____
Plate, 14" sandwich	70	40	30	____
Plate, 14" sandwich w/2 handles	80	50	30	____
Platter, 12"	45	40	30	____
Powder jar w/3 feet	400	350	250	____
Saucer	10	8	5	____
Sherbet, 2.5"	20	18	15	____
Sherbet, 4.5"	40	30	25	____
Sugar, 2.75"	20	18	15	____
Sugar, 4"	22	18	15	____
Tray, 7.5" for 2.75" creamer & sugar	50	40	30	____
Tumbler, 2.75" whiskey	20	18	15	____
Tumbler, 2.75" whiskey w/handle	20	18	15	____
Tumbler, 3.75" w/foot	20	18	15	____
Tumbler, 3.75" flat	18	15	12	____
Tumbler, 4.25", 7 & 8 oz.	20	18	15	____
Tumbler, 4.75" w/handle	35	30	20	____
Tumbler, 4.75"	25	20	15	____
Tumbler, 5.25"	40	35	20	____
Vase, 7.75"	80	75	65	____
Vase, 8.5" ("rocket")	300	275	200	____
Vase, 9.25" ("rocket")	275	250	175	____

MOONSTONE
(1942-1946 Hocking Glass Company)

Moonstone was introduced during World War II and made for only four years, but Hocking Glass Company must have produced huge quantities of this pattern as it is still readily available. It is amazing how often a collection of Moonstone ends up in a central Pennsylvanian auction house. Obviously Moonstone was a pattern heavily distributed in this part of the country. It is an extremely durable pattern with no thin, delicate edges.

There is an assortment of occasional pieces in this pattern: bowls, candlesticks, boxes, and more. Often a piece of Moonstone is bought to be used singularly as an accent piece, as something to hold decorative soaps or pot pourri, as a candy container, etc.

Fenton also made opalescent hobnail glass, so if you find a piece that appears to be Moon-

Back row: 6.5" crimped edge bowl w/ handles, 9.5" crimped edge bowl; *front row:* 5.5" crimped edge dessert bowl, 7.5" crimped edge bowl. *Courtesy of Connie & Bill Hartzell.*

Back row: cloverleaf bowl, 10.75" sandwich plate; *front row:* bonbon, 5.5" vase, 7.75" divided relish bowl. *Courtesy of Connie & Bill Hartzell.*

stone but isn't on the list, you may have something that is not Hocking. Some sellers also confuse Moonstone with Hobnail. Remember, Hobnail is not opalescent.

Back: 5.5" berry bowl, sugar; *front row:* candle holders, creamer. *Courtesy of Connie & Bill Hartzell.*

Back row: sherbet on 6.25" sherbet plate, 8.25" luncheon plate;
front row: cup, saucer & goblet. *Courtesy of Connie & Bill Hartzell.*

Back: 4.75" round puff box w/ cover; *front:* cigarette jar w/ cover, candy jar w/ cover. *Courtesy of Connie & Bill Hartzell.*

MOONSTONE	Crystal w/bluish white	Qty
Bonbon, heart-shaped w/one handle	15	____
Bowl, 5.5" berry	18	____
Bowl, 5.5" dessert, crimped edge	12	____
Bowl, 6.5" crimped edge w/handles	10	____
Bowl, 7.75", crimped edge	12	____
Bowl, 7.75" relish, divided	12	____
Bowl, 9.5" crimped edge	25	____
Bowl, cloverleaf (3 sections)	12	____
Candleholder, ea.	9	____
Candy jar w/cover	30	____
Cigarette jar w/cover	25	____
Creamer	8	____
Cup	8	____
Goblet	18	____
Plate, 6.25" sherbet	5	____
Plate, 8.25" luncheon	15	____
Plate, 10.75" sandwich	30	____
Puff box w/cover, 4.75" round	30	____
Saucer	5	____
Sherbet	7	____
Sugar	8	____
Vase, 5.5"	12	____

Note: Items in green 4 times prices of crystal

MOROCCAN AMETHYST
(1960s HAZEL Ware by Continental Can)

There were many requests to include Moroccan Amethyst in the second edition of *Mauzy's Depression Glass* as there are no books showing **and** identifying the huge array of pieces in Moroccan Amethyst. We hope the presentation offered will take some of the guesswork out of this pattern. A huge thank you goes to Scott & Rhonda Hackenburg / Blue Jay Antiques & Collectibles for sharing both their glassware and their knowledge.

The prices and pieces are arranged by the shape of the glass. First are "Colony" items, which have square or rectangular bases. Listed and pictured for the first time is the 9.5" rectangular bowl with a white overlay. The 8" square ashtray was made from the Colony 8" square dinner plate and sold in pairs as "Moderne 8" Ash Trays" by HAZEL Ware. This plate was also made with a cup rest and paired with a cup in sets of four creating the "Colony C-409 Amethyst Vanity 8 Piece Snack Set."

Next are "Octagonal" pieces; as the name suggests they are eight-sided. Often when people think of Moroccan Amethyst it is the Octagonal dinnerware that comes to mind. Shown in Octagonal dinnerware are a 7.25" salad plate, 9.5" dinner plate, cup and saucer with a pebble rim. The eating surface on these pieces is smooth; the pebble rim is on the underside.

The third grouping is "Scalloped" as these pieces have a scalloped edge. A variety of bowls including the punch bowl, the fan snack plate with cup, and the shakers make up the pieces in this style. A pair of Moroccan-like shakers (they were probably Imperial) sold on eBay in September 2000 for over $200 and the lids were even worn. Collectors need and want purple shakers if attempting to do an entire dinner set. The "Seashell Snack Set" consists of fan trays and cups. When the cups are crystal this set

is called "Informal," when the cups are white this set is called "Alpine," and when the cups are amethyst this set is called "Moroccan." The punch bowl box indicates the contents are "The Alpine 15 Piece Punch Set." Whenever white is used with the amethyst it is labeled "alpine," but when the white is alone it is labeled "opaque white." The 7.25" bowl is also serves as the punch bowl base.

Finally, "Swirled" pieces are (you guessed it) swirled with lines or ridges that curve upward and around the shape of each item. Swirled Moroccan Amethyst is made up of hollowware and tumblers. These are among the most difficult to find and desirable items in this pattern.

Moroccan Amethyst has a variety of miscellaneous glassware including round, square, triangular, and flower-shaped ashtrays. Flower-shaped (coaster) ashtrays are available in three sizes, 3.25", 4.25", and 5.25." The largest one is also found in green. The candleholders are shaped like five pointed stars. Apple-shaped bowls are found in crystal (clear) and amethyst and have an apple blossom in the bottom. Actually, the crystal bowls are from the "Orchid Crystal Line." The 10.25" bowl has only been found in crystal while the smaller one is found in both crystal and amethyst. The triangular bowl with the pressed design is very rare, and a prize for serious Moroccan Amethyst collectors.

All goblets and some sizes of tumblers are challenging to find. A set of 24 Colony tumblers in three sizes with the original box sold on eBay in April 2000 for $1,025. The box was marked, "Colony Vanity 24 Piece Tumbler Set" with a stock number of C-414.

In the second edition of *Mauzy's Comprehensive Handbook of Depression Glass Prices* we presented three go-along possibilities. When these pieces were placed under the lights in the studio it was obvious that the purple hue was wrong so they are no longer included.

Octagonal (8-sided) style. *Back row:* 6" dessert plate, 7.25" salad plate, 9.5" dinner plate w/ original sticker; *front row:* 4.75" fruit bowl, cup & saucer, 9.5" dinner plate (with center handle). *Courtesy of Scott & Rhonda Hackenburg / Blue Jay Antiques & Collectibles.*

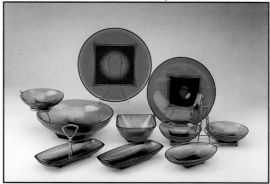

Colony (square base) style. *Back row:* 12" plate, 11" bowl; *middle row:* chip & dip, 5.75" square bowl, 4.5" dessert bowl, 6" bowl; *front row:* 9.5" x 4.25" rectangular bowl (with center handle), 9.5" x 4.25" rectangular bowl, 8" oval bowl. *Courtesy of Scott & Rhonda Hackenburg / Blue Jay Antiques & Collectibles.*

Bottom left: 4.75" candy w/lid, 7.75" candy w/lid, 5" ice bucket, 8.5" ruffled vase, 6.5" cocktail stirrer, 8.25" cocktail shaker w/ original sticker. *Courtesy of Scott & Rhonda Hackenburg / Blue Jay Antiques & Collectibles.*

Bottom right: Octagonal (8-sided) style 3-tier tidbits with gold or silver handles consist of 9.5" dinner plates, 7.25" salad plates, & 6" dessert plates; 2-tier tidbit on *left:* 7.25" salad plate & 6" dessert plate; 2-tier tidbit on *right:* 9.5" dinner plate & 4.75" fruit bowl. *Courtesy of Scott & Rhonda Hackenburg / Blue Jay Antiques & Collectibles.*

Opposite page, center left: *Back row:* 8 piece "Vanity" snack set consisting of 8" square plates w/cup rest & cups, 8" square ashtray, 8" square dinner plate; *middle row:* 5.75" under plate for 4.5" dessert bowl, *front row:* cup & saucer, 4.5" dessert bowl. *Courtesy of Scott & Rhonda Hackenburg / Blue Jay Antiques & Collectibles.*

Bottom left: *Back row:* Opaque cup, Colony cup, crystal cup; *front row:* octagonal cup, amethyst punch cup, amethyst punch cup. *Courtesy of Scott & Rhonda Hackenburg / Blue Jay Antiques & Collectibles.*

Colony design (square or rectangular base)	Amethyst	Qty
Bowl, dessert, 4.5"	20	_____
Bowl, 5.75" square	20	_____
Bowl, 6" round	18	_____
Bowl, 8" oval	30	_____
Bowl, 9.5" x 4.25" rectangle	18	_____
Bowl, 9.5" x 4.25" rectangle w/white overlay	25	
Bowl, 11"	40	_____
Chip & dip (11" & 6" bowls w/metal holder)	65	_____
Cup	5	
Plate, square dinner	14	_____
Plate, square snack w/cup rest	20	_____
Plate, 12" round	20	_____
Saucer	3	_____
Tray	20	_____
Tumbler, 4 sizes	10	_____

Note: Bowls may be found with metal handles or holders or used in combinations which will increase the price by a few dollars.

Octagonal (8-sided)	Amethyst	Qty
Bowl, 4.75" fruit	20	_____
Cup	5	_____
Plate, 6" dessert	8	_____
Plate, 7.25" salad	12	_____
Plate, 9.5" dinner	14	_____
Saucer, 6"	3	_____
Tidbit, 2-tier (6" & 7.25" plates)	25	_____
Tidbit, 3-tier (6", 7.25", 9.5" plates)	40	_____

Note: Dinner plate may be found with metal handle which will increase the price by a few dollars

Scalloped	Amethyst	Qty
Bowl, 4.75"	20	_____
Bowl, 8" (same as Punch base)	60	_____
Bowl, 14-piece Punch Set	155	_____

	Amethyst	Qty
Punch bowl, 10.75" (white)	35	_____
Base, 8"	60	_____
Cup	5	_____
Plate, 10" fan w/cup rest	12	_____
Salt & pepper	125	_____
Snack set (4 fan plates & 4 milk glass swirled cups), 10" x 6.5"	50	_____

Swirled	Amethyst	Qty
Candy w/lid, 4.75"	35	_____
Candy w/lid, 7.25"	35	_____
Cocktail, 6.5" w/lip	45	_____
Cocktail shaker w/lid, 8.25"	65	_____
Cocktail stirrer	12	_____
Ice bucket, 5"	45	_____
Tumbler, 2.5"	10	_____
Tumbler, 3"	10	_____
Tumbler, 3.25"	10	_____
Tumbler, 3.75"	10	_____
Tumbler, 4.5" water	10	_____
Tumbler, 6.25" iced tea	15	_____
Vase, ruffled 8.5"	45	_____

Miscellaneous	Amethyst	Qty
Ashtray, 3.25" triangle	10	_____
Ashtray, 3.75" round	10	_____
Ashtray, 5" triangle	15	_____
Ashtray, 7" triangle	15	_____
Ashtray, 8" square	15	_____
Bowl, 6.75" triangle w/3 feet and pressed design	15	_____
Candle holder, 5-pointed star 4.5" diam., ea.	25	_____
Goblet, 4" wine	10	_____
Goblet, 4.25" juice	10	_____
Goblet, 4.25" sherbet	10	_____
Goblet, 5.5" water	12	_____
Tumbler, 3.75" juice w/crinkled bottom	15	
Tumbler, 4.25" water w/crinkled bottom	18	

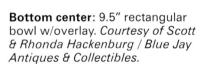

Top center: Octagonal pieces with a "pebble rim." *Courtesy of Scott & Rhonda Hackenburg / Blue Jay Antiques & Collectibles.*

Bottom center: 9.5" rectangular bowl w/overlay. *Courtesy of Scott & Rhonda Hackenburg / Blue Jay Antiques & Collectibles.*

Bottom right: 6.75" triangular bowl w/3 feet & pressed design. *Courtesy of Scott & Rhonda Hackenburg / Blue Jay Antiques & Collectibles.*

MT. PLEASANT
(Early 1930s L.E. Smith Glass Company)

Cobalt blue is the primary color choice of Mt. Pleasant collectors. Black amethyst is the second most favorite color, with pink and green trailing far behind.

Black amethyst is so called because at first glance the color appears to be black, however when it is held up to a bright light a definite purple (amethyst) hue is visible. The condition of black amethyst is very important as any surface scratching is easily seen.

Some pieces of Mt. Pleasant, particularly the blue, were trimmed in gold with single or multiple lines. This detailing must have survived in good condition or collectors usually pass.

The 11.25" leaf plate has been removed from the list as many dealers have commented that this is a piece that they had never seen. If you are aware of its existence please let us know!

One new item has been added to the list and is also pictured in black amethyst: a 5.75" bowl with three feet. Also shown side by side are the two sherbets so you can see the minute differences. The caption provides exacting measurements.

L.E. Smith Glass Company created many lines of glassware similar to Mt. Pleasant including Do-Si-Do, No. 55, and Kent. They also produced a plethora of unnamed footed bowls, vases, ashtrays, and more that were reminiscent of Mt. Pleasant, but not officially part of the line. Collectors of this pattern rarely care whether or not an item is actually Mt. Pleasant. If it is L.E. Smith glassware in their chosen color there is a good chance a purchase will be made.

Back row: 9" grill plate, 6" mint plate w/ center handle; *front row:* 6" square bowl w/ handles on 8" plate w/ handles, tumbler, cup & saucer, shaker.

Double candlestick, single candlestick, 8" leaf plate, bonbon w/ 2 handles and foot.

Back row: 8" luncheon plate, 7" plate w/2 handles; *front row:* 8.75" center-handled serving tray, 5.75" x 7.25" bonbon w/ rolled-up handles. *Courtesy of Bill Quillen.*

Back row: 8" bowl w/2 handles, cup & saucer; *front row:* creamer & sugar. *Courtesy of Bill Quillen.*

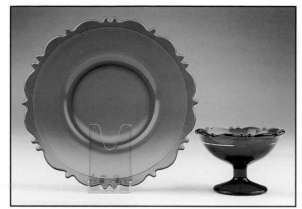

8" plate, sherbet.

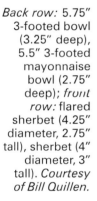

8" square bowl w/ handles.

Back row: 5.75" 3-footed bowl (3.25" deep), 5.5" 3-footed mayonnaise bowl (2.75" deep); *front row:* flared sherbet (4.25" diameter, 2.75" tall), sherbet (4" diameter, 3" tall). *Courtesy of Bill Quillen.*

MT. PLEASANT	Cobalt	Other colors	Qty
Ashtray	30	25	____
Bonbon w/2 handles & foot	35	25	____
Bonbon, 7" w/rolled-up edges & handles	30	20	____
Bowl, 4" opening w/rolled -in edges (rose bowl)	35	25	____
Bowl, 4.75" square w/foot	30	20	____
Bowl, 5.5" mayonnaise w/3 feet	35	20	____
Bowl, 5.75" w/3 feet		25	____
Bowl, 6" square w/handles	35	20	____
Bowl, 7" rolled-out edge w/3 feet	30	20	____
Bowl, 8" scalloped w/2 handles	40	20	____
Bowl, 8" square w/2 handles	40	20	____
Bowl, 9" scalloped w/foot	40	20	____
Bowl, 9.25" square w/foot	45	25	____
Bowl, 10" scalloped	50	35	____
Bowl, 10" rolled-up edge w/2 handles	50	35	____
Candlestick, single ea.	25	15	____
Candlestick, double ea.	35	20	____
Creamer	25	15	____
Cup	15	10	____
Plate, 6" mint w/center handle	30	20	____
Plate, 7" scalloped w/2 handles	15	10	____
Plate, 8" scalloped (no handles)	15	10	____
Plate, 8" square (no handles)	15	10	____
Plate, 8" w/2 handles	15	10	____
Plate, 8" leaf	25		____
Plate, 8.25" square w/cup indent	15	10	____
Plate, 9" grill	15	10	____
Plate, 10.5" cake w/2 handles	35	15	____
Plate, 10.5" cake, 1.25" high	45	15	____
Plate, 12" w/2 handles	45	15	____
Plate, sandwich server w/ center handle, 8.75"	45	15	____
Salt & pepper, 2 styles	65	45	____
Saucer	10	5	____
Sherbet, 2 styles	20	12	____
Sugar	25	15	____
Tumbler, 5.75"	30		____
Vase, 7.25"	35	15	____

NATIONAL (2200 Line)

(1940s-1950s Jeannette Glass Company)

Most collectors know Jeannette Glass Company's 2200 Line as National, so we have listed it by this name rather than by number. Janice Johnston / Behind The Green Door was kind enough to bring unused boxes of National to the studio. The results of opening and inventorying this glassware was the discovery of several previously undocumented pieces including a grand total of four tumblers, a sherbet, three different pitchers and a 4" coaster. Unfortunately we did not get to photograph the coaster in time for this edition.

If you haven't handled National you are missing something really wonderful. The pieces are substantial and well-made. There are no rough edges, sloppy molds, or uneven seams. A dinner plate hasn't been discovered yet, but there is a wonderful array of serving pieces with an 8" plate that would makes this suitable for luncheons, teas, and desserts. Certain pieces may be found with gold trim including the sugar, creamer, 8" tray, and more. The shakers have white plastic lids.

Here is a description of the boxed sets. First there is the Juice Set consisting of one 4.75" juice or milk pitcher, four 4" flat tumblers, and an 8" tray with handles. This is such a useful set we have one for ourselves! Next is the 24-piece Refreshment Set consisting of eight 5" footed tumblers, eight 3.5" footed tumblers, and eight 3" sherbets. The Berry Set has one 8.75" berry bowl and eight 4.5" bowls. The 18-piece Luncheon Set consists of four 8" luncheon plates, four 5" footed tumblers, four cups, four saucers, a creamer, and a sugar. The fewest pieces of all are found in the Relish Set, which has one 12.5" 6-part relish and the 4.5" condiment jar with lid. The circular indent in the center of the relish is designed to hold the condiment jar. Finally, the cigarette set consists of four 3" individual ashtrays, two 5" ashtrays, and one cigarette box. When reading the numbers on a box of Jeannette glassware, the first number is the product line and the second number is the quantity of items contained therein.

Just to clarify some measurement information, the pitchers were measured at the side. The juice pitcher was 4.75" along the side although it was 6" to the very top. Likewise, the larger pitchers were both 7" at the side.

If you are looking for versatile serving pieces or a gift with a bit of age, National is worth your consideration. In fact National was promoted by Jeannette as giftware.

Back row: 12.5" 6-part relish, 8" luncheon plate; front row: 3.5" footed tumbler, 3" sherbet, 5" footed tumbler, 4.5" jar, cup & saucer, sugar, creamer. Courtesy of Janice Johnston / Behind The Green Door.

Back row: 15" console bowl; middle row: 2.75" candlestick holders w/3 feet, 5" x 4" cigarette box, front row: 3" ashtray, 5" ashtray. Courtesy of Janice Johnston / Behind The Green Door.

Back row: 7" pitcher w/ice lip, 7" pitcher w/out ice lip, 4.75" juice pitcher. Courtesy of Janice Johnston / Behind The Green Door.

NATIONAL	Crystal	Qty
Ashtray, 3"	3	____
Ashtray, 5" (indents for 4 cigarettes)	5	____
Bowl, 4.5" small berry	5	____
Bowl, 8.75" large berry	12	____
Bowl, 12" low	18	____
Bowl, 12" punch	35	____
Bowl, 15" console	20	____
Box w/lid, cigarette, 5" x 4", 2.25" deep	18	____
Candlestick holder, 2.75" w/3 feet, ea.	10	____
Candy jar w/lid	25	____
Coaster, 4"	5	____
Creamer	10	____
Cup, coffee	5	____
Cup, punch	3	____
Jar w/lid, 4.5" tall (condiment)	20	____
Lazy Susan, complete	65	____
15" tray	15	____
outer inserts, ea.	8	____
center insert	10	____
Pitcher, 4.75" juice/milk	25	____
Pitcher w/ice lip, 7"	22	____
Pitcher w/out ice lip, 7"	20	____
Plate, 8" luncheon	8	____
Relish, 12.5" 6-part (14.75" handle to handle)	12	____
Salt & pepper	15	____
Saucer	3	____
Sherbet, 3"	5	____
Sugar	10	____
Tray, 8" w/handles (13" handle to handle)	8	____
Tumbler, 3.5" w/foot	8	____
Tumbler, 5" w/foot	8	____
Tumbler, 4" flat	5	____
Tumbler, 6" flat	5	____
Vase	12	____

NEW CENTURY

(late 1920s-early 1930s Hazel-Atlas Glass Company)

There is nothing new about New Century as it is one of the older patterns of Depression Glass. Primarily found in cobalt blue and green, New Century amethyst and pink are hard to find. Crystal (clear) is not only not seen but also not collected. After reviewing the input of many dealers the pricing for green and crystal has been separated; the overall consensus is that crystal is simply worth less than green. No one seems to be able to sell crystal as no one seems to be looking for it.

There are many reasonably priced items in this Hazel-Atlas pattern. If you are looking for a green pattern, New Century is one you may wish to consider. Keep in mind that lower prices usually mean higher availability; this is not the case with New Century. Many pieces are quite difficult to find as you can see from our layout.

If you have a collection of New Century we would love the opportunity to feature it in our third edition.

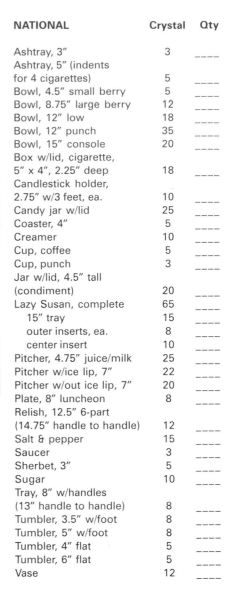

Back: 11" platter, 5.5" flat tumbler; front: 6" sherbet plate, shaker, sugar base.

NEW CENTURY	Green	Amethyst & Pink	Cobalt	Qty
Ashtray/coaster, 5.25"	30			----
Bowl, 4.75" berry	35			----
Bowl, 4.75" cream soup	25			----
Bowl, 8" berry	30			----
Bowl, 9" casserole base	30			----
Bowl, 9" casserole w/lid	75			----
Butter dish base	30			----
Butter dish lid	45			----
Butter dish complete	75			----
Creamer	12			----
Cup	10	15	20	----
Decanter w/stopper	85			----
Goblet, 2.5 oz. wine	45			----
Goblet, 3.25 oz. cocktail	45			----
Pitcher, 7.75" w/or w/out ice lip	45	45	60	----
Pitcher, 8" w/or w/out ice lip	45	45	70	----
Plate, 6" sherbet	5			----
Plate, 7.25" breakfast	12			----
Plate, 8.5" salad	12			----
Plate, 9" dinner	25			----
Plate, 10" grill	15			----
Platter, 11.75"	30			----
Salt & pepper	45			----
Saucer	5	10	15	----
Sherbet	10			----
Sugar base	12			----
Sugar lid	28			----
Tumbler, 2.5" whiskey, 1.5 oz. flat	35			----
Tumbler, 3.5", 5 oz. flat	15	20	22	----
Tumbler, 3.5", 8 oz. flat	25			----
Tumbler, 4", 5 oz. footed	30			----
Tumbler, 4.25", 9 oz. flat	15	20	22	----
Tumbler, 4.75", 9 oz. footed	30			----
Tumbler, 5", 10 oz. flat	20	25	28	----
Tumbler, 5.25", 12 oz. flat	30	35	40	----

Note: Items in crystal 1/2 of green.

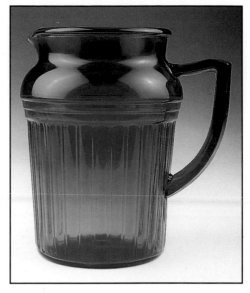

Left: 8" pitcher w/ no ice lip. *Courtesy of Diefenderfer's Collectibles & Antiques.*

Below: 3.5" 5 oz. flat tumbler, 5" flat tumbler, 3.5" 5 oz. tumbler. *Courtesy of Marie Talone & Paul Reichwein.*

NEWPORT

(mid-1930s Hazel-Atlas Glass Company)

Amethyst Depression Glass is getting more popular so it is particularly nice that we can feature Bill Quillen's collection. It is much harder to find Newport in amethyst than in cobalt. The current trend may create some frustrated collectors and an increase in prices. Fired-on pieces are rarely seen, but there is limited demand for these.

In general serving pieces are the most difficult items to find. This includes bowls, the platter, and the 11.5" sandwich plate. Newport has a great deal of surface space with plain, undecorated glass, and any scratching whatsoever becomes very apparent. Collectors normally seek glassware that appears to be unused, so this causes additional problems.

There is no Newport butter dish or pitcher, but virtually everything else needed to set the table and serve the meal is available even though there are only sixteen different items for this pattern.

Back row: 11" round sandwich platter, 11.75" platter; *front row:* 9" dinner plate, 8.5" salad plate, 6" sherbet plate. *Courtesy of Bill Quillen.*

8" berry bowl & 4.75" berry bowl

Shakers in two colors. *Courtesy of Michael Rothenberger/Mike's Collectibles.*

Back row: sugar & creamer; *middle row:* cup & saucer, 4.75" cream soup bowl; *front row:* sherbet & 4.75" berry bowl. *Courtesy of Bill Quillen.*

NEWPORT	Cobalt	Amethyst	Fired-on colors	Qty
Bowl, 4.25" berry	25	22	8	____
Bowl, 4.75" cream soup	25	25	10	____
Bowl, 5.25" cereal	45	45		____
Bowl, 8.25" berry	50	50	15	____
Creamer	20	18	8	____
Cup	15	12	8	____
Plate, 6" sherbet	10	8	5	____
Plate, 8.5" luncheon	20	15	8	____
Plate, 8.75" dinner	35	35		____
Plate, 11.5" sandwich	50	50	15	____
Platter, 11.75"	50	50	15	____
Salt & pepper	75	75	30	____
Saucer	5	5	2	____
Sherbet	18	18	8	____
Sugar	20	18	8	____
Tumbler, 4.5"	50	50	15	____

Note: Pink pieces ½ price of Amethyst. Crystal pieces ½ price of fired-on colors.

4.25" berry bowls in fired-on colors. *Courtesy of Charlie Diefenderfer.*

NORMANDIE
(1933-1939 Federal Glass Company)

Some things don't change. Two years after making the statement that iridescent Normandie is found throughout New England this still hold true. We passed through early in the summer of 2000 and found piles of iridescent Normandie in shop after shop. Much of it was in wonderful condition with a deep rich color indicating virtually no use at all. The conclusion one has to draw is few wanted to use it in the 1930s and few want to use it in the new millennium. Normandie is available in three colors, and iridescent (originally called "Sunburst") is the least favorite.

Normandie is one of the more popular amber (originally called "Golden Glow") patterns, joining the ranks of Madrid and Patrician. The availability of Normandie is high with the sugar lid being the most difficult item to locate. Even the pitcher, though pricey compared to the rest of this pattern, is not too challenging to find. The pieces are durable and many have survived in great condition since their manufacture in the 1930s.

Pink is not as popular as amber and a lot more difficult to find. Cups are very common and are often seen without saucers. Luncheon plates and 5" berry bowls are also abundant. Finding the rest of this pattern in pink will require time to hunt and search. The dinner plates are quite rare and many people are not willing to invest large sums of money into dinners. Assuming one is building a service for eight, pink Normandie dinner plates become a serious, if not prohibitive, investment. The rarity of this color has not created a greater demand as is sometimes the case. Normandie is primarily a pattern collected in amber.

11" dinner plate, 9.75" luncheon plate, 7.75" salad plate.

5" tumbler &
4.5" tumbler.

NORMANDIE	Amber	Pink	Iridescent	Qty
Bowl, 5" berry	8	14	4	____
Bowl, 6.5" cereal	20	35	8	____
Bowl, 8.5" berry	25	40	15	____
Bowl, 10" oval vegetable	25	50	15	____
Creamer	15	20	10	____
Cup	10	15	8	____
Pitcher	95	195		____
Plate, 6" sherbet	8	12	4	____
Plate, 7.75" salad	25	15	50	____
Plate, 9.25" luncheon	25	15	10	____
Plate, 11" dinner	65	150	10	____
Plate, 11" grill	18	45	8	____
Platter, 11.75"	40	35	15	____
Salt & pepper	65	100		____
Saucer	8	12	2	____
Sherbet	7	10	5	____
Sugar base	15	20	10	____
Sugar lid	125	500		____
Tumbler, 4"	50	125		____
Tumbler, 4.5"	40	90		____
Tumbler, 5"	65	150		____

Back: 8" mint tray, 7.25" vase; *front:* 6" olive dish, 4.5" bowl, 6.5" bowl. *Courtesy of Michael Rothenberger/Mike's Collectibles.*

OLD CAFE
(1936-1938 Hocking Glass Company)

Some Old Café prices are slowly moving upward. Even though this is a pattern with few options, what was made in pink and Royal Ruby is liked by many. The big surprise is the common 8" mint tray. These appear on eBay all the time with many different labels and descriptions, often with no pattern named or the wrong pattern listed. They often sell for more than $20. Factor in the shipping cost and one can determine that these are worth close to $25 to many buyers. By the way, very little else in the way of Old Café seems to be online.

Old Café pitchers are very rare and dinner plates are getting more difficult to find. It is hard to serve a meal without dinner plates. A collector may only need one pitcher, but chances are good that at least eight dinner plates need to be purchased.

There is only a ruby lid for the candy jar. Last edition the candy jar was pictured with a pink base, so this time it is presented with a crystal (clear) base. This is one of the only crystal pieces of any consequence as few collectors are interested in crystal Old Café.

Back: 6" sherbet plate, 10" dinner plate; *front:* sherbet, 3" juice tumbler, 4" tumbler. *Courtesy of Michael Rothenberger/Mike's Collectibles.*

Candy jar w/lid.

OLD CAFÉ	Pink	Ruby	Crystal	Qty
Bowl, 3.75" berry	10	15	5	____
Bowl, 4.5" w/handles	12		6	____
Bowl, 5.5" cereal	25	20	10	____
Bowl, 6.5" w/handles	30			____
Bowl, 9" w/handles	20	30	8	____
Candy jar w/lid (crystal or pink base, ruby lid), 7"	34		20	____
Cup	10	12	5	____
Lamp	135	150	125	____
Mint tray, 8" low & flared	18	20	6	____
Olive dish, 6" oval	12			____
Pitcher, 6", 36 oz.	100			____
Pitcher, 80 oz.	125			____
Plate, 6" sherbet	15		2	____
Plate, 10" dinner	65			____
Relish set				
15" crystal base, 5 ruby inserts, 7" candy jar w/lid		100		____
Relish set w/rotating base		140		____
Saucer	8		2	____
Sherbet, 3.75"	18	20	5	____ Tumbler,
3" juice	20	25	8	____
Tumbler, 4"	22	30	8	____
Vase, 7.25"	35	45	20	____

Note: Mint tray, 8", add $5 for metal handle.

OLD COLONY

(1935-1938 Hocking Glass Company)

One of Hocking Glass Company's most popular Depression Glass patterns, Old Colony, continues to attract new collectors. Because there is a great deal of interest in the pattern prices are stable or slowing rising. This is not a pattern seen in any quantity, as there is a reasonable amount of competition among buyers, especially for hard-to-find pieces and items in perfect condition.

Condition is a real factor when assessing a piece of Old Colony because the lacy loops have a tendency to crack. As these lines in the glass are often difficult to discern, some collectors actually use a jeweler's loupe to examine a piece under consideration. To get "full book price" for Old Colony an item must be able to withstand the most thorough scrutiny. Because the elusive pieces are in such demand, even if they have a line or two collectors are often interested if the price is adjusted downward. We sold a candleholder with chips in the base and a line in a loop for $85 on eBay and a cracked sherbet realized about $40. This is one of a few patterns whose pieces retain some value despite damage.

The satinized cookie jar with gold trim was found in the middle of nowhere in western Pennsylvania. Satinized Old Colony is less popular that transparent pink, but isn't this an interesting piece? Other variations in Old Colony include the fact that some pieces have ribs and some do not; some loops are open and some are closed; and the flat tumblers don't even look like they belong with this pattern. Be sure to examine the footed Old Colony tumbler and the footed Coronation tumbler to avoid any confusion, as the Old Colony tumbler is considerably more expensive.

If you find a piece of glass that appears to be Old Colony but is not on the list you may have a piece of Imperial, Lancaster, or Westmoreland glass as all three companies produced similar glassware.

Back row: 10.5" dinner plate, 10.5" grill plate, 8.25" luncheon plate; *front:* cup & saucer. *Courtesy of Bryan & Marie James.*

Back row: 13" 4-part solid lace plate, 10.5" 3-part relish, 12.75" 5-part platter; *front:* 7.5" 3-part relish. *Courtesy of Bryan & Marie James.*

Back: 9.5" salad bowl w/ ribs, 9.5" smooth bowl; *front:* 6.5" cereal bowl, 10.5" bowl w/ 3 feet. *Courtesy of Bryan & Marie James.*

4.25" flat tumbler, 5" footed tumbler that resembles Coronation tumbler. *Courtesy of Staci & Jeff Shuck/Gray Goose Antiques & Neil McCurdy - Hoosier Kubboard Glass.*

Back: 12.75" platter; *front:* ribbed flower bowl w/ crystal frog, sherbet, 7" comport. *Courtesy of Bryan & Marie James.*

Butter, ribbed candy jar w/ lid, 7" comport w/ lid, cookie jar w/ lid. *Courtesy of Bryan & Marie James.*

Satin-finished cookie jar and lid with gold embellishment.

Candleholder. *Courtesy of Scott & Rhonda Hackenburg / Blue Jay Antiques & Collectibles.*

OLD COLONY	Pink	Qty
Ashtray	trtp*	____
Bowl, 6.5" cereal	30	____
Bowl, 6.5" cereal satin finish	20	____
Bowl, 7.75" salad w/ribs	40	____
Bowl, 8.25" (in crystal)	12	____
Bowl, 9.5" smooth	30	____
Bowl, 9.5" w/ribs	38	____
Bowl, 9.5" satin finish	25	____
Bowl, 10.5" w/3 feet	350	____
Bowl, 10.5" w/3 feet satin finish	55	____
Bowl, ribbed flower w/crystal frog, 3.5" tall, 7" diam.	50	____
Bowl, fish (in crystal; similar to cookie jar base)	40	____
Butter dish base	45	____
Butter dish lid	65	____
Butter complete	110	____
Candle holder, ea.	225	____
Candle holder, ea. satin finish	30	____
Candy jar w/lid, ribbed	100	____
Comport, 7"	40	____
Comport, 7" satin finish	25	____
Comport w/lid, 7"	80	____
Comport, 9"	trtp*	____
Cookie jar w/lid	100	____
Cookie jar w/lid satin finish	50	____
Creamer	40	____
Cup	35	____
Plate, 7.25" salad	35	____
Plate, 8.25" luncheon	30	____
Plate, 10.5" dinner	40	____
Plate, 10.5" grill	25	____
Plate, 13" solid lace	65	____
Plate, 13" solid lace, 4-part	65	____
Plate, 13" solid lace w/satin finish, 4-part	30	____
Platter, 12.75"	50	____
Platter, 12.75", 5-part	45	____
Relish, 7.5", 3-part	100	____
Relish, 10.5", 3-part	35	____
Saucer	18	____
Sherbet	165	____
Sugar	50	____
Tumbler, 3.5" flat	225	____
Tumbler, 4.25" flat	40	____
Tumbler, 5" w/foot	100	____
Vase, 7"	850	____
Vase, 7" satin finish	65	____

Note: 6.5" green cereal bowl, $100. White sherbet, $8.

*trtp = too rare to price

OLD ENGLISH

(1926-1929 Indiana Glass Company)

The finely ribbed design of Old English distinguishes it from other Depression Glass patterns, even Homespun. Found predominantly in green, note that the egg cup is made only in crystal (clear).

This is a pattern with few collectors. Perhaps that is why this is a difficult pattern to find. When patterns become popular often pieces have a way of showing up in the marketplace. When there is limited demand, dealers hesitate to invest space and money in glassware that will be difficult to sell. In the meantime, if you have a collection to bring to the studio we would love the chance to improve our presentation of Old English.

5.5" tumbler, 4.5" tumbler, sherbet.

Far left: 5.5" & 4.5" tumbler. *Courtesy of Staci & Jeff Shuck/Gray Goose Antiques.*

Left: Sugar w/ lid. *Courtesy of Vic & Jean Laermans.*

OLD ENGLISH	All colors	Qty
Bowl, 4"	25	____
Bowl, 9" w/foot	35	____
Bowl, 9.5" flat	50	____
Bowl, 11" fruit, w/foot	50	____
Candlestick, ea.	30	____
Candy jar w/lid	75	____
Comport, 3.5", 2 styles	35	____
Creamer	25	____
Egg cup (only in crystal)	12	____
Goblet, 5.75"	40	____
Pitcher	80	____
Pitcher cover	120	____
Sandwich server w/ center handle	75	____
Sherbet, 2 styles	25	____
Sugar base	25	____
Sugar lid	40	____
Tumbler, 4.5"	30	____
Tumbler, 5.5"	40	____
Underplate for comport	30	____
Vase, 5.25" fan	60	____
Vase, 8"	60	____
Vase, 8.25"	60	____
Vase, 12"	75	____

9.5" bowl. *Courtesy of Charlie Diefenderfer.*

Egg cup.

11" bowl, pair of candlesticks. *Courtesy of Debora & Paul Torsiello, Debzie's Glass.*

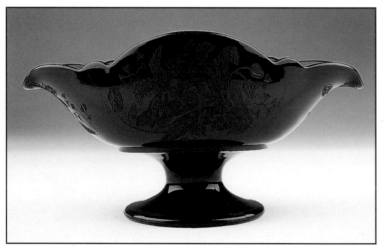

6.75" comport. *Courtesy of Debora & Paul Torsiello, Debzie's Glass.*

Two 10" vases, 5" vase, 8.25" elliptical vase. *Courtesy of Debora & Paul Torsiello, Debzie's Glass.*

ORCHID
(1929-1930s Paden City Glass Manufacturing Company)

The exquisite quality of Paden City Glass is evident in the beautiful Orchid pattern. As with other lines of glass manufactured by Paden City during the 1930s, the Orchid shapes were used elsewhere. The basic mold was advertised as "Line No. 300." Etchings were applied to these pieces thus creating masterpieces like Orchid. There are several orchid designs that have been applied by Paden City artists, and most collectors are content with any design they are fortunate enough to discover.

Time to clarify the vases and offer a big "Oops! The tallest vases pictured are twelve inches tall (not ten as we erroneously stated). The cobalt blue one is much rarer than the other colors and worth about $1800. The five-inch vase is an elliptical vase. Another five-inch elliptical vase is pictured in Peacock and Rose. The red vase in the back is thought to be the only one in existence. It is a cupped nine-inch vase whose bottom half is done in a corrugated style. We have listed this as trtp (too rare to price).

Finding any piece of Orchid can be a challenge. Most collectors are happy to own any one of the beautifully bold colors: Cheri-glo (pink), crystal (clear), Golden Glow (amber), green, amethyst, black, cobalt blue, and red.

ORCHID	Black, Cobalt blue, & Red	Other colors	Qty
Bowl, 4.75"	65	30	____
Bowl, 8.5" w/handles	150	100	____
Bowl, 8.75"	150	100	____
Bowl, 10" w/foot	200	125	____
Bowl, 11"	200	100	____
Cake stand	175	100	____
Candlestick, 5.75" ea.	220	120	____
Candy box w/cover (square shape)	220	120	____
Candy box w/cover (3-leaf clover shape)	220	120	____
Comport, 3.25" tall	65	30	____
Comport, 6.75" tall	150	75	____
Creamer	100	60	____
Ice Bucket, 6"	220	120	____
Mayonnaise, 3-piece set	200	120	____
Plate, 8.5"	85		____
Sandwich server w/ center handle	125	75	____
Sugar	100	60	____
Vase, 5" elliptical	400		____
Vase, 8.25"	280	120	____
Vase	400	150	____
Vase, 9" cut	*trtp		____
Vase, 12"	1800		____

*trtp = too rare to price

OVIDE
(1930-1935 Hazel-Atlas Glass Company)

There seems to be no end to the Ovide possibilities. Whatever colors are needed to compliment a kitchen, Ovide seems to be able to provide a match. Despite all its versatility, few collectors seem to pay any attention to this pattern. In the first edition of *Mauzy's Depression Glass* we presented three color combinations, and in this edition there are three new ones. The pink and black is also available in turquoise and black. Place black Bakelite utensils by either of these combinations and the look would be pure vintage fun!

The colors are fired-on so care must be taken when washing Ovide. Pieces should not be placed in a dishwasher and abrasive cleansers are inappropriate.

Ovide may be worth your consideration if you are interested in a colorful table with only a moderate investment. As long as shoppers pass this by the prices will remain quite affordable.

Back row: 9" dinner plate; *middle row:* 5.5" cereal bowl, sugar; *front row:* cup & saucer, creamer.

Variations of creamers & sugars.

OVIDE	Decorated	Deco	Black	Green	Qty
Bowl, 4.75" berry	10				____
Bowl, 5.5" cereal	15				____
Bowl, 8" berry	25				____
Candy dish w/lid	40		50	30	____
Cocktail, stemmed			8	4	____
Creamer	15	85	10	4	____
Cup	10	60	8	3	____
Plate, 6" sherbet	5			3	____
Plate, 8" luncheon	10	45		4	____
Plate, 9" dinner	20				____
Platter, 11"	25				____
Salt & pepper	35		35	30	____
Saucer	5	18	5	3	____
Sherbet	12	50	8	3	____
Sugar	15	85	10	4	____
Tumbler	25	85			____

Cup.

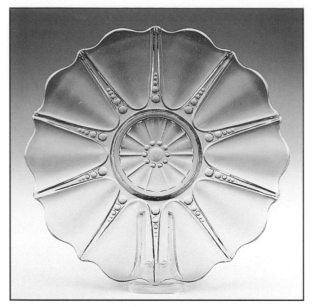

OYSTER AND PEARL

(1938-1940   Anchor Hocking Glass Corporation)

Oyster and Pearl offers a small but pleasing array of bowls, some serving plates, candle holders, and that's all. If you are looking for a dinnerware pattern this is one to pass by as there are no cups, saucers, tumblers, or plates smaller than 13.5". Pink and the more elusive Royal Ruby Oyster and Pearl pieces are extremely popular. They enhance Depression Glass collections and work nicely as single items or in small groupings. The 10.5" console bowl with a pair of candle holders looks great on a dining room table or buffet table.

13.5" sandwich plate. *Courtesy of Joan Kauffman.*

Back: two 10.25" oval 2-part relishes; *front row:*
two 6.5" bonbons. *Courtesy of Jane O'Brien.*

Candle holders, 10.5" console bowl. *Courtesy of Jane O'Brien & Tanya Poillucci.*

OYSTER & PEARL	Ruby	Pink	Crystal, other colors, & fired-on	Qty
Bowl, 5.25" jelly, heart-shaped w/1 handle	25	15	8	____
Bowl, 5.5" round w/1 handle	25	15		____
Bowl, 6.5" bon bon, deep	30	18		____
Bowl, 10.5" console	60	30	15	____
Candle holder, 3.5" ea.	30	20	10	____
Plate, 13.5" sandwich	60	35	12	____
Relish, 10.25" oval, 2-part		18		____
Tray, 10.5" x 7.75"			15	____

Fired-on pieces: 10.5" console bowl, 10.5" x 7.75" tray, candle holders.

PARK AVENUE

(1941-early 1970s Federal Glass Company)

There is little interest in this little pattern. However, Park Avenue tumblers are fairly common and you may have questions as to what you are looking at. Like Peanut Butter Glasses and Swanky Swigs, some Park Avenue tumblers were marketed with a food product inside. The pry-off top was removed, the contents consumed, and a "free" glass was added to the cupboard. Collectors buying Park Avenue usually either have a sentimental attachment to these tumblers or appreciate buying something reasonably priced with a bit of age to it.

4.75" dessert bowls in a variety of colors.
Courtesy of Charlie Diefenderfer.

PARK AVENUE	Crystal & Amber	Qty
Ashtray, 3.5"	5	____
Ashtray, 4.5"	5	____
Bowl, 4.75" dessert	5	____
Bowl, 8.5" vegetable	10	____
Candle holder, 5" each	10	____
Tumbler, 2.25" whiskey, 1.25 oz.	4	____
Tumbler, 3.5" juice, 4.5 oz.	4	____
Tumbler, 3.75", water 9 oz.	4	____
Tumbler, 4.75", water 10 oz.	6	____
Tumbler, 5.25" iced tea, 12 oz.	6	____

Note: 4.75" dessert bowls in frosted colors $8 each.

8.5" vegetable bowl,
4.75" dessert bowl,
3.5" 4.5 oz. tumbler.

PATRICIAN

(1933-1937 Federal Glass Company)

Both amber ("Golden Glow") and green ("Springtime Green") are extremely popular colors in Patrician. Once a pattern for amber collectors, green lovers have stepped forward and the pendulum has swung. Both colors are fairly easy to find although amber continues to be a bit more plentiful. Pink is the color that is difficult to find. In fact, pink dinner plates seem to have disappeared.

Patrician is a very popular pattern for several reasons. First of all, there are many options from which to select. There are five plates, four tumblers, and six bowls. The dinner plates are 10.5" making them almost two inches larger than many patterns. Patrician has not been reproduced, allowing collectors to shop with confidence.

Some changes and additions have been made to the list. Pictured is a 6.75" jam bowl in amber. Let us know if you have one in another color. The overwhelming message from dealers was that crystal (clear) Patrician is worth far less than amber and should not share the same values. That adjustment has been made.

Patrician plates were molded with a severe edge where the rim and eating surface meet. The inner edge of this rim is susceptible to damage. A fingernail should be taken across this area to determine if the condition is acceptable.

PATRICIAN	Green	Pink	Amber	Qty
Bowl, 4.75" cream soup	25	20	17	____
Bowl, 5" berry	15	14	14	____
Bowl, 6" cereal	30	26	26	____
Bowl, 6.75" jam			65	____
Bowl, 9" berry	45	35	45	____
Bowl, 10" oval vegetable	40	35	30	____
Butter dish base	75	150	65	____
Butter dish lid	50	75	35	____
Butter complete	125	225	100	____
Cookie jar/lid	600		100	____
Creamer	18	15	12	____
Cup	12	14	10	____
Jam dish, 6"	50	40	35	____
Pitcher, 8" molded handle	150	130	120	____
Pitcher, 8.25" applied handle	175	160	160	____
Plate, 6" bread & butter	12	12	10	____
Plate, 7.5" salad	18	18	18	____
Plate, 9" luncheon	15	20	15	____
Plate, 10.5" dinner	45	35	14	____
Plate, 10.5" grill	20	18	14	____
Platter, 11.5"	35	35	30	____
Salt & pepper	75	100	65	____
Saucer	12	12	10	____
Sherbet	18	15	12	____
Sugar base	18	15	12	____
Sugar lid	70	70	70	____
Tumbler, 4" flat	35	35	30	____
Tumbler, 4.5" flat	30	30	30	____
Tumbler, 5.25" w/foot	80		70	____
Tumbler, 5.5" flat	45	40	45	____

Note: Crystal 1/2 of Amber EXCEPT: complete butter, $125; 8.25" pitcher w/applied handle, $175; 10.5" dinner plate, $25.

10.5" grill plate, 10.5" dinner plate, 9" luncheon plate, 7.5" salad plate. *Courtesy of Bill Quillen.*

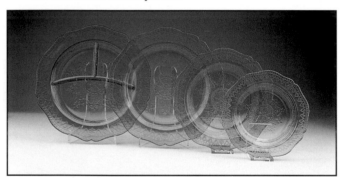

Back row: 9" berry bowl, 10" oval vegetable bowl; *front row:* 4.75" cream soup bowl, 6.75" jam bowl, 5" berry bowl. *Courtesy of Bill Quillen.*

Back row: 8" pitcher, cookie jar w/lid; *front row:* sugar & creamer. *Courtesy of Bill Quillen.*

5.25" tumbler w/foot, 4.5" flat tumbler, 4" flat tumbler.

Back row: 11.5" platter, salt & pepper; *front row:* cup & saucer, sherbet, butter dish. *Courtesy of Bill Quillen.*

PATRICK
(1930s Lancaster Glass Company)

It is easy to identify Lancaster glass, especially in yellow. Lancaster Glass Company produced a "signature" pure, bright yellow that was called topaz. Pink (rose) was also produced and is even more difficult to find than yellow. Glassware made by this company has smooth rims and edges. There are no troubling edges of extra glass as seen in Lorain and Horseshoe.

If you are a frustrated Patrick collector we feel your pain! We can't find any either, and even Internet auction searches come up empty. Likewise, if you have a collection we again extend an invitation to have your pieces featured our third edition.

Frustrated Patrick collectors will occasionally buy other Lancaster Glass Company items such as Jubilee just for the gratification of making a purchase. Conversely, Jubilee collectors rarely buy Patrick. Of course, there is very little Patrick to be found.

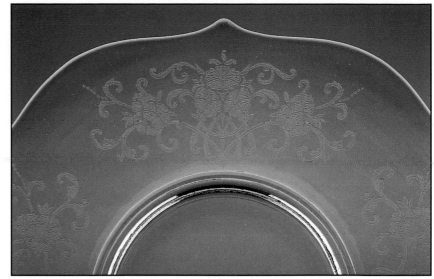

Detail of pattern. *Courtesy of Michael Rothenberger/Mike's Collectibles.*

PATRICK	Pink	Yellow	Qty
Bowl, 9" fruit w/handles	200	150	____
Bowl, 11.5" low console	180	140	____
Candlestick, ea.	85	85	____
Candy bowl w/cover	200	175	____
Cheese & cracker	200	175	____
Creamer	90	50	____
Cup	85	50	____
Goblet, 4" stemmed cocktail	100	100	____
Goblet, 4.75" juice	100	100	____
Goblet, 6" water	100	100	
Mayonnaise, 3-piece set	240	220	____
Plate, 7" sherbet	30	20	____
Plate, 7.5" salad	40	30	____
Plate, 8" luncheon	60	40	____
Plate, 9"	60		____
Plate, 11" sandwich w/handles	100	85	____
Saucer	25	15	____
Sherbet, 4.75" w/stem	80	65	____
Sugar	90	50	____
Tray, 11" sandwich w/center handle	175	140	____

Above: Creamer, two sugars, 8" luncheon plate, cup & saucer. *Courtesy of Vic & Jean Laermans.*

PEACOCK & ROSE
(1928-1930s Paden City Glass
Manufacturing Company)

Paden City Glass Manufacturing Company used blanks Line No. 300 for Peacock and Rose. As these blanks were used for other Paden City glassware the shapes should begin to look familiar. Pieces come in amber, black, cobalt blue, blue, crystal (clear), green, pink, and red. Peacock and Rose is difficult to find, so we were delighted to have some magnificent examples to share thanks to Mike Rothenberger.

Added to the list and pictured in black are two vases: the 5" elliptical #182 Vimmer Vase and the 6.5" vase. The 6.5" vase is also found in green and in green Peacock Reverse. Another addition is the green 10" bowl with two handles. This is actually the Crow's Foot blank with the Peacock and Rose design. There are two comports to consider. The green comport has an 8" inch diameter and is rolled and scalloped at the edge while the amber comport has a 7.75" diameter and is flared and scalloped at the rim. Two additional new pieces were seen on the Internet including

Detail of pattern. *Courtesy of Debora & Paul Torsiello, Debzie's Glass.*

Back: 8.5" oval bowl; *front:* 10" footed bowl w/ rolled edge, 9.5" footed bowl. *Courtesy of Michael Rothenberger/Mike's Collectibles.*

a crystal 11" x 7.5" footed dish. This is not the cake dish as it is an oval and sold for $158 in February 2000. Also found online during the same month is a 10" eight-sided plate in amber which sold for $108.

The cup and saucer pictured were found on a tray lot at an auction along with three other yellow cups and saucers. All had the same blank with four distinctly different designs.

12" vase. *Courtesy of Debora & Paul Torsiello, Debzie's Glass.*

6.25" vase. *Courtesy of Mike Rothenberger / Mike's Collectibles.*

PEACOCK & ROSE	Any color	Qty
Bowl, 8.5" flat	130	____
Bowl, 8.5" oval	200	____
Bowl, 8.75" w/foot	200	____
Bowl, 9.5" w/center handle	175	____
Bowl, 9.5" w/foot	200	____
Bowl, 10" w/foot	200	____
Bowl, 10" w/2 handles	275	____
Bowl, 10.5" w/center handle	175	____
Bowl, 10.5" w/foot	200	____
Bowl, 10.5" flat	200	____
Bowl, 11" console, rolled edge	180	____
Bowl, 14" console, rolled edge	220	____
Cake plate, 11" w/foot	150	____
Candlestick, 5" across, ea.	85	____
Candy box w/lid, 7"	200	____
Cheese and cracker	200	____
Comport, 3.25" tall	130	____
Comport, 6" tall	150	____
Comport, 7.75" diam., flared & scalloped	150	____
Comport, 8" diam., rolled & scalloped	150	____
Ice bucket, 6"	200	____
Ice tub, 6.25"	200	____
Mayonnaise, 3 piece set	130	____
Pitcher, 5"	265	____
Plate, 10" w/8 sides	100	____
Plate, 11" x 7.5" w/foot	150	____
Relish, 6.25"	130	____
Tray, 10" sandwich	150	____
Tray, 10.75" oval w/foot	200	____
Tumbler, 2.25"	100	____
Tumbler, 3"	80	____
Tumbler, 4"	80	____
Tumbler, 4.75" ftd.	80	____
Tumbler, 5.25"	100	____
Vase, 5", elliptical	500	____
Vase, 6.5"	400	____
Vase, 8.25", elliptical	400	____
Vase, 10" 2 styles	275	____
Vase, 12" 2 styles	300	____

Note: 12" vase in Ruby, yellow, or cobalt, $500 each.

Three elliptical vases: 8.25" vase, #182 5" Vimmer vase, 8.25" vase. *Courtesy of Mike Rothenberger / Mike's Collectibles.*

Back row: #182 Vimmer vase, 6" comport w/rolled & scalloped edge; *front row:* 10" 2-handled bowl on Crow's Foot blank, 10" server w/center handle. *Courtesy of Mike Rothenberger / Mike's Collectibles.*

Cup & saucer.

Pieces on the "Mrs. B. blank:" *Back row:* 9.5" footed bowl, 6" comport w/scalloped edge; *front row:* 10" server w/center handle, 6.25" ice bucket, 11.75" console bowl w/rolled edge. *Courtesy of Mike Rothenberger / Mike's Collectibles.*

PEACOCK REVERSE
(1930s Paden City Glass Manufacturing Company)

Back: 6" vase; *front:* 5" candlesticks, 9.25" bowl w/ center handle.
Courtesy of Michael Rothenberger/Mike's Collectibles.

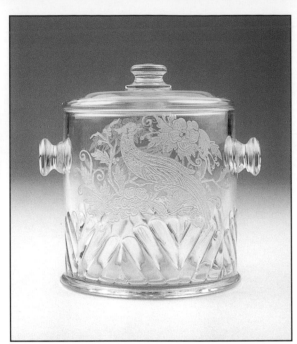

Biscuit jar w/lid. Note: this is missing the reed handle. 5.5" to top of base. *Courtesy of Mike Rothenberger / Mike's Collectibles.*

Peacock Reverse is a motif that is etched on Paden City blanks from Crow's Foot and "Penny" Line, No. 991. Like Peacock and Rose, Peacock Reverse is a beautiful pattern on a superior quality of glass that is found in a spectrum of colors, when found at all! Colors include amber, black, cobalt blue, blue, crystal (clear), green, pink, red, and yellow.

Two new items are being added to Peacock Reverse. First is a crystal biscuit jar with lid. It is 5.5" tall to the top of the base with a 5.25" diameter and should have a reed handle. This piece was on eBay without the lid but with the handle in May 2000 and sold for $406.51. The seller had listed it as an "ice tub." The second piece, a crystal bowl, was found in December 2000. It measures 6.5" from side to side, 7.5" across the diagonal, and 2" deep.

Cheese & cracker. *Courtesy of Debora & Paul Torsiello, Debzie's Glass.*

Sugar & creamer. *Courtesy of Vic & Jean Laermans.*

PEACOCK REVERSE	Any color	Qty
Biscuit jar w/lid	600	____
Bowl, 4.75"	50	____
Bowl, 6.5", 2" deep	75	____
Bowl, 8.75"	125	____
Bowl, 8.75" w/handles	125	____
Bowl, 9.25" w/center handle	150	____
Bowl, 11.75", console	150	____
Candlestick, ea., 5" tall	85	____
Candy box w/lid	200	____
Cheese & cracker	200	____
Comport, 3.25" tall	85	____
Comport, 4.25" tall	85	____
Creamer, 2.75"	95	____
Cup	85	____
Plate, 5.75" sherbet	25	____
Plate, 8.5" luncheon	70	____
Plate, 10.5" w/handles	100	____
Plate, sandwich w/center handle	85	____
Saucer	25	____
Sherbet, 2 sizes	75	____
Sugar, 2.75"	95	____
Tumbler, 4"	100	____
Vase, 6.5"	400	____
Vase, 10"	225	____

PEBBLE OPTIC (formerly called RAINDROPS)

(1927-1932 Federal Glass Company)

Incorrectly called Raindrops in the past, we are returning this pattern to its correct name, Pebble Optic. This was one of the earliest Depression Glass patterns and typical of the time was only made in green. Manufactured by Federal Glass Company, some of the pieces were molded with Federal's signature mark, an F inside a shield. Bowls have the mark, plates do not.

This is an interesting pattern. There are only nineteen items made and seven of them are tumblers. Yet, the tumblers are among the hardest pieces to find! The sugar lid is also a challenge to locate and we have never seen the shakers. Let us know if you own a pair!

Collectors new to this pattern and to Depression Glass in general sometimes have difficulty discerning the differences between Pebble Optic, Hex Optic, and Thumbprint. All three patterns are pictured, but here are some additional points to consider. The surface texture of Hex Optic resembles a honey-comb having hexagonal indents. (Hence the name Hex Optic.) Pebble Optic has round indents. The Thumbprint design favors that of Pebble Optic with oval indents shaped like an actual thumbprint. Again, pattern names often relate to their designs.

Top right: 6" cereal bowl. *Courtesy of Neil McCurdy-Hoosier Kubboard Glass.*

Right: *Back row:* 6" sherbet plate, 4.5" fruit bowl; *front row:* sugar w/ lid, creamer, 3" tumbler.

PEBBLE OPTICS	Green	Qty
Bowl, 4.5" fruit	8	____
Bowl, 6" cereal	12	____
Bowl, 7.5" berry	40	____
Creamer	10	____
Cup	8	____
Plate, 6" sherbet	4	____
Plate, 8" luncheon	8	____
Salt & pepper	trtp*	____
Saucer	4	____
Sherbet	10	____
Sugar base	10	____
Sugar lid	125	____
Tumbler, 1.75" whiskey	10	____
Tumbler, 2.25"	10	____
Tumbler, 3"	10	____
Tumbler, 3.75"	12	____
Tumbler, 4.25"	12	____
Tumbler, 5"	12	____
Tumbler, 5.25"	15	____

3.75" tumbler, sherbet, 1.75" whiskey tumbler.

*trtp = too rare too price

Note: Crystal items half those in green.

PETALWARE

(1930-1940 Macbeth-Evans Glass Company)

From the *Macbeth Monax Petalware Catalog 405* come some statements describing their product: "In the new, modern Monax Petalware, Macbeth has achieved the ultimate in eye appeal. It is truly a bargain in beauty in its graceful petal pattern, in its ever-popular, translucent blue-white tint. This latest in tableware is predestined for large sales volume…Adding sales appeal to this lovely line is a subtle, flame-tinted undertone visible under various lighting conditions…pictures could never do justice to the jewel-like coloring of Macbeth Monax Petalware…In tune with the times and blending artistically with the finest of table service, Macbeth Monax Petalware will find universal acceptance… Women everywhere will want the complete ensemble."

Above: *Back row:* 7" soup bowl, 13" platter; *front row:* cream soup bowl, 6" dessert/cereal bowl, 9" berry bowl. *Courtesy of Bob & Cindy Bentley.*

Left: 3-tier & 2-tier tidbits. *Courtesy of Bob & Cindy Bentley.*

You are in for a treat! Lorain Penrod sent her complete ensemble to the studio, and she had so many fantastic pieces some will be unveiled in our third edition. There was simply too much for one book!

Among the most popular of the Petalware designs are Petalware pieces with flowers, and particularly flowers **and** a red trim. These are surface decorations that can wear off or be damaged by abrasive cleaning, dishwashers, rough use, and stacking. We recommend a coffee filter or paper plate between all stacked glassware.

Shown are nine 8.25" salad plates with fruit decorations: Roseberry Strawberry, Florence Cherry, Lucretic Dewberry, Muscat, Ord Apple, Knight's Peach, Hungarian Plum, and Souvenir D'espe'ren. Do these actually grown in Charleroi, Pennsylvania?

The 5.75" cereal bowl used to create a decorative wall hanger is also a unique piece.

Depression Glass was often a premium that was given away with the purchase of a good or service. The unopened box of Nu Bora Borax Soap Granules has more space devoted to the Petalware saucer packed inside than to the soap itself. But not *every* piece was free, and shown is a letter dated November 5, 1937 from Corning Glass Works providing pricing information for Petalware. Just imagine cream soup bowls for twelve cents each!

A Monax 5.75" cereal bowl was used to create a decorative wall hanger. *Courtesy of Lorraine Penrod.*

Lampshade (one of many shapes). *Courtesy of Charlie Diefenderfer.*

Gold trimmed Petalware. *Courtesy of Lorraine Penrod.*

This 1937 Corning Glass Works letter provides pricing information for Petalware. *Courtesy of Lorraine Penrod.*

Back: 9" dinner plate, 6" bread & butter plate, 9" berry bowl; *front:* cream soup bowl, condiment.

Left center top: 8.25" salad plates w/fruit decorations. Notice the Cremax pear plate next to a Monax pear plate has a distinctly different color. *Courtesy of Lorraine Penrod.*

Left center middle: Flowers without red trim. *Back row:* 8.5" berry bowl, 9" dinner plate, 12" salver; *front row:* 5.75" cereal bowl, cup & saucer, sugar, creamer. *Courtesy of Lorraine Penrod.*

Right: A Petalware saucer was a free premium with the purchase of Nu Bora Borax Soap. *Courtesy of Lorraine Penrod.*

Red trim w/flowers. *Back row:* creamer, 6.25" bread & butter plate, 8.25" salad plate, 9" dinner plate, 12" salver; *front row:* sugar, cup & saucer, 5.75" cereal bowl, sherbet. *Courtesy of Lorraine Penrod.*

PETALWARE	Pink	Monax & Cremax (plain)	Decorated & Ivrene	Crystal	Qty
Bowl, cream soup, 4.5"	20	15	15	5	____
Bowl, 5.75" dessert/cereal	15	10	15	5	____
Bowl, 7" soup		60	75		____
Bowl, 8.5" berry	30	25	35	12	____
Creamer, 3.25"	15	10	15	5	____
Cup	10	8	10	5	____
Lamp shade (multiple shapes)		25			____
Pitcher				25	____
Plate, 6.25" bread & butter	8	8	12	4	____
Plate, 8.25" salad	12	10	15	4	____
Plate, 9" dinner	20	15	24	6	____
Plate, 11" salver	20	15	25	8	____
Plate, 12" salver	20	20			____
Platter, 13"	25	20	30	10	____
Saucer	5	5	5		____
Sherbet, 4"		22			____
Sherbet, 4.25"	15	15	18	5	____
Sugar, 3.5"	15	10	15	5	____
Tidbits, 2- or 3-tier servers, several sizes	30	25	25	15	____
Tumbler, 3 sizes				12	____

Note: Cobalt Blue condiment, $10; add $5 for metal lid with wooden knob; add $8 for metal lid with Bakelite knob. Cobalt 9" berry bowl, $50; 4.5" sherbet, $30. Red trim with flowers twice prices of pink. Monax with gold trim 1/2 price of plain.

"PHILBE"
FIRE-KING DINNERWARE
(1940 Hocking Glass Company)

Philbe continues to be an impossible pattern to find regardless of color. Pieces don't seem to be for sale in virtually any brick and mortar situation. You can occasionally discover a piece online; on rare instances in a cyber-auction but more likely in a website devoted to Depression Glass.

The prices shown are realistically what one can expect to pay. The competition for Philbe is fierce as it is a trophy among serious glass aficionados.

Philbe was only produced for one year using resurrected Cameo molds. (Cameo was terminated in 1934). There are considerably less offerings in Philbe as its period of production was so brief, but what was made is now highly desirable.

Collectors of Philbe are usually happy to find any color. The reward of a actually adding to a collection is usually gratifying enough. As for colors, the blue is more of an ice blue, a color rarely used in Depression Glass. Crystal Philbe has the least value but it is still very difficult to find. As shown on the value guide, pink and green fall in the middle.

Above: Two 10" oval vegetable bowls, 4" water tumbler, 4.75" stemmed sherbet. *Courtesy of Staci & Jeff Shuck/Gray Goose Antiques.*

Left: Creamer. *Courtesy of Neil McCurdy - Hoosier Kubboard Glass.*

PHILBE	Blue	Pink & Green	Crystal	Qty
Bowl, 5.5" cereal	180	100	35	____
Bowl, 7.25" salad	300	120	50	____
Bowl, 10" oval vegetable	500	200	100	____
Candy jar w/lid, 4"	2000	1500	500	____
Cookie jar w/lid	trtp*	trtp*	trtp*	____
Creamer, 3.25"	300	200	65	____
Cup	300	200	100	____
Goblet, 7.25"	600	300	150	____
Pitcher, 6" juice	2200	1200	500	____
Pitcher, 8.5"	4000	2500	600	____
Plate, 6" sherbet	200	100	50	____
Plate, 8" luncheon	180	100	40	____
Plate, 10" heavy sandwich	350	200	50	____
Plate, 10.5" salver	250	125	50	____
Plate, 10.5" grill	250	125	50	____
Plate, 11.5" salver	300	125	50	____
Platter, 12" w/tab handles	500	300	80	____
Saucer/sherbet plate	200	100	50	____
Sherbet, 4.75" stemmed	1500	500		____
Sugar	300	200	65	____
Tumbler, 3.5" juice w/foot	500	350	80	____
Tumbler, 4" water, no foot	400	300	80	____
Tumbler, 5.25" w/foot	300	200	80	____
Tumbler, 6.5" iced tea w/foot	300	200	80	____

*trtp = too rare to price

Cup, 11.5" salver, 6.5" footed iced tea tumbler.

PIECRUST

(1940s Pyrex, Macbeth-Evans Division of
Corning Glass Works)

If you've ever baked a pie with a crust on top and had to push this down with a fork to seal the lid to the bottom crust... If you can imagine the impression the tines of the fork made as they sank into the soft dough...

Piecrust is so named for the ridges of glass encircling each piece. These ridges are reminiscent of the lines in a piecrust before it is baked.

This wonderful Canadian Depression Glass pattern is found in a pleasing blue color that is similar to Delphite. There are sixteen items in the line, just enough to set a lovely table. Pieces of Piecrust have been filtering south, perhaps Americans are hungry for the color. Piecrust is marked "Made in Canada PYREX" providing a definitive way to assist in identification, and as a Pyrex product this glassware will be quite durable.

Shown are two plates with floral embellishments. Hand painted decorations will require extra care when cleaning. One must also consider the possibility of lead being in any old paint prior to using anything for dining.

PIECRUST	Blue	Qty
Bowl, 5" small berry	4	____
Bowl, 6" oatmeal	8	____
Bowl, 7.75" soup	16	____
Bowl, 9" large berry	20	____
Bowl, 9.25" rimmed soup	25	____
Creamer	8	____
Cup	5	____
Mug	25	____
Pitcher, 5.25"	25	____
Plate, 6.75" sherbet	4	____
Plate, 7" salad	8	____
Plate, 9" dinner	8	____
Plate, 12" salver	13	____
Saucer	2	____
Sherbet	6	____
Sugar	8	____

Back row: 12" salver, 9" dinner plate, 7" salad plate, decorated 7" salad plate; *front row:* cup & saucer. *Courtesy of Walter Lemiski / Waltz Time Antiques.*

Back row: large berry bowl, *middle bowl:* rimmed soup bowl, soup bowl; *front row:* berry bowl, oatmeal bow. *Courtesy of Walter Lemiski / Waltz Time Antiques.*

Back row: decorated 12" salver, 12" salver; *front row:* sherbet, sugar, creamer, milk pitcher, mug. *Courtesy of Walter Lemiski / Waltz Time Antiques.*

PINEAPPLE AND FLORAL
Reproduced
(1932-1937 Indiana Glass Company)

For simplification purposes, No. 618 by Indiana Glass Company is listed by its commonly used nickname.

Pineapple and Floral is a pattern that very few collectors are seeking. For that reason, an equally few number of dealers keep it in stock. The relatively low prices make this an affordable line of glassware but the pieces are heavy, the pattern is very busy, and it is most often available only in crystal (clear).

The 7.5" berry bowl is listed as being reproduced. This was actually reissued by Indiana.

9.5" plate w/ center indent, 4" water tumbler.
Courtesy of Diefenderfer's Collectibles & Antiques.

Back: platter, 3-part relish; *front:* sugar, creamer, diamond-shaped comport.

Back: 9.5" dinner plate, 6" sherbet plate, sherbet; *front:* cream soup bowl.

PINEAPPLE & FLORAL	Crystal, Fired-on red, & Amber	Qty
Ashtray, 4.5"	10	____
Bowl, cream soup	14	____
Bowl, 4.75" berry	12	____
Bowl, 6" oatmeal	25	____
Bowl, 7.5" berry *R*	5	____
Bowl, 10" oblong vegetable	10	____
Comport, 6.25" diamond shaped *R*	4	____
Creamer	5	____
Cup	5	____
Plate, 6" sherbet	3	____
Plate, 8.5" salad	5	____
Plate, 9.5" dinner	15	____
Plate, 9.5" w/center indent	10	____
Plate, 11.5" cake	8	____
Plate, 11.5" w/center indent	10	____
Platter	8	____
Relish, 11.5" 3-part, 11.5" x 7.25"	10	____
Saucer	2	____
"Servitor" 2-tier 8" & 11" plates	15	____
"Servitor" 2-tier 6" & 9" plate	15	____
Sherbet	10	____
Sugar	5	____
Tumbler, 4"	20	____
Tumbler, 4.5" iced tea	25	____
Vase, 12"	35	____
Vase holder (metal)	35	____

Reproduction information: Other fired on colors, light pink.

Note: Green dinner plate, $15

PRETZEL

(1930s-1970s Indiana Glass Company)

For simplification purposes, No. 622 by Indiana Glass Company is listed by its commonly used nickname.

For years Pretzel was a pattern overlooked by virtually everyone, however times may be changing. There is a renewed interest in this pattern. Iris and Manhattan have been the primary crystal (clear) patterns being sought by collectors, but a growing number of people are asking for Pretzel. When the demand increases prices usually follow, so we'll just have to wait and see.

The 10.25" celery bowl is extremely common, while pieces in teal are extremely rare. Indiana added several pieces to this line in the 1970s including the celery, 8.5" pickle bowl. And the 7" leaf plate.

Most pieces of Pretzel are plain in the center. Shown is a 8.25" salad plate with the fruit design in center. Pieces so decorated are worth twice as much as the same undecorated item. Most collectors want either one style or the other and its seems not to be a matter of money but simply a matter of taste.

PRETZEL	Crystal	Qty
Bowl, 4.5" fruit cup	10	____
Bowl, 7.5" soup	12	____
Bowl, 8.5" oblong pickle w/handles	8	____
Bowl, 9.5" berry	20	____
Bowl, 10.25" oblong celery	5	____
Creamer	10	____
Cup	8	____
Leaf, 7" olive	8	____
Pitcher	trtp*	____
Plate, 6"	4	____
Plate, 6.25" w/tab (fruit cup plate or cheese plate)	12	____
Plate, 7.25" square snack plate w/cup indent	12	____
Plate, 7.25" 3-part square	12	____
Plate, 8.25" salad	8	____
Plate, 9.25" dinner	12	____
Plate, 11.5" sandwich/cake	15	____
Saucer	2	____
Sugar	10	____
Tray, 10.25" oblong celery	5	____
Tumbler, 3.5"	75	____
Tumbler, 4.5"	75	____
Tumbler, 5.5"	100	____

*trtp = too rare to price

Note: Teal cup, $125; saucer, $45. Plates with center design twice those with plain center.

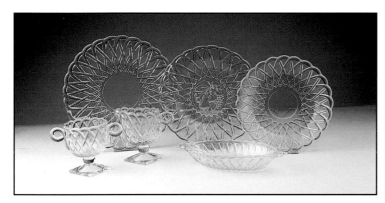

Back row: 9.25" dinner plate, 8.25" salad plate w/fruit design in center, 7.5" soup bowl; *front row:* sugar, creamer, 8.5" oblong pickle bowl w/handles.

6" plate w/tab.

PRIMO

(1932 United States Glass Company)

United States Glass Company manufactured Primo for one year. There are few pieces in the pattern and these are difficult to find. However, we were able to add a new discovery to the list: a 10" grill plate with an indent for a cup is shown in yellow. We don't know if it was made in green.

When doing an Internet search for Primo it is best to use the nickname "Paneled Aster."

Our third edition could really benefit from the help of a Primo collector!

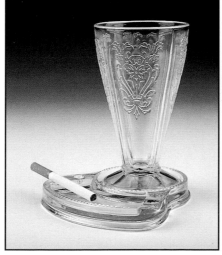

5.75" tumbler on 5.25" x 4.75" coaster/ashtray. *Courtesy of Staci & Jeff Shuck / Gray Goose Antiques.*

10" grill plate w/indent for cup. *Courtesy of David G. Baker.*

10" grill plate, cup & saucer.

PRIMO	Yellow	Green	Qty
Bowl, 4.5"	22	18	____
Bowl, 7.75"	35	30	____
Bowl, 11" footed console bowl	45	35	____
Cake plate, 10"	35	30	____
Coaster or ashtray, 5.25" x 4.75"	15	12	____
Creamer	20	15	____
Cup	15	12	____
Plate, 6.25"	12	10	____
Plate, 7.5"	12	10	____
Plate, 9.5" grill w/cup ring	50		____
Plate, 10" dinner	25	22	____
Plate, 10" grill	20	15	____
Saucer	5	4	____
Sherbet	18	15	____
Sugar	20	15	____
Tumbler, 5.75"	30	25	____

PRINCESS
Reproduced
(1931-1934 Hocking Glass Company)

Equally collected in both pink and green, Princess continues to be one of the most popular of patterns. There are many items from which to select and most of them are found without a great deal of legwork, although amassing the complete array of tumblers with take some energy. Topaz (yellow) is more difficult to find, and few people are collecting apricot.

Princess shakers come in two sizes. Shown are the salt and pepper shakers. The spice shakers are 5.5" tall and often come with flat lids, rather than the dome ones that are pictured. Be aware of the fact that Princess shakers are being reproduced.

Also newly discovered are more colors of new candy jars. Dark green and cobalt blue have been around for a while, but now there is a dark amber (almost brown) candy jar on the market. No Princess was ever originally made in this color. Sadly, some are being sold as if old, similarly priced as the green and pink jars.

The 5.5" plate is the most common of all the plates. This piece was designed to be a sherbet plate and a saucer. There is no Princess saucer with a cup ring.

Satinized items are in low demand at this time. The following pieces may be found with a satinized finish: 9.5" orange or flower bowl, candy jar and lid, cookie jar and lid, creamer, 10.25" sandwich plate with two closed handles, salt and pepper shakers, sugar and lid, and 8" vase. Some of these items have become relatively scarce, and tastes change, so it is always possible that in the future the value of these pieces could increase dramatically.

Above: 5.5" oatmeal bowl, 8.25" salad plate, 9.5" dinner plate, 6.5" footed iced tea tumbler. *Courtesy of Diefenderfer's Collectibles & Antiques.*

Right: Candy jar w/ lid. *Courtesy of Bryan & Marie James.*

PRINCESS	Pink & Green	Topaz & Apricot	Qty
Ashtray, 4.5"	85	120	____
Bowl, 4.5" berry	30	50	____
Bowl, 5.5" oatmeal	45	40	____
Bowl, 9" salad, octagonal	65	150	____
Bowl, 9.5" orange or flower (hat shaped)	80	160	____
Bowl 10" vegetable	40	65	____
Butter dish base	50	*trtp	____
Butter dish lid	75	*trtp	____
Butter complete	125	*trtp	____
Cake stand, 10"	50		____
Candy jar w/lid *R*	70		____
Coaster	85	120	____
Cookie jar/lid	75		____
Creamer	20	20	____
Cup	15	10	____
Pitcher, 6" no foot	70	700	____
Pitcher, 7.5" w/foot	750		____
Pitcher, 8" no foot	60	125	____
Plate, 5.5" sherbet or saucer	10	6	____
Plate, 8.25" salad	20	20	____
Plate, 9" dinner	30	25	____
Plate, 9.5" dinner	30	25	____
Plate, 9.5" grill	16	8	____
Plate, 10.25" sandwich w/closed handles (add 1" if measuring handles)	30	175	____
Plate, 10.5" grill w/closed handles	15	10	____
Platter, 12"	30	65	____
Relish, 7.5" divided	30	100	____
Relish, 7.5"	200	250	____
Salt & pepper, 4.5" *R*	70	90	____
Spice shaker, 5.5" ea	25		____
Saucer or sherbet plate	10	5	____
Sherbet	25	35	____
Sugar base	20	20	____
Sugar lid	25	20	____
Tumbler, 3" juice	35	35	____
Tumbler, 4" water	32	30	____
Tumbler, 4.75" square foot	65		____
Tumbler, 5.25" iced tea	40	30	____
Tumbler, 5.5" round foot	30	25	____
Tumbler, 6.5" iced tea, round foot	125	175	____
Vase, 8"	55		____

Reproduction information: Candy jar in green: crude & foot missing rays. In pink the new foot is smooth & missing rays. Old knobs have 2 flat sides & two round sides; new knobs are flat on all 4 sides. All blue candy jars or other odd colors or shades of colors are new. Shakers new crude, low quality glass may have bubbles, odd colors and shades of colors. Anything in cobalt blue is new. The candy jar is reproduced in dark amber.

Note: Satinized pieces 1/2 value of transparent items in same color.

*trtp = too rare to price

Note: Items in	Ice Blue	Qty:
Cookie jar w/lid	1000	____
Cup	175	____
Plate, 5.5" sherbet/saucer	175	____
Plate, 9.5" grill	175	____

Back: 10" cake plate; *middle:* 8" pitcher, 9.5" orange or flower bowl (hat shaped), 8" pitcher; *front:* 5.5" tumbler, sherbet, cookie jar w/ lid. *Courtesy of Marie Talone & Paul Reichwein.*

4.5" ashtray. *Courtesy of Charlie Diefenderfer.*

Reproduction candy jar w/ lid.

4.5" shakers in various colors. *Courtesy of Michael Rothenberger/Mike's Collectibles.*

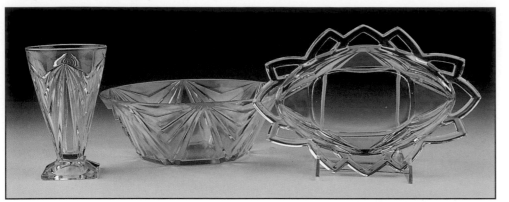

5.5" 8 oz. tumbler, 8.5" berry bowl, 9.5" oval bowl.

PYRAMID
Reproduced
(1928-1932...see note below Indiana Glass Company)

For simplification purposes, No. 610 by Indiana Glass Company is listed by its commonly used nickname, Pyramid.

This dramatic pattern with angular drapes of glass and pointed loops of glass has no plates. Pyramid provides companion pieces and serving pieces. There are four bowls, a sugar and creamer with tray, ice tub, relish, pitcher, and two sizes of tumblers. These pieces could supplement another pattern or be used simply for serving purposes. With tumblers and a pitcher one could assemble a water set. Plates from the Indiana pattern Tearoom would be a possibility to use with Pyramid, as they are also geometric.

There is a strong demand for Pyramid, but once acquiring the creamer, sugar, and tray this pattern gets to be a challenge as none of the other pieces are particularly easy to find.

The 5.5" tumbler is available in two styles: a 2.25" square foot and a 2.5" square foot. If consistency is important to you, make note as to the size you are collecting.

PYRAMID	Green	Pink	Yellow	Crystal	Qty
Bowl, 4.75" berry *R*	30	30	35	15	____
Bowl, 8.5" berry	45	45	75	25	____
Bowl, 9.5" oval	45	45	65	25	____
Bowl, 9.5" oval pickle w/handles & rounded edges	50	50	65	25	____
Creamer	30	35	45	20	____
Ice tub	125	125	250	50	____
Ice tub cover				trtp*	____
Pitcher	350	350	550	550	____
Relish, 4-part *R*	60	60	75	25	____
Sugar	30	35	45	20	____
Tray w/center handle for creamer & sugar	30	30	65	30	____
Tumbler, 8 oz., 5.5" tall w/2.25" or 2.5" base *R*	60	60	95	95	____
Tumbler, 11 oz.	80	80	120	120	____

*trtp = too rare to price

Reproduction information: Items marked as reproduced were part of Indiana Glass Company's Tiara line in the 1970s and were issued in the new colors of blue and black.

Creamers & sugars on center-handled trays. *Courtesy of Debora & Paul Torsiello, Debzie's Glass.*

QUEEN MARY
(1936-1939 Hocking Glass Company)

Queen Mary is most popular in pink, but there are many interested in crystal (clear). Although not as popular as Iris and Manhattan, crystal Queen Mary does have a good following. The simple geometric design particularly in crystal makes a strong Deco statement that many find appealing. We suggest that you pair crystal Queen Mary with black Bakelite utensils.

A meal can't be served without dinner plates, and Queen Mary dinners are difficult to find in either color. As a result, both pink and crystal dinners continue to rise in price.

Back row: 12" 3-part relish, 14" 4-part relish; *front row:* sherbet on 6" sherbet plate, 5" x 10" celery/pickle, 5.75" comport. *Courtesy of Eunice A. Yohn.*

Back row: 6" sherbet plate, 10" dinner plate;
front row: 5.25" bowl w/handles, sugar.
Courtesy of Dave & Jamie Moriarty.

Back row: 14" sandwich plate, 12" sandwich plate, 10" dinner plate;
front row: 4" bowl, cup & saucer. *Courtesy of Eunice A. Yohn.*

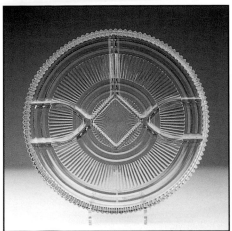

14" 6-part relish.

6.5" plate, 6" sherbet plate, creamer & sugar.
Courtesy of Eunice A. Yohn.

Although this pattern was only produced for a few years there is an extensive assortment of pieces from which to select. Added to this list and shown for the first time is a Queen Mary 14" 6-part relish in crystal. As most pieces in this pattern are made in both colors, one must suspect that a pink 14" relish is "out there."

Queen Mary has edges everywhere and a great deal of care must be taken to examine each item thoroughly prior to making a purchase.

Clarification of cups, creamers, and sugars should also be helpful. It is important to note that there are two creamers and two sugars. The flat creamer and sugar are easy to find and are much less valuable than those with a foot. Note that although there is a metal lid for the butter base, a glass one worth considerably more money is also available. Most collectors opt for an all-glass butter and delay making a purchase until they find one.

There are two cup sizes, one being a bit larger than the other. Some collectors don't care which cup they buy as long as it is consistent with the size they already have. Because the smaller cups fit well on the saucer, and the larger ones rest on the 6" sherbet plate some collectors prefer the smaller cups. The arrangement with the larger cup is the same as the Princess cups and saucers, another Hocking pattern.

As a note of interest, a candy jar with lid sold on eBay in October 2000 for $82.

The Queen Mary tumbler was resurrected in 1942 to make the Stars and Stripes tumbler.

Back: candy jar w/ lid, butter, 5" footed tumbler; *front:* cigarette jar (missing lid), 3.5" round coaster/ashtray, ashtray, salt & pepper. *Courtesy of Eunice A. Yohn.*

6" cereal bowl, 8.75" berry bowl, 4.5" berry bowl,
7" bowl. *Courtesy of Eunice A. Yohn.*

Candlesticks, 5.5" bowl w/ handles.
Courtesy of Eunice A. Yohn.

Butter w/ metal lid. *Courtesy of Michael
Rothenberger/Mike's Collectibles.*

Shakers in various colors. *Courtesy of Michael
Rothenberger/Mike's Collectibles.*

QUEEN MARY	Pink	Crystal	Qty
Ashtray, 2 styles	7	5	____
Bowl, 4" w/ or w/out single handle	8	5	____
Bowl, 4.5" berry	8	5	____
Bowl, 5" berry	15	8	____
Bowl, 5.25" w/handles	15	8	____
Bowl, 6" cereal	30	10	____
Bowl, 7"	15	8	____
Bowl, 8.75" berry	20	10	____
Butter dish base	30	10	____
Butter dish metal lid	35		
Butter complete w/metal lid	65		____
Butter dish glass lid	120	20	____
Butter complete w/glass lid	150	30	____
Candy Dish, 7" cloverleaf		15	____
Candy Jar w/lid	65	25	____
Candlestick, 4.5" ea.		15	____
Celery/pickle, 5" x 10"	40	15	____
Cigarette Jar, 2" x 3" oval w/metal lid	25	15	____
Coaster, 3.5" round	12	5	____
Coaster/ashtray, 4.25" sq.	12	5	____
Comport, 5.75"	30	15	____
Creamer w/foot	75	25	____
Creamer, flat	15	8	____
Cup, 2 sizes	12	6	____
Plate, 6" sherbet	10	4	____
Plate, 6.5"	10	4	____
Plate, 8.5" salad		6	____
Plate, 10" dinner	65	28	____
Plate, 12" sandwich	30	15	____
Plate, 12" 3-part relish	40	20	____
Plate, 12.75" 6-part relish		40	____
Plate, 14" sandwich	40	25	____
Plate, 14" 4-part relish	40	25	____
Punch Bowl Set:Ladle & bowl w/metal ring on which rests 6 cups	trtp*	trtp*	____
Salt & pepper		28	____
Saucer	10	4	____
Sherbet	15	8	____
Sugar w/foot	75	25	____
Sugar, flat	15	8	____
Tumbler, 3.5" juice	20	8	____
Tumbler, 4" water	22	8	____
Tumbler, 5" w/foot	80	30	____

*trtp = too rare to price

Note: Royal Ruby: candlesticks, trtp*; 3.5"
round ashtray, $10. Forest Green: 3.5" round
ashtray, $10.

RADIANCE

(1936-1939 New Martinsville Glass Company)

Once again beautiful glassware from the collection of Debora and Paul Torsiello, Debzie's Glass, is featured in this presentation of Radiance. New Martinsville created some of the most spectacular pieces of Depression Glass with a combination of vivid colors and bold design.

Radiance is usually found without surface decoration, as the loveliness of the glass needs nothing more. Some pieces were etched and listed in the New Martinsville Glass Company catalogue as "Etched No. 26 Pattern."

Added to the list is the 10" tray shown with the decanter. Remember, cobalt blue Radiance is the most elusive color as well as the most valuable color.

The pricing reflects the challenge one will have in locating Radiance. Items with multiple parts such as lids and stoppers command high prices. Finding both pieces of any two-part glassware can be extremely difficult. The candlesticks with prisms are extremely rare as few survived. Please note the pricing for all candlesticks in this book is for each and not for a pair.

Top right: 2.75" cordials & 8.5" decanter w/ stopper on 10" tray. Courtesy of Debora & Paul Torsiello / Debzie's Glass.

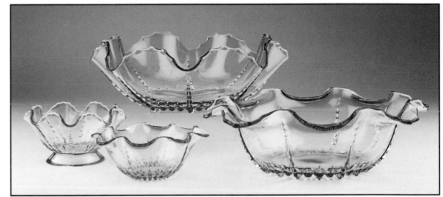

Back: 10" crimped bowl; *front:* 6" crimped footed compote, 6" crimped open bonbon, 12" crimped bowl. *Courtesy of Debora & Paul Torsiello, Debzie's Glass.*

Ladle, pickle bowl on Farberware stem ($55), punch bowl, 4.5" tumbler. *Courtesy of Debora & Paul Torsiello / Debzie's Glass.*

Back row: cheese & cracker, 8" salad plate; *front row:* 6" crimped open bonbon, 9 oz. tumbler, 5" mint w/ handles. *Courtesy of Debora & Paul Torsiello, Debzie's Glass.*

RADIANCE

	Pink, Red, Ice Blue	Amber	Qty
Bon Bon, 6" ftd. open	50	25	____
Bon Bon, 6" flared open	50	25	____
Bon Bon, 6" crimped open	50	25	____
Bon Bon, 6" highly crimped open	50	25	____
Bon Bon, 6" covered	130	60	____
Bowl, 5" nut	30	15	____
Bowl, 10" flared w/foot	60	30	____
Bowl, 10" crimped	60	30	____
Bowl, 10" w/short stem crimped	60	30	____
Bowl, 10" w/short stem flared	60	30	____
Bowl, 12" crimped, 2 styles	60	30	____
Bowl, 12" flared (shallow)	60	30	____
Bowl, 12" flared fruit	60	30	____
Bowl, Punch	250	150	____
Butter/Cheese base	200	80	____
Butter/Cheese lid	300	170	____
Butter/Cheese complete	500	250	____
Candelabra, 2 lights w/prisms ea.	250	100	____
Candlestick, 6" ruffled ea.	120	60	____
Candlestick, 8" 1 light w/prisms ea.	200	75	____
Candlestick, 2 lights, no prisms ea.	80	40	____
Candy Box w/ cover	250	150	____
Celery, 10"	40	20	____
Cheese & Cracker	90	60	____
Compote/Mint 5" stemmed	60	30	____
Compote, 6" crimped ftd.	60	30	____
Compote, 6"	60	30	____
Condiment set, 5 pieces: tray, 2 cruets, salt & pepper	295	165	____
Creamer	30	20	____
Cruet	80	40	____
Cup, coffee	30	14	____
Cup, punch	16	10	____
Decanter w/stopper, 8.5"	200	120	____
Goblet, 1 oz. Cordial, 2.75"	50	30	____
Honey jar w/lid	250	150	____
Ladle (for Punch Bowl)	150	120	____
Lamp, 12"	125	75	____
Mayonnaise w/under plate and spoon	120	80	____
Mint, 5" w/handles, 2 styles	30	15	____
Pickle, 8.5" x 5"	45	30	____
Pitcher	300	200	____
Plate, 8" salad	20	12	____
Plate, 8" ftd salver	60	30	____
Plate, 11"	60	30	____
Plate, 14"/Punch bowl liner	90	50	____
Relish, 7" 2-part crimped	45	25	____
Relish, 7" 2-part flared	45	25	____
Relish, 7" 2-part flat rim	45	35	____
Relish, 8" 3-part	50	30	____
Relish, 8" 3-part crimped	50	30	____
Relish, 8" 3-part flared	50	30	____
Salt & pepper	125	75	____
Saucer	10	7	____
Service Set, 5 pieces: tray, creamer, sugar, salt & pepper	195	125	____
Sugar	30	20	____
Tray for sugar & creamer	35	20	____
Tray, 10"	60		____
Tumbler, 4.5"	50	35	____
Vase, 10" crimped	100	80	____
Vase, 10" flared	100	80	____
Vase, 12" crimped	125	100	____
Vase, 12" flared	125	100	____

Note: Cobalt Blue is twice the price of Red, Pink, and Ice Blue.
Emerald Green: 9" punch bowl, $200; 14" punch bowl liner, $150.
Crystal: 1/2 amber values.

12" crimped vases. *Courtesy of Debora & Paul Torsiello / Debzie's Glass.*

Back row: creamer & sugar on tray; *front row:* cup & saucer, decanter w/stopper, cordial, salt & pepper. *Courtesy of Debora & Paul Torsiello / Debzie's Glass.*

"Service Set" consisting of tray, sugar & creamer, salt & pepper, and 2-light candlesticks. *Courtesy of Debora & Paul Torsiello, Debzie's Glass.*

6" compote, 8" salad plate, cup & saucer, honey jar w/ lid. *Courtesy of Debora & Paul Torsiello, Debzie's Glass.*

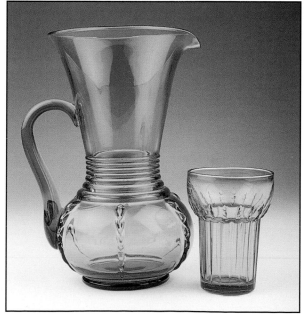

Pitcher & tumbler. *Courtesy of Mike Rothenberger / Mike's Collectibles.*

6" ruffled candlesticks, cruets, 12" flared fruit bowl. *Courtesy of Debora & Paul Torsiello, Debzie's Glass.*

RIBBON

(1930-1931 Hazel-Atlas
Glass Company)

There are many Ribbon look-alike pieces, but true Ribbon has a strong indent to the pattern and not just a weak indication of some design. Ribbon is predominantly a green pattern and many of the pieces that cause confusion are also green. It is certainly fine to purchase them, but disappointing if one intended to buy Ribbon and later discovers an error. Not all sellers of glass are Depression Glass dealers, so take care and depend on your own knowledge and intelligence as glassware does get unintentionally incorrectly identified on price tags.

Keeping this thought in mind, there has been a plethora of green salt and pepper shakers offered on the Internet that are being labeled as Ribbon, but are not. If you have a pair of these shakers we would love to get a picture of them for our third edition so we can clarify this for everyone!

Ribbon plates, sherbets, creamers, and sugars are still fairly easy to find. Bowls, however, are another story and the 4" berry bowl is particularly elusive. Black and pink are rarely seen, but Ribbon is a pattern collected in green with just the perfect assortment of pieces to use as a luncheon set.

Back row: 8" luncheon plate, 6.25" sherbet plate; *front row:* sugar, creamer, cup & saucer, 3" sherbet.

RIBBON	Green	Black	Pink	Qty
Bowl, 4" berry	40			____
Bowl, 5" cereal	40			____
Bowl, 8"	40	40		____
Candy jar w/cover	40			____
Creamer, 3.5"	18			____
Cup	5			____
Plate, 6.25" sherbet	4			____
Plate, 8" luncheon	5	10		____
Salt & pepper	35	50	50	____
Saucer	3			____
Sherbet, 3"	5			____
Sugar, 3.5"	18			____
Tumbler, 5.5"	30			____

RING

(1927-1933 Hocking Glass Company)

Ring is one of the earliest Depression Glass patterns. At the time of publication of the first edition of *Mauzy's Depression Glass* this was a pattern that was particularly desirable if the pieces had decorated bands of color. It's been just a few years and tastes are changing. New collectors are now also looking for crystal (clear) Ring, particularly with the platinum trim. Decorated Ring is not less popular; Ring in general is simply gaining favor with a greater number of people.

As for the decorated bands, there are several color combinations. If a consistent look is important, it would behoove you to write down the color arrangement you have and thus avoid confusion.

There is a wonderful assortment of goblets and tumblers in this pattern. For collectors interested in barware, this pattern, complete with a cocktail shaker and a decanter, really satisfies.

The 7.75" open candy with three feet has now been documented in three colors: black amethyst (shown in our first book), pink (shown in this presentation), and yellow. This yellow piece is particularly interesting as this is the first yellow Ring to be

Back row: 5.5" ice bucket, 8" luncheon plate, 6.5" sherbet plate with off-center indent; front row: 11.75" sandwich server w/center handle, cup.

3.5" 3 oz. cone-shaped footed juice tumbler, 8" luncheon, 4.75" 10 oz. flat tumbler, 7.25" goblet, 6.5" 14 oz. cone-shaped footed iced tea tumbler. *Courtesy of David G. Baker.*

Ice bucket, 4.25" 9 oz. flat tumbler, cocktail shaker w/ aluminum top, 3" 3 oz. flat tumbler. *Courtesy of Michael Rothenberger/ Mike's Collectibles.*

identified. If you know of other pieces in yellow please get in touch with us.

Take note of the significant price increase of the shakers. A pair with yellow, red, and black stripes sold on *eBay* in April 2000 for $104.

Here are some clarifications on two patterns often confused by collectors: distinguish Ring by groupings of four rings; Circle has only one larger group of rings encircling each piece. The shapes of many of the pieces in these two patterns are not the same even though Hocking Glass Company produced them both. Green Ring is much harder to find than green Circle. So, if one locates a quantity of green glass with some kind of circles or rings, it will probably be Circle. Both patterns have been presented in this reference and examining the photographs should prove helpful.

7.25" goblet, 4.75" goblet, 6.5" sherbet, 3" flat tumbler.

8" luncheon plate, 8.5" pitcher.

RING	Crystal w/ Colors	Green	Crystal	Qty
Bowl, 5" berry	16	6	2	____
Bowl, 5.25" divided	60	35	15	____
Bowl, 7" soup	40	15	8	____
Bowl, 8"	30	15	8	____
Butter tub/ice bucket	60	35	20	____
Cocktail shaker w/ aluminum top	60	30	25	____
Creamer	30	8	5	____
Cup	20	6	2	____
Decanter w/stopper	100	40	30	____
Goblet, 4.5" wine	40	15	8	____
Goblet, 4.75" cocktail plain foot	40	15	8	____
Goblet, 7.25"	40	15	8	____
Ice bucket, 5.5"	60	25	15	____
Pitcher, 8"	80	35	25	____
Pitcher, 8.5"	80	35	25	____
Plate, 6" sherbet	14	5	2	____
Plate, 6.5" sherbet w/off-center indent	16	6	3	____
Plate, 8" luncheon	16	6	2	____
Plate, 11" sandwich	30	14	8	____
Salt & pepper	85	60	20	____
Sandwich server w/center handle, 11.75"	40	24	18	____
Saucer	10	3	2	____
Sherbet (fits 6.5" sherbet plate)	30	12	5	____
Sherbet, 5" stemmed	25	8	4	____
Sugar	30	8	5	____
Tumbler, 2" whiskey, 1.5 oz.	20	12	5	____
Tumbler, 3" flat, 3 oz.	25	7	3	____
Tumbler, 3.5" flat, 5 oz.	25	7	3	____
Tumbler, 3.5" footed juice (cone-shaped), 3 oz.	25	10	5	____
Tumbler, 4.25" flat, 9 oz.	25	10	3	____
Tumbler, 4.75" flat, 10 oz.			5	____
Tumbler, 5.25" flat iced tea, 10 oz.	25	7	5	____
Tumbler, 5.5" footed water (cone-shaped), 10 oz.	30	10	5	____
Tumbler, 6.5" footed iced tea (cone-shaped), 14 oz.	30	15	7	____
Vase, 8"	50	30	20	____

Note: Distinguish this pattern from similar ones by looking for bands of **4** rings.

Note: Pink pitcher, $35. Red & Blue: cup, $65; 8" luncheon, $25. Green salt & pepper, $60 for the pair. Open candy, 7.75", w/3 feet, black amethyst, $50, pink, $35, yellow, $35. Iridescent vase, 8", $15. Ruby: 8" luncheon plate, $30; 3" tumbler, $25; 4" tumbler, $25; 5" tumbler, $25.

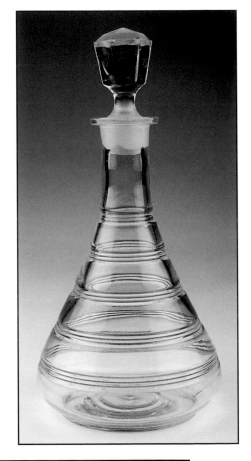

Decanter w/ stopper. *Courtesy of Diefenderfer's Collectibles & Antiques.*

7.75" candy dish w/3 feet.

ROCK CRYSTAL FLOWER

(1922-1931 McKee Glass Company)

If you like choices, if you want a pattern in a variety of colors and with an assortment of pieces, Rock Crystal Flower may be for you. This pattern has one of the longest lists of glassware as McKee Glass Company produced it for almost ten years. It was originally issued in crystal (clear), which explains why this color is the more prevalent than the others (amber, amethyst, blue, green, milk glass, pink, yellow, red).

Speaking of color, shown is an 8.5" (3.25" deep) scalloped edge bowl in a really unusual blue. Susie Thompson found this fabulous, possibly one-of-a-kind piece in a flea market! You never know where a treasure will be found. When we visited with Susie and Rick Hirte in their Maine home and saw the bowl we knew it had to be included in our next book. They graciously shipped it to the studio.

Rock Crystal Flower is heavy but well-made glassware. The pieces are finished neatly with no rough mold seams or bits of extra glass. Because the pieces are so thick they are not prone to damage. For people hesitant to collect delicate glass (perhaps suffering from the "Bull in the China Shop Syndrome") this a pattern worth consideration.

The original McKee Glass Company catalog designated the two different edges as "s.e." for scalloped edge and "p.e." for plain edge. The same abbreviations are used in the pricing lists.

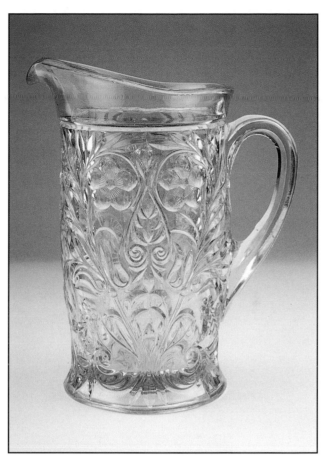

Above: 8.5" (3.25" deep) scalloped edge bowl in unusual blue. *Courtesy of Rick Hirte / Sparkle Plenty Glassware.*

Top right: Fancy tankard. *Courtesy of Bill Quillen.*

Back: 12 oz. iced tea tumbler, creamer; *middle:* 6 oz. low footed sundae, 9 oz. tumbler, sugar; *front:* cup & saucer. *Courtesy of Marie Talone & Paul Reichwein.*

ROCK CRYSTAL FLOWER

ROCK CRYSTAL FLOWER	Red	Cobalt	Other Colors	Crystal	Qty
Bon bon, 7.5" s.e.	60	50	30	20	----
Bowl, 4" s.e., sauce	35	30	20	10	----
Bowl, 4.5" s.e., fruit	35	30	20	10	----
Bowl, 5" s.e., fruit	45	35	25	15	----
Bowl, 5" p.e., finger	60	50	40	20	----
Bowl, 7" s.e., salad	65	55	35	25	----
Bowl, 8" s.e., salad	80	60	40	30	----
Bowl, 8.5" p.e., open center handle	250				----
Bowl, 9" s.e., salad	120	100	50	25	----
Bowl, 10.5" s.e., salad	100	80	50	25	----
Bowl, 12.5" s.e., "Center Bowl", ftd.	300	200	150	75	----
Butter dish base				200	----
Butter dish lid				150	----
Butter complete				350	----
Cake stand, 11"	125	100	60	40	----
Candelabra, 2-lite, ea.	150	75	60	20	----
Candelabra, 3-lite, ea.	185	85	70	30	----
Candlestick, flat w/stem, ea.	70	60	40	20	----
Candlestick, 5.5", ea.	100	70	40	20	----
Candlestick, 8.5", ea.	225	175	80	40	----
Candy w/lid, 7"	250	200	80	60	----
Candy w/lid, 9.25"	275	225	100	70	----
Comport, 7"	100	80	50	40	----
Creamer, s.e., flat				30	----
Creamer, s.e., ftd., 4.25"	70	50	30	20	----
Cruet w/stopper, 6 oz.				100	----
Cup	70	50	20	15	----
Devilled egg plate				65	----
Goblet, 4 oz., 3.75"				15	----
Goblet, 7.5 oz	60	50	25	15	----
Goblet, 8 oz.	60	50	25	15	----
Goblet, 8 oz., "Large Footed"	60	50	25	15	----
Goblet, 11 oz. iced tea	70	50	20	15	----
Ice Dish, 3 designs				35	----
Jelly, 5" s.e.	50	40	30	15	----
Lamp	750	600	350	225	----
Parfait, 3.5 oz.	80	60	40	20	----
Pitcher, 1 qt., s.e., "Squat Jug"			250	175	----
Pitcher, ½ gal., 7.5" s.e., "Squat Jug"			200	130	----
Pitcher, fancy tankard, 8.5"	1000	800	600	250	----
Pitcher, 9" covered	750	600	325	200	----
Plate, 6" s.e., bread & butter	20	18	12	8	----
Plate, 7" p.e., under plate for finger bowl	20	18	12	8	----
Plate, 7.5" p.e. & s.e., salad	20	18	12	8	----
Plate, 8.5" p.e. & s.e., salad	30	20	18	10	----
Plate, 9" s.e., cake	65	45	25	20	----
Plate, 10.5" s.e., cake (small center design)	65	45	35	25	----
Plate, 10.5" s.e., dinner (large center design)	180	100	80	60	----
Plate, 11.5" s.e., cake	60	40	30	20	----
Punch bowl, 14", 2 styles				400	----
Punch bowl base, 2 styles				225	----
Relish, 11.5" p.e., 2-part		70	60	40	----
Relish, 14" p.e., 6-part			100	80	----
Relish, 7-part w/closed handles, p.e.				80	----
Salt & pepper			140	85	----
Salt dip				30	----
Sandwich server, center handle	150	100	60	40	----
Saucer	20	18	12	8	----
Sherbet/Egg, 3 oz.	70	50	30	15	----
Spooner				50	----
Stemmed 1 oz. cordial	70	50	50	25	----
Stemmed 2 oz. wine	60	40	30	20	----
Stemmed 3 oz. wine	60	40	30	20	----
Stemmed 3.5" cocktail	50	30	25	20	----
Stemmed 6 oz. champagne/tall sundae, 4.5"	40	30	25	20	----
Stemmed 7 oz. goblet	60	40	30	20	----
Stemmed 8 oz. goblet	60	40	30	20	----
Sugar base	50	40	30	20	----
Sugar lid	150	120	50	40	----
Sundae, 6 oz., low foot	40	30	20	15	----
Syrup w/metal lid	800			200	----
Tray, 7" s.e., Pickle or Spoon				70	----
Tray, 12" s.e., Celery	90	60	50	30	----
Tray, 13" p.e., Roll	125	100	75	35	----
Tumbler, 2.5 oz. whiskey	70	50	30	20	----
Tumbler, 5 oz. tomato juice	60	50	30	20	----
Tumbler, 5 oz. old fashioned	60	50	30	20	----
Tumbler, 9 oz., 2 styles	60	50	30	20	----
Tumbler, 12 oz., 2 styles, iced tea	70	60	40	30	----
Vase, cornucopia			100	80	----
Vase, 11"	200	175	125	65	----
Vase, 12" w/square top	200	175	125	65	----

Right: 6 oz. low footed sundae. *Courtesy of Charlie Diefenderfer.*

Below: *Back:* 6" scalloped edge bread & butter plate, 8.5" salad plate; *front:* butter, 3 oz. sherbet/egg. *Courtesy of Charlie Diefenderfer.*

Below right: 14" 6-part relish, 13" roll tray. *Courtesy of Michael Rothenberger/Mike's Collectibles.*

Note: Red slag 12.5" footed bowl, $450. Cobalt: 12.5" footed bowl, $450; 2-light candelabra, $450.

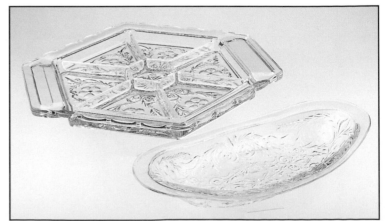

3.5" cocktail, 11.5" 2-part relish, 4.5" fruit bowl
on 7" under plate for finger bowl.

4.5" 6 oz. champagne/tall sundae
w/ unusual round foot. *Courtesy
of Charlie Diefenderfer.*

ROMANESQUE

(Late 1920s L.E. Smith Glass Company)

This L. E. Smith pattern is gaining a following of collectors, as people are discovering and desiring the octagonal pattern, Romanesque. Pieces were manufactured in amber, crystal (clear), canary, green, and pink, with green and amber seen most frequently. The 8" octagonal plates are common; sherbets, bowls, and the vase are more difficult to locate.

The web-like design is found on the underside of the plates thus preventing damage from eating utensils. To preserve this design we recommend either a coffee filter or paper plates between stacked pieces.

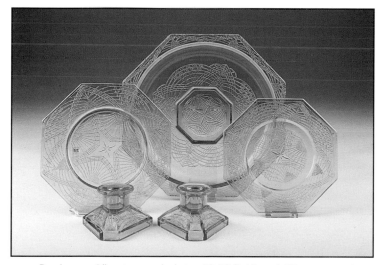

Back row: 8" octagonal plate, 10.5" flat bowl, 7" octagonal plate; *front row:* candlesticks.

7" octagonal plate, 10.5" flat bowl, 7" octagonal plate.
Courtesy of Dave & Jamie Moriarty.

ROMANESQUE	All colors*	Qty
Bowl, 10.5" flat	40	____
Bowl, 10.5" w/foot	50	____
Cake plate w/2 open handles	30	____
Candlestick, ea., 2.5"	20	____
Plate, 5.5", octagonal	10	____
Plate, 7", octagonal	10	____
Plate, 8", octagonal	12	____
Plate, 8", round	12	____
Plate, 10", octagonal	20	____
Sherbet, round rim	12	____
Sherbet, crimped rim	12	____
Tray, snack	20	____
Vase, 7.5" fan	45	____

*Made in Amber, Black, Crystal, Green, & Yellow.

ROSE CAMEO

(1931 Belmont Tumbler Company)

Six pieces make up this lovely pattern, Rose Cameo. The "cameo" or medallion on this pattern features a rose, a detail that distinguishes it from Cameo and Georgian Lovebirds. Rose Cameo can be used with these patterns as they mix and match nicely even though different companies make them all. As there are no serving pieces or dinner plates, Rose Cameo is perfect for desserts and luncheons if used alone.

The 5" footed tumbler may or may not have a flare at the rim. Discerning collectors will want the style that matches their previous purchases.

ROSE CAMEO	Green	Qty
Bowl, 4.5" berry	15	____
Bowl, 5" cereal	20	____
Bowl, 5.5", straight sided	35	____
Plate, 6.75" luncheon	18	____
Sherbet	15	____
Tumbler, 5", 2 styles	25	____

5" footed tumbler, 7" luncheon plate, 5.5" straight sided bowl, sherbet.

ROSEMARY

(1935-1936 Federal Glass Company)

Rosemary evolved from Federal Glass Company's Mayfair pattern. Federal Glass created and advertised Mayfair in 1934 not realizing that Hocking Glass Company already had a patent on the Mayfair name. Federal's Mayfair pattern was simplified and renamed Rosemary; it enjoyed a two-year production period in 1935 and 1936. Transitional pieces are available that show a lovely blending of the two Federal Glass patterns, as seen on the tumbler. Other transitional items are provided in Mayfair "Federal."

Most often seen and collected in amber, Rosemary is not a particularly popular pattern. The glass is heavy and there aren't many pieces from which to select. There is also a great deal of undecorated glass on the plates and the platter. Whatever the damage or wear, no matter how little, it becomes very obvious. Collectors usually want dinnerware to appear to have never been used. Green is harder to find than amber, and in the eastern U.S. pink is rarely seen. Although not often found, Rosemary prices have remained relatively unchanged. This pattern is worth your consideration if you are looking for Depression Glass that will require a relatively modest investment. It is unlikely that the prices will see any dramatic increases in the near future.

Above: *Back:* 6" cereal bowl, 10" oval bowl; *front:* 5" berry bowl, cup & saucer, cream soup bowl. *Courtesy of Connie & Bill Hartzell.*

Left: 12" platter. *Courtesy of Neil McCurdy - Hoosier Kubboard Glass.*

ROSEMARY	Amber	Green	Pink	Qty
Bowl, 4.75" cream soup	15	25	35	____
Bowl, 5" berry	7	10	15	____
Bowl, 6" cereal	35	35	40	____
Bowl, 10" oval	15	30	40	____
Creamer	8	14	20	____
Cup	5	7	10	____
Plate, 6.75" salad	6	8	12	____
Plate, 9.5" dinner	9	16	24	____
Plate, 9.5" grill	10	16	24	____
Platter, 12"	20	30	38	____
Saucer	5	5	5	____
Sugar, 4", no handles	8	14	20	____
Tumbler, 4.25"	30	35	60	____

Above: *Back:* 12" platter, 9.5" dinner plate, 9.5" grill plate; *front:* 6.75" salad plate, creamer & sugar. *Courtesy of Connie & Bill Hartzell.*

Right: 4.5" transitional tumbler as Federal changed their Mayfair pattern to Rosemary. *Courtesy of Connie & Bill Hartzell.*

ROULETTE

(1936-1937 Hocking Glass Company)

Roulette is usually collected in green. Crystal (clear) is rare, but in no real demand. Only the pitcher and tumblers were made in pink, allowing one to create water or beverage sets with these pieces. It is important to note that this shade of green is different from most other Depression Glass dinnerware, as it is a yellow green. Colonial "Knife and Fork," another Hocking Glass Company pattern, was also made in this odd shade that doesn't mix well with most green Depression Glass. The production period for these patterns overlapped which may account for the duplication of this shade.

Roulette prices are increasing as collectors experience greater frustration in satisfying their needs. The pitcher, fruit bowl, and tumblers are particularly troublesome while the 12" sandwich plate, 8.5" luncheon plate, and sherbet remain common.

Above: Saucer, sherbet.

Right: 9.5" fruit bowl. *Courtesy of Charlie Diefenderfer.*

ROULETTE	Green	Pink	Crystal	Qty
Bowl, 9.5" fruit	25		7	____
Cup	8		5	____
Pitcher, 8"	50	50	30	____
Plate, 6" sherbet	8		3	____
Plate, 8.5" luncheon	8		4	____
Plate, 12" sandwich	20		8	____
Saucer	5		2	____
Sherbet	8		3	____
Tumbler, 2.5" whiskey, 1.5 oz.	20	20	10	____
Tumbler, 3.25" old-fashioned, 7.5 oz.	45	45	20	____
Tumbler, 3.5" juice, 5 oz.	35	35	12	____
Tumbler, 4" water, 9 oz.	35	35	10	____
Tumbler, 5" iced tea, 12 oz.	35	35	10	____
Tumbler 5.5" footed, 10 oz.	37		10	____

Above: 8" pitcher. *Courtesy of Diefenderfer's Collectibles & Antiques.*

Left: 4" 9 oz. water tumbler, 2.5" whiskey tumbler. *Courtesy of Diefenderfer's Collectibles & Antiques.*

ROUND ROBIN

(Late 1920s Unknown manufacturer)

An unknown manufacturer created this charming luncheon set commonly called Round Robin. There are two unique features worth noting. First, the cup has a foot, a design element rarely seen in Depression Glass. Second, as abbreviated as this pattern is, a Domino tray was included. Cameo has two Domino trays, but this particular item is a piece not found in other patterns. Finding the Domino tray will be the greatest challenge in assembling this set.

Most Round Robin pieces were made in green and iridescent; however, green is the color in greatest demand. As for iridescent round Robin, there is little interest and therefore it remains extremely low in value.

Cup & saucer, sherbet.

ROUND ROBIN	Green	Iridescent	Qty
Bowl, 4" berry	10	3	____
Creamer	10	4	____
Cup	5		____
Domino tray (Sugar cube tray), 7.5" w/3" indent	55		____
Plate, 6" sherbet	5	2	____
Plate, 8" luncheon	10	3	____
Plate, 12" sandwich	15	5	____
Saucer	2		____
Sherbet	10	4	____
Sugar	10	4	____

7.5" domino tray. *Courtesy of Vic & Jean Laermans.*

Right: 5.5" plate, sherbet.

Below: Saucer, 4.5" x 2.5" bowl.

ROXANA
(1932 Hazel-Atlas Glass Company)

Depression Glass patterns with extremely limited offerings were often made in green. Aurora is an exception as it is primarily found in cobalt, and Roxana is another exception as it is basically a yellow pattern. Produced for only one year, Roxana's seven items provide just enough to serve dessert.

This is not a commonly seen pattern. The sherbet and 6" sherbet plate are the easiest pieces to locate and they are not particularly easy to find in any quantity. The bowls and 4" tumbler are downright difficult to find, but as there is minimal interest in Roxana the prices stay the same.

The shade of yellow used for Roxana is different from the yellow used in the Florentines, two other Hazel-Atlas patterns commonly collected in yellow. Roxana would be a poor match to accessorize these patterns.

ROXANA	Yellow	White	Qty
Bowl, 4.5" x 2.5"	25	20	____
Bowl, 5" berry	15		____
Bowl, 6" cereal	20		____
Plate, 5.5"	12		____
Plate, 6" sherbet	12		____
Sherbet	12		____
Tumbler, 4"	25		____

Console bowls & candle holders in all three styles: straight edge, rolled edge, ruffled edge. *Courtesy of Donna L. Cehlarik.*

ROYAL LACE
Reproduced
(1934-1941 Hazel-Atlas Glass Company)

Here's the latest reproduction news, as this is valuable information to collectors. Initially when Royal Lace tumblers were reproduced there was no design (some call it a medallion) on the bottom as would be found on old tumblers. This has changed. Counterfeiters have corrected the design of new tumblers and they are now decorated on the bottom. Cobalt blue tumblers are a bit cruder and the color is too dark. If you don't trust your own eye be sure to deal with a knowledgable and reputable seller. (Check our "Dealer Directory"). Initially reproduction cookie jars were only made in cobalt blue, but that has also changed. Shown is a new cookie jar in teal. Although lovely, it is brand new! Hazel-Atlas never made Royal Lace in this color.

There are some new finds and confirmed finds, thanks to Fran and Tom Inglis. First of all, shown are pink juice tumblers with a gold overlay. The photograph doesn't do these justice, as they are really magnificent. The mysterious 68 oz. water pitcher with ice lip IN GREEN is pictured, so we all know this does exist! We understand that our friends in

Back row: cup & saucer, 9.75" dinner plate; *front row:* butter dish, cookie jar w/lid. *Courtesy of Donna L. Cehlarik.*

Royal Lace

Canada have several more of these hidden to our north. Aren't they lucky? Finally, Tom and Fran have the sherbet with the chrome base on a chrome plate. The plate has an off-center indent sized perfectly for the Royal Lace sherbet. Hopefully we can picture it in the third edition. For those of you preferring the all-glass sherbet, this awesome combination may convert you!

In the first edition of *Mauzy's Depression Glass* cobalt blue Royal Lace was featured as many consider it to be the epitome of Depression Glass. This time we are offering pink for your consideration. For many items, pink can be more difficult to find than cobalt.

No matter what the color, there are some points to consider regarding this pattern. All plates, including the saucer, share a design feature that makes finding 100% perfect pieces an extra challenge. There is an inner edge of glass where the eating surface and rim meet. This is a hard edge with a minute upward roll that is highly susceptible to damage, especially if the pieces get stacked. Collectors of Royal Lace are often willing to overlook minor "inner rim damage" if the rest of the plate is chip-free. A perfect outer edge is much more important than this inner rim.

Nut bowls continue to be a challenge and a trophy. They look like the 10" round bowl in a scaled down size. Here's a story you may find interesting. A dealer/friend made a house call to buy a collection of Royal Lace. The owner had everything inventoried and a price she expected to realize. "Here," she said to my friend. "You can just have these for free. They forgot to put the holder part in the center of these candleholders. I don't want them and maybe you can sell them." Our friend thanked her and walked out with a pair of nut bowls.

After all this time, people are still buying cookie jar bottoms hoping to find the top. Remember, the cookie jar bottom was used in the toddy set, so more bottoms than tops were made. Lids of all kinds (sugar, candy, etc.) normally suffer damage through use and misuse and many simply did not survive. It is unlikely that a dealer will have a cookie jar lid for sale, ever, plus the lid is now being reproduced. If you want a cookie jar, buy it complete.

Back row: sugar, 13" platter; *front row:* sherbet, 4.5" cream soup bowl, shaker, creamer. *Courtesy of Donna L. Cehlarik.*

5.25" tumbler, 4.75" tumbler, 4" tumbler, 3.5" tumbler. *Courtesy of Donna L. Cehlarik.*

Toddy set. *Courtesy of Donna L. Cehlarik.*

Juice tumblers w/gold overlay.
Courtesy of Fran & Tom Inglis.

Back row: 8.5" 96 oz. pitcher w/ ice lip, 8" 86 oz. pitcher w/
no ice lip; *front:* 8" 68 oz. pitcher w/ ice lip, 8" 64 oz. pitcher
w/ no ice lip, straight pitcher. *Courtesy of Donna L. Cehlarik.*

68 ounce pitcher. *Courtesy of*
Fran & Tom Inglis.

ROYAL LACE

	Blue	Green	Pink	Crystal	Qty
Bowl, nut	trtp*	trtp*	trtp*	trtp*	____
Bowl, cream soup, 4.5"	50	40	28	15	____
Bowl, 5" berry	135	100	75	50	____
Bowl, 10" round	85	75	65	30	____
Bowl, 10" straight edge	100	80	65	45	____
Bowl, 10" rolled edge	1200	400	200	400	____
Bowl, 10" ruffled edge	1400	300	200	100	____
Bowl, 11" oval	95	85	75	45	____
Butter dish base	450	250	150	75	____
Butter dish lid	350	200	100	50	____
Butter complete	800	450	250	125	____
Candle holder, ea., straight edge	110	80	70	40	____
Candle holder, ea., rolled edge	250	150	140	85	____
Candle holder, ea., ruffled edge	300	150	140	75	____
Cookie jar/lid *R*	450	125	75	40	____
Creamer	65	45	25	15	____
Cup	40	30	20	10	____
Pitcher, straight	180	150	120	375	____
Pitcher, 64 oz., 8" no ice lip	350	225	125	75	____
Pitcher, 68 oz., 8" with ice lip	500	trtp*	125	100	____
Pitcher, 86 oz., 8" no ice lip	500	300	200	125	____
Pitcher, 96 oz., 8.5" with ice lip	600	275	225	150	____
Plate, 6" sherbet	18	15	12	8	____
Plate, 8.5" luncheon	60	40	35	20	____
Plate, 9.75" dinner	45	40	35	25	____
Plate, 9.75" grill	35	30	25	15	____
Platter, 13"	75	65	50	30	____
Salt & pepper	350	200	125	75	____
Saucer	18	15	12	8	____
Sherbet, all glass	55	45	30	20	____
Sherbet w/chrome base	40			8	____
Sugar base	65	45	25	15	____
Sugar lid	200	150	100	75	____
Toddy set, cookie jar w/metal lid & tray, 8 plain cobalt roly-polies, ladle	400				____
Tumbler, 3.5" *R*	65	60	60	25	____
Tumbler, 4" *R*	50	45	35	20	____
Tumbler, 4.75"	225	125	125	75	____
Tumbler, 5.25"	150	95	110	75	____

Reproduction information: Tumblers: new may have smooth bottoms; some have no design; color too dark. Cookie jar lid: new missing mold seam across knob & down 2 sides. Cookie jar base: new missing circular mold mark on bottom. Cobalt too dark, green too light, pink difficult to discern.

*trtp = too rare to price

Note: Amethyst: 10" rolled edge console bowl, $2000; rolled edge candlesticks, $1000 ea.; sherbet w/chrome base, $65; Toddy set, $500.

This reproduction tumbler DOES have the correct design on the bottom. *Courtesy of Fran & Tom Inglis.*

Reproduction cookie jar lid missing mold seams across the knob and down two sides. *Courtesy of Marie Talone.*

Reproduction cookie jar w/ crude design and slightly darker color. *Courtesy of Marie Talone.*

Reproduction cookie jar. *Courtesy of Fran & Tom Inglis.*

Nut bowl, 10" round bowl. (Note: the design is the same less the medallion not found in the center base of the nut bowl.) *Courtesy of Donna L. Cehlarik.*

ROYAL RUBY
(1938-1960s, 1977 Anchor Hocking Glass Company)

Many users of *Mauzy's Depression Glass* requested the addition of Royal Ruby and Forest Green, so here you are! We have attempted to give you a complete listing of the pieces and prices in this edition. Be sure to cross reference Bubble, Fire-King Charm, and Oyster & Pearl, as these patterns are available in Royal Ruby.

Remember, Royal Ruby is a color, not a pattern, so the format of this list is a bit different than the others in this book. We hope this presentation will be useful. Again, let us know what you think as this book is designed to be helpful to YOU!

Royal Ruby is not uncommon. Tumbler, cups, saucers, and vases, oh those vases, are everywhere. The search begins when one looks for dinnerware, and especially bowls. The challenge culminates with the punch bowl base.

Some interesting pieces have been discovered. We sold a flower frog that really and truly appeared to be Royal Ruby for more than $150 on eBay. In December 1999 some coasters showed up on eBay. Again, these were thought be Royal Ruby. The seller was kind enough to share the information he had regarding these unique pieces. "To look an them and touch them you would absolutely say they are Royal Ruby, and the color is all the way through and not fired on." He received an e-mail from another individual indicating "these coasters were a salesman's sample that they passed out to store owners." Help! If anyone can add information on either piece, please let us know.

Square dinnerware is Fire-King Charm. Not shown is Charm dinnerware with the etched tulips. These pieces come from Canada. An array of American glassware ended up in Canada where it was given lovely embellishments. There are two round dinnerware lines and an example of each is pictured with side-by-side saucers. The R-4000 line has a modern look with plates that resemble Frisbees. The eating area is entirely flat and the edges of the plates curl up. (Shown on the left.) Turquoise Fire-King dinnerware has the same design as the R-4000 line. No documentation can be found for the time of production of the R-4000 line, but Fire-King Turquoise Blue was manufactured from 1956-1958. The R-1700 line was introduced in the 1940s and features a shape that is similar to ceramic or china dinnerware. There is a flat eating area in the center of the plate with an elevated rim. (Shown on the right.)

Sales of Royal Ruby are quite seasonal, and during the Christmas season pieces are in greatest demand. Some collectors put entire sets together; others look to make a table more festive with accents of red glassware. There are many sizes and shapes from which to collect, as Royal Ruby production was not short-lived.

Back row: 6.5" sherbet plate, 9.25" dinner plate, 7.75" salad plate; *front row:* cup & saucer, punch cup.

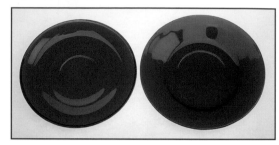

R-4000 saucer & R-1700 saucer.

Balled stem sherbet & Baltic 2.25" tall sherbet.

Newport 6" iced tea tumbler, Newport 5" water tumbler, Newport 4" juice tumbler, Newport 3" old fashioned tumbler.

Windsor 4" tumbler, Windsor 3.25" tumbler, Georgian 4.5" tumbler, Georgian 3.5" tumbler.

Baltic 4.5" water tumbler, Baltic 3.5" cocktail tumbler, Baltic 2.5" juice tumbler, 3.25" footed wine.

ROYAL RUBY	Qty	
Ashtrays		
3.25" square	10	____
4.25" square	10	____
4.5" square	10	____
5.75" square	10	____
Leaf	15	____
Bowls		

Baltic (rounded foot/base), 4.75" — 10 — ____
Burple (vertical rows of
balls & lines)
    Dessert, 4.5" — 8 — ____
    Berry, 8" — 25 — ____
Charm (square)
    Dessert, 4.75" — 8 — ____
    Salad, 7.25" — 25 — ____
Whirly Twirly (series of
    horizontal bulges), 3.75" — 14 — ____
Other bowls
    4.25" dessert — 6 — ____
    5.25" popcorn — 18 — ____
    6.75" cereal — 18 — ____
    7.5" soup — 15 — ____
    8.25" vegetable — 20 — ____
    10" punch — 30 — ____
Boxes
    Cigarette (rectangular 4.5"
    crystal base, ruby lid) — 20 — ____
    Puff (round 4.5" crystal
    base, ruby lid) — 20 — ____
Cocktail Glasses (metal stems) — 15 — ____
Cocktail Shaker, 5.5" — 35 — ____
Cocktail Shaker, 9.5" — 85 — ____
Creamers
    Flat (no foot) — 8 — ____
    Footed, 2 styles — 10 — ____
Cups
    Bubble — 10 — ____
    Charm (square) — 5 — ____
    Coffee, 2 styles — 5 — ____
    Punch — 3 — ____
Ice Bucket — 70 — ____
Maple Leaf (spoon rest) — 10 — ____
Moskeeto-lites, ea. — 25 — ____
Mint tray w/center handle, 7.5" — 10 — ____
Pitchers
    Bubble (large bubbles that
    just touch each other) — 60 — ____
    Georgian (honeycomb-like bottoms) — 50 — ____
    High Point (vertical ribs
    w/series of 3 circular
    shapes in between,
    tapered in at base) — 85 — ____
    Hobnail (small bumps that
    do not touch one another) — 35 — ____
    Roly Poly (flat bottom,
    smooth sides curve
    inward at base) — 35 — ____
    Swirl, 2 styles — 60 — ____
    Tilted, 2 styles — 50 — ____
    Whirly Twirly (series of
    horizontal bulges) — 85 — ____
    Windsor (small cube-like
    design at bottom) — 40 — ____
Plates
    Sherbet, 6.5" — 8 — ____
    Salad, 2 styles, 7.75" — 8 — ____
    Snack w/cup indent, 8.25" — 40 — ____
    Luncheon, Charm (square) 8.25" — 12 — ____
    Dinner, 2 styles, 9.25" — 14 — ____
Platter, 10" x 6" oval
    w/tab handles — 200 — ____
Punch bowl, 10" — 30 — ____
Punch bowl base — 50 — ____
Salt & Pepper (Georgian) — 60 — ____
Saucers
    Bubble — 5 — ____
    Charm (square) — 3 — ____
    Round, 2 styles — 3 — ____
Sherbets
    Baltic (rounded foot/base),
    2.25" tall, 2.5" diam., — 7 — ____
    Balled Stem — 10 — ____
    Smooth Stem — 8 — ____
Spoon rest (Maple Leaf) — 10 — ____
Sugar bases
    Flat (no foot) — 8 — ____
    Footed, 2 styles — 10 — ____

Sugar Lid — 20 — ____
Tumblers
    Baltic (rounded foot/base)
        Juice, 2.5" — 7 — ____
        Cocktail, 3.5" — 5 — ____
        Water, 4.5" — 5 — ____
    Bubble (large bubbles that
    just touch each other)
        Old Fashioned, 3.25" — 16 — ____
        Juice, 3.75" — 12 — ____
        Water, 4.5" — 12 — ____
        Iced Tea, 5.75" — 18 — ____
    Clear "bubble" foot
        Berwick (single row of "balls")
            Sherbet, 3.5" — 14 — ____
            Cocktail, 3.75" — 16 — ____
            Juice/wine, 4.5" — 16 — ____
            Goblet, 5.5" — 16 — ____
        Early American (rows
        of "balls" w/largest ones
        at outer edge)
            Cocktail, 3.25" — 16 — ____
            Sherbet, 4" — 16 — ____
            Juice, 4.25" — 16 — ____
            Goblet, 5.25" — 16 — ____
    Georgian (honeycomb-like bottoms)
        3.25" — 10 — ____
        3.5" — 8 — ____
        4.5" — 8 — ____
        5" — 8 — ____
        5.5" (flat) — 8 — ____
        5.5" (pedestal) — 15 — ____
    High Point (vertical ribs
    w/series of 3 circular
    shapes in between, tapered
    in at base)
        Fruit, 3.25" — 15 — ____
        Table, 4.25" — 15 — ____
        Iced Tea, 5.5" — 40 — ____
    Hobnail (small bumps that
    do not touch one another) — 8 — ____
    Newport (straight sides,
    sharp inward taper near base)
        Old fashioned, 3" — 6 — ____
        Juice, 4" — 6 — ____
        Water, 5" — 6 — ____
        Iced Tea, 6" — 8 — ____
    Roly Poly (flat bottom,
    smooth sides curve inward
    at base)
        Juice, 3.25" — 5 — ____
        Table, 4.25" — 6 — ____
        Water, 4.75" — 6 — ____
        Iced Tea, 5" — 8 — ____
    Whirly Twirly (series of
    horizontal bulges)
        3.25" — 10 — ____
        4" — 10 — ____
        5" — 10 — ____
    Windsor (small cube-like
    design at bottom)
        3.25" — 7 — ____
        4" — 7 — ____
    Other Tumblers
        Hoe Down, 2 sizes — 5 — ____
        3.25" footed wine — 15 — ____
        4.75" footed iced tea — 10 — ____
        4.75" flat w/gold trim — 5 — ____
Vases
    Bud, 3.75" — 5 — ____
    Bud, 5.75" — 10 — ____
    Coolidge, 6.75" — 6 — ____
    Harding, 6.75" — 6 — ____
    Hoover, 9" (plain) — 15 — ____
    Hoover, 9" (decorated) — 20 — ____
    Ivy ball, two styles, 4" — 5 — ____
    Ivy ball, 6" — 7 — ____
    Square textured bottom,
    flared top w/or w/out
    crimped top, 9" — 20 — ____

"S" PATTERN

(1930-1932 & Fired-on red 1934-1935
Macbeth-Evans Glass Company)

The thinness of the glass and slightly uneven outer rim of the plates help to identify this as another Macbeth-Evans Glass Company pattern. As with Petalware, "S" Pattern is quite underrated and somewhat overlooked by many collectors at this time. Most pieces were never produced in pink or green, so "S" Pattern is a bit out of the mainstream for collectors. Topaz is a midway shade that is neither light enough to be yellow nor deep enough to be amber, which limits the options for mixing it with other colored glass. The crystal (clear) both with and without decorations receives minimal attention from collectors. With only five items in fired-on red, one can't create much of a collection or place setting, but if you are doing a vintage kitchen and red is one of your colors, consider using fired-on red "S" Pattern to either decorate or supplement your décor. The pieces are a true red, unlike Royal Ruby, which is really a burgundy color, and will nicely enhance your look.

When searching on eBay for this pattern we suggest you use "s pattern depression" as the wording that will most effectively eliminate extraneous auctions.

Back row: 8" luncheon plate w/ platinum trim, 8" luncheon plate; *front row:* cup & saucer w/ platinum trim, cup & saucer, 4" water tumbler. *Courtesy of Charlie Diefenderfer.*

8.5" berry bowl.

4.75" tumbler, sherbet.

"S" PATTERN	Topaz	Crystal w/variations	Crystal	Red (Fired-on)	Qty
Bowl, 5.5" cereal	8	4	2	16	____
Bowl, 8.5" berry	18	9	5		____
Creamer, 2.75" thin & 3" thick	8	4	3	16	____
Cup, 2 styles	6	3	2	12	____
Pitcher, round sides		60	50		____
Pitcher, straight sides	125	50	40		____
Plate, 6" bread & butter	4	2	1		____
Plate, 8" luncheon	6	3	2	40	____
Plate, 9.25" dinner	8	6			____
Plate, 10.5" grill	8	4	3		____
Plate, 11.75" cake	40	20	15		____
Plate, 13" cake	60	30	20		____
Saucer	4	2	1		____
Sherbet	6	3	2		____
Sugar, 2.5" thin & 3" thick	8	4	3	16	____
Tumbler, 3.5" juice	10	5	5		____
Tumbler, 4" water	8	4	4		____
Tumbler, 4.75"	8	4	4		____
Tumbler, 5"	12	6	6		____

Note: Monax: 6" sherbet plate, $8; 8" luncheon, $10. Amber 11.75" cake plate, $80. Green & Pink: Pitcher, $600; 4" tumbler, $65.

SAGUENAY
(1945-1950 Dominion Glass Company)

Attention jade-ite lovers! Take a look at this wonderful pattern from Dominion Glass Company! Saguenay has offerings of pieces in crystal (clear) plus a rainbow of fired-on colors. Traditionally American collectors have shied away from fired-on glassware, but perhaps after seeing Canada's Saguenay tastes may change with choices of yellow, pink, red, blue, teal, and a pastel green that really looks like jade-ite.

Here are some particulars. Molds for this glassware are thought to have been made by Toledo Mold Company. Saguenay has similar design features to Jeannette Glass Company's Homespun. All of the pieces were produced in crystal and then colors applied. No fired-on shakers have been found at this time, the only teal items seem to be cups and saucers, and the sherbet may be the only red piece. Blue, green, pink, and yellow were fired-on to the entire line.

As you familiarize yourself with Saguenay take a good look at the pastel green. Now you tell us, wouldn't it look great with jade-ite?!

Saguenay	Fired-on colors	Crystal	Qty
Bowl, 4.25" berry w/handles	8	5	____
Butter dish base	12	6	____
Butter dish lid	13	7	____
Butter complete	25	13	____
Creamer	8	5	____
Cup	5	3	____
Egg cup, 2.5"		7	____
Plate, 6" sherbet	6	4	____
Plate, 8" luncheon	7	5	____
Salt & pepper		12	____
Saucer	3	1	____
Sherbet	6	4	____
Sugar	8	5	____
Tumbler, 3.5", 5 oz. juice	7	5	____
Tumbler, 4.25", 9 oz. water	12	8	____

Back row: 9 oz. tumbler, 8" luncheon plate, butter dish, 4.25" handled berry bowl; front row: 5 oz. tumbler, cup & saucer, sherbet, 2.5" egg cup, creamer, salt & pepper, sugar. Courtesy of Walter Lemiski / Waltz Time Antiques.

Sherbets in a variety of colors. *Courtesy of Ian Warner & Mike Posegay and Walter Lemiski / Waltz Time Antiques.*

Fired-on green. *Back row: creamer, sherbet & 6" sherbet plate, 8" luncheon plate; front row: sugar, butter dish, 5 oz. tumbler, 4.25" handled berry bowl, cup & saucer. Courtesy of Ian Warner & Mike Posegay and Walter Lemiski / Waltz Time Antiques.*

SANDWICH
Reproduced
(1940s-1960s Anchor Hocking Glass Company)

The Sandwich glass produced by Anchor Hocking was available in a rainbow of colors, but today's collectors are primarily interested in Forest Green. Collectors of Forest Green glass tend to be purists. If Sandwich is the chosen pattern, it is unlikely that another line such as Charm will also be collected. Forest Green was not a successful color when originally introduced as the overall consensus was food was unattractive and unappetizing when served on this color. Today Forest Green is in demand, particularly for use at Christmas time.

The most common Forest Green pieces, 4.25" bowl with a smooth rim, custard with a smooth rim, custard liner/under plate, 3.5" 5 ounce juice tumbler, and 4" 9 ounce water tumbler, were given away free inside a package of oatmeal. The quantity made was tremendous and availability today continues to be fine so prices have remained low. The remainder of the Forest Green pieces increases in value somewhat dramatically. Dinner plates are very much in demand and certainly essential if one intends to use these dishes. The two pitchers are rarely seen, especially the half-gallon water pitcher. The green cookie jar resembles a vase, but, as noted in the pricing, it is open and never had a lid. There is no vase in this pattern.

Crystal (clear) Sandwich is one of the most recognized pattern-color combinations. It was available in Woolworth's for pennies apiece and many items became part of households particularly in the late 1940s and 1950s. Bowls are the most frequently seen commodity; however, the 6.5" scalloped cereal bowl is particularly rare, and the 4.75" crimped dessert is also difficult to find. As with Forest Green, crystal pitchers are not common, but they are much easier to locate than green. The punch bowl and salad bowl are one and the same. Adding the elusive punch bowl stand transforms the salad bowl into a punch bowl.

Amber Sandwich is less in demand than green and crystal, partially because there are fewer pieces available with which to create a table setting. The hue is deeper and somewhat browner than the amber of many Depression Glass lines.

Pink, white, and ivory pieces are few and far between. Pink sells well as shoppers are often drawn to unique pink items as gifts. Ivory and white punch bowls are abundant and often overlooked.

Shown is a reproduction cookie jar next to an old one. The measurement differences are provided but seeing them side-by-side allows one to see the much larger size of the new one.

Sold online for $25 was an unlisted 2-tier tidbit in Amber. This was made of a 6.75" cereal bowl above a 12" sandwich plate. The posts were made of gold-colored metal.

Back row: open cookie jar, 9" dinner plate; *front row:* creamer, sugar, custard w/ smooth rim & custard liner/ under plate, cup & saucer. *Courtesy of Wes & Carla Davidson.*

8.25" bowl w/scalloped rim, 7.5" salad bowl w/scalloped rim, 6.25" bowl w/scalloped rim, 4.25" bowl w/smooth rim. *Courtesy of Wes & Carla Davidson.*

8.5" two quart pitcher, 7" juice pitcher, 4" flat water tumbler, 3.5" flat juice tumbler. *Courtesy of Wes & Carla Davidson.*

Boxed 9-piece Water Set consisting of one 2 quart pitcher & eight 4" drinking glasses which originally sold for $1.39. *Courtesy of Mike Rothenberger / Mike's Collectibles.*

Reproduction cookie jar w/lid , original cookie jar w/lid & box. *Courtesy of David G. Baker.*

Back: 12" sandwich plate; *middle:* 9" dinner plate, 8" plate; *front:* 7" dessert plate. *Courtesy of Connie & Bill Hartzell.*

3.25" juice tumbler, 3.5" juice tumbler, 4" water tumbler, 9 oz. footed water tumbler. *Courtesy of Connie & Bill Hartzell.*

SANDWICH (Anchor Hocking)	Crystal	Forest green	Amber	Qty
Bowl, 4.25" w/smooth rim	6	5		____
Bowl, 4.75" dessert w/ crimped rim	25		5	____
Bowl, 4.75" w/smooth rim	6		6	____
Bowl, 5" w/scalloped rim	8			____
Bowl, 5.25" w/scalloped rim	8			____
Bowl, 6.25" scalloped	8		30	____
Bowl, 6.5" w/smooth rim	8		6	____
Bowl, 6.75"cereal w/scalloped rim	100	50		____
Bowl, 6.75" cereal	35		14	____
Bowl, 7" salad	8			____
Bowl, 7.5" salad w/scalloped rim	8	60		____
Bowl, 8.25" w/scalloped rim	10	80		____
Bowl, 8.25" oval w/scalloped rim	12			____
Bowl, 9" salad	25		30	____
Bowl, 9.75" punch/salad	30			____
Butter dish base	20			____
Butter dish lid	25			____
Butter complete	45			____
Cookie jar open, never had lid		20		____
Cookie jar w/lid *R*	40		45	____
Creamer	8	40		____
Cup, coffee	4	20	5	____
Cup, punch	4			____
Custard w/ smooth rim	4	4		____
Custard w/crimped rim	15	25		____
Custard liner/under plate	20	4		____
Pitcher, 7" juice	70	185		____
Pitcher, 8.5", half gallon	90	475		____
Plate, 7" dessert	14			____
Plate, 8"	7			____
Plate, 9" dinner	30	140	12	____
Plate, 9" w/indent for cup	8			____
Plate, 12" sandwich	25		15	____
Punch bowl (salad bowl), 9.75"	30			____
Punch bowl stand	40			____
Saucer	3	18	4	____
Sherbet	8			____
Sugar base	8	40		____
Sugar lid	18			____
Tidbit, 2-tier, 6.75" cereal bowl & 12" sandwich plate			25	____
Tumbler, 3" juice, 5 oz., flat	8	8		____
Tumbler, 3.25" juice, 3 oz., flat	20			____
Tumbler, water, 9 oz., flat, 4"	8	12		____
Tumbler, water w/foot, 9 oz.	35		250	____

Reproduction information: New cookie jar is taller & wider than old. New measures 10.25" tall; old measures 9.75" tall. New measures 5.5" across at opening; old measures 4.75".

Note: Ruby items: 4.75" bowl, $20; 5.25" bowl, $25 (smooth or scalloped); 6.5" bowl, $30; 8.25" bowl, $80. Pink items: 4.75" bowl, $8; 5.25" bowl, $10; 8.25" bowl, $20; 6" juice pitcher, $300. Ivory & white: punch bowl, $20; punch bowl base, $25; punch cup, $3.

SANDWICH
Reproduced
(1920s-1980s Indiana Glass Company)

Indiana Sandwich glass is available in a variety of colors and pieces, but many have been reproduced using original molds. This has created a great deal of frustration for collectors. Old green Sandwich will glow under a black light. If you are going to be buying green Sandwich a portable, battery operated black light should be carried when you shop. The following items are all recent additions: creamers, cups, saucers, sugars, and water goblets.

Other colors have also had newer production runs. Red was made in 1969, amber was made in 1970, and crystal (clear) was made in 1978. Because the same molds were used, discerning old from new becomes exceedingly challenging. The new wine goblet is a different mold and the dimensions are provided in the reproduction information. These later additions and reissues have severely damaged the collectibility of Indiana's Sandwich.

Back: 10.5" dinner plate; *front row:* 6" bowl, salt & pepper, 12 oz. footed iced tea tumbler. *Courtesy of Charlie Diefenderfer.*

SANDWICH (Indiana)	Amber & Crystal	Teal	Red	Pink & Green	Qty
Ashtrays shaped in 4 suits for bridge parties	5				____
Basket, 10"	35				____
Bowl, 4.25" berry	4				____
Bowl, mayonnaise w/foot	15			30	____
Bowl, 6" round	4				____

Creamer. *Courtesy of Vic & Jean Laermans.*

Diamond-shaped creamer & sugar on tab-handled tray. *Courtesy of Vic & Jean Laermans.*

Reproduction butter dish. *Courtesy of Charlie Diefenderfer.*

	Amber & Crystal	Teal	Red	Pink & Green	Qty
Bowl, 6", hexagonal	5	20			____
Bowl, 8.5"	10				____
Bowl, 9" console	22			40	____
Bowl, 11.5" console	18			50	____
Butter dish base *R*	10	75			____
Butter dish lid *R*	20	100			____
Butter complete *R*	30	175			____
Candlestick, 3.5" ea.	10			25	____
Candlestick, 7" ea.	15				____
Celery	18				____
Creamer	10		50		____
Creamer, diamond-shaped	10	12			____
Cruet w/stopper	30	150		175	____
Cup	4	9	30		____
Decanter w/stopper (R in green)	75		85	125	____
Goblet, 4 oz. wine, 3" *R*	8		15	28	____
Goblet, 9 oz., 5.75"	14		50		____
Pitcher	30		130		____
Plate, 6" sherbet	4	8			____
Plate, 7" bread & butter	4				____
Plate, 8" oval w/cup indent	5	12			____
Plate, 8.25" luncheon	5		20		____
Plate, 10.5" dinner	12			30	____
Plate, 13" sandwich	14	28	38	28	____
Puff box	18				____
Salt & pepper	30				____
Sandwich server w/center handle	24		50	35	____
Saucer	3	5	8		____
Sherbet	7	15			____
Sugar base	10		50		____
Sugar, diamond-shaped	10	12			____
Sugar lid	20				____
Tray w/tab handles for diamond-shaped creamer & sugar	10				____
Tumbler, 3 oz. cocktail w/ft.	10				____
Tumbler, 8 oz. water w/foot	10				____
Tumbler, 12 oz. iced tea w/foot	10				____

Reproduction information: Green & pink items that are too light in color are new. Items not shown in this list are new. Wine goblet: old measures 2" across top; new is larger, about 2.75" across top. Butter dish, as well as other items, made new using old molds. Beware! Old green will glow under black light. Cookie jars in cobalt and pink are new.

Back: cake plate; *front row:* butter, sherbet, candy jar w/ lid. *Courtesy of Sylvia A. Brown.*

SHARON
Reproduced
(1935-1939 Federal Glass Company)

Rose of Sharon, Cabbage Rose, Sharon. Whatever the name, Sharon is one of the most recognized Depression Glass patterns. Distribution for Sharon must have been throughout the United States as it is found in all colors wherever one travels.

Collected in three colors, there are many enthusiastic collectors of this pattern. The pink has a slight orange cast to it, so it does not mix well with some pink Depression Glass. Amber is common and green can be a challenge once you get the very basics.

The pieces in this pattern tend to be heavy. Interestingly, there are thick tumblers, which are about the same thickness as the rest of the collection, and thin tumblers. Thin ones are more delicate and almost seem to not belong with the set. Flat tumblers were part of the original line and footed tumblers were added a year after production began. Sharon glassware has no delicate edges with which to be concerned, but scratching is an issue. With an abundance of dinner plates in the marketplace, collectors can still be fussy. This is quite a luxury as collectors of some patterns may go months or even years between finding a single dinner plate.

Sugar bowls were marketed with and without lids; therefore, there are more bases than lids. If owning a sugar lid is important to you, then you may want to buy the two pieces together. Most dealers do not sell lids separately. If they gain possession of a lid, they normally match it to a base they may already have in stock or may wait to acquire the appropriate bottom. As a result, if you purchase only a bottom, it is unlikely that you will find the lid for sale.

When reproductions are first produced there is normally a negative impact on the original line of glassware. Collectors and dealers alike get wary and the decline in demand often causes a decline in values. As Sharon reproduction information has had a chance to get well publicized few are concerned to the point of avoiding Sharon altogether. Shown is a reproduction butter dish (left) next to an original one. The hard edge to fit the lid in the new butter dish is very obvious. Old butter dishes (right) have a smooth, rounded rim. With knowledge should come confidence.

Back row: 12.5" platter, 9" pitcher w/ no ice lip; *front row:* 8.5" berry bowl, cream soup bowl, 5" berry bowl. *Courtesy of Sylvia A. Brown.*

Back row: 9.5" dinner plate, 6" bread & butter plate, sugar w/ lid; *front:* cup & saucer, creamer. *Courtesy of Sylvia A. Brown.*

Shakers in various colors. *Courtesy of Michael Rothenberger/Mike's Collectibles.*

SHARON	Green	Pink	Amber	Qty
Bowl, 5" berry	18	15	10	____
Bowl, cream soup	60	50	30	____
Bowl, 6" cereal	30	30	25	____
Bowl, 7.75" flat soup		55	55	____
Bowl, 8.5" berry	38	35	5	____
Bowl, 9.5" oval	38	35	22	____
Bowl, 10.5" fruit	50	50	28	____
Butter dish base *R* 7.5" x 1.5"	45	25	15	____
Butter dish lid *R*	75	40	30	____
Butter complete *R*	120	65	45	____
Cake plate	65	45	20	____
Candy jar w/ lid *R*	180	65	50	____
Cheese dish base *R* 7.25" x .75" w/rim		1500	200	____
Cheese dish lid *R* (Butter dish lid)		40	30	____
Cheese dish complete		1540	230	____
Creamer *R*	25	20	16	____
Cup	20	15	7	____
Jam dish, 7.5"	75	250	50	____
Pitcher, 9" ice lip	450	200	150	____
Pitcher, 9" no ice lip	500	180	150	____
Plate, 6" bread & butter	10	8	5	____
Plate, 7.5" salad	28	28	18	____
Plate, 9.5" dinner	25	24	12	____
Platter, 12.5"	35	30	22	____
Salt & pepper *R*	70	70	30	____
Saucer	12	12	5	____
Sherbet	38	18	14	____
Sugar base *R*	25	20	16	____
Sugar lid *R*	45	35	25	____
Tumbler, 4" thick, flat	75	50	35	____
Tumbler, 4" thin (blown), flat	80	50	35	____
Tumbler, 5.25" thick, flat	100	100	65	____
Tumbler, 5.25" thin (blown), flat	120	50	55	____
Tumbler, 6.5" footed		65	150	____

Note: Items in Crystal: 11.5" cake plate, $10; 7.5" salad plate, $10; 6.5" footed tumbler, $15.

Reproduction information: Butter: new lid has easy-to-grasp knob as it is about 1"; new base has true rim with a hard edge in which lid fits. Old lid's knob is about .75" high and the base has rounded, smooth rim for lid. No blue butters are old. Cheese dish: new base too thick, not flat enough but rather bowl shaped. Creamer: new pink is too pale, mold seam is not centered on spout. Sugar: new handles meet bowl in a circle; new lid missing extra glass from mold seam around the middle. Shakers: crude flowers with 4 petals rather than a bud with 3 leaves. Candy dish: thick glass, poor quality. Old foot is 3.25" in diameter; new foot is just under 3". If you find a piece of Sharon in an odd color, beware!

*trtp = too rare to price

6.5" footed tumbler, 5.25" thin flat tumbler, 4" thick flat tumbler, 4" thin flat tumbler. *Courtesy of Diefenderfer's Collectibles & Antiques.*

Butters in various colors. *Courtesy of Michael Rothenberger/Mike's Collectibles.*

Reproduction butter showing knob on lid that protrudes higher than on older lids making lid easier to grasp. *Courtesy of Charlie Diefenderfer.*

Reproduction butter dish, original butter dish. *Courtesy of Charlie Diefenderfer.*

SIERRA
(1931-1933 Jeannette Glass Company)

The availability of Sierra is on the decline, but the interest in this pattern inexplicably also seems to be waning. Sierra is a unique design with an uneven, almost serrated edge that is unlike any of the other Depression Glass patterns. It is apparent how it earned the nickname "Pinwheel."

Some patterns have luncheon plates but no dinner plates. Sierra has only a 9" dinner plate; there are no other sizes of plates available. With a tumbler, a variety of bowls, and just a few additional items one can serve a one course meal.

Care must be taken when selecting any Sierra as the pointy edges are susceptible to damage. We recommend that you run a fingernail on each edge with the piece right side up and upside down. In fact, the reason this pattern was only manufactured for two years is that it became apparent to Jeannette Glass Company that the design was simply too fragile. In an industry that used and reused molds, Sierra molds were permanently retired in 1933.

Here is a description of the Adam-Sierra combination butter dish. The bottom of the butter dish will be either Sierra or Adam. The key is the top which has both the Sierra motif and the Adam motif. The Sierra pattern is on the inside of the lid and the Adam pattern is on the outside of the lid. This item is too rare to price.

9" dinner plate, 6.5" pitcher. *Courtesy of Diefenderfer's Collectibles & Antiques*.

SIERRA	Pink	Green	Qty
Bowl, 5.5" cereal	20	25	____
Bowl, 8.5" berry	40	40	____
Bowl, 9.25" oval vegetable	80	175	____
Butter dish base	40	50	____
Butter dish lid	40	50	____
Butter complete	80	100	____
Butter w/Sierra bottom & Adam/Sierra lid	trtp*		____
Creamer	28	28	____
Cup	15	15	____
Pitcher, 6.5"	120	150	____
Plate, 9" dinner	30	30	____
Platter, 11" oval	60	70	____
Salt & pepper	60	60	____
Saucer	10	10	____
Sugar base	28	28	____
Sugar lid	28	28	____
Tray, 10.25" sandwich w/2 open handles	25	25	____
Tumbler, 4.5"	70	90	____

Note: Ultra-marine: cup, $175; 5.5" cereal bowl, $225.

*trtp= too rare to price

Back row: 10.25"
sandwich tray w/
open handles, sugar
w/ lid; *front:* saucer,
creamer.

8.5" berry bowl, 5.5" cereal bowl. *Courtesy
of Marie Talone & Paul Reichwein*.

Back row: 9.25" oval vegetable bowl, 9" dinner plate; *front:*
butter. *Courtesy of Diefenderfer's Collectibles & Antiques*.

Shakers in both colors. *Courtesy of Michael
Rothenberger/Mike's Collectibles.*

SPIRAL

(1928-1930 Hocking Glass Company)

Back row: 3" flat tumbler, 8" luncheon plate, pitcher; *front row:* sherbet, cup & saucer, creamer. *Courtesy of Charlie Diefenderfer.*

Earliest Depression Glass patterns featured simple designs and were often produced in at least green glass, and Spiral fits this generalization. This is Hocking Glass Company's offering of spiraling glass. To confuse matters, Imperial Glass created Twisted Optic and U.S. Glass Company made U.S. Swirl during the same time period.

To further muddy the waters of identification there is a myriad of miscellaneous spiraling glassware that is not any of these named patterns.

Several Spiral pieces resemble Cameo items, which is a clue for identification. Spiral production ended in 1930, the year that Hocking introduced Cameo. One can easily determine that at least some Spiral molds became Cameo molds.

Luncheon plates and sherbet plates continue to be abundant. This is amazing when considering the fact that Spiral was only manufactured for a relatively brief period. Values are a good indication of the level of difficulty one will experience when building a collection. At $5 apiece, luncheon plates and sherbet plates are a real bargain!

Pink Spiral is rare. If you have a collection we would be honored to feature it in our next book.

SPIRAL	Green	Qty
Bowl, 4.75" berry	7	____
Bowl, 8" berry	14	____
Bowl, batter w/spout & 1 handle	50	____
Candy w/lid	35	____
Creamer, 2.5" & 3"	10	____
Cup	6	____
Ice bucket	35	____
Pitcher, 3 styles	45	____
Plate, 6" sherbet	5	____
Plate, 8" luncheon	5	____
Platter, 12"	30	____
Preserve w/notched lid (for spoon)	50	____
Salt & pepper	80	____
Sandwich server w/open center handle	18	____
Saucer	3	____
Sherbet	5	____
Sugar, 2.5" & 3"	10	____
Syrup pitcher	65	____
Tumbler, 3" flat	8	____
Tumbler, 5" flat	10	____
Tumbler, flat iced tea	15	____
Tumbler, 5.75" footed	18	____
Vase, 5.75"	50	____

Note: Pink pieces worth twice green, crystal pieces worth 1/4.

Ice bucket. *Courtesy of Michael Rothenberger/Mike's Collectibles.*

Shaker. *Courtesy of Michael Rothenberger/Mike's Collectibles.*

STARLIGHT
(1938 Hazel-Atlas Glass Company)

Demand for Starlight continues to be very low, and the net result is that values remain suppressed. There are few people looking for this pattern even though it is quite attractive and offers an interesting array of nicely proportioned pieces. The cobalt bowl sells because of the color, not because of being a piece of Starlight.

Starlight was only made for one year. Pieces are not common. It's hard to tell if this is because little was made or that the demand is so low few dealers keep it in stock.

2 dinners, 4.75" bowl w/ closed handles.

Creamer & sugar. *Courtesy of Diefenderfer's Collectibles & Antiques.*

Salt & pepper. *Courtesy of Michael Rothenberger/Mike's Collectibles.*

STARLIGHT	Pink	Cobalt	White, Crystal	Qty
Bowl, 4.75" w/closed handles			10	____
Bowl, 5.5" cereal w/closed handles	14		7	____
Bowl, 8.5" w/closed handles	20	40	10	____
Bowl, 11" salad			20	____
Bowl, 12"			20	____
Creamer			7	____
Cup			7	____
Plate, 6" bread & butter			4	____
Plate, 8.5" luncheon			4	____
Plate, 9" dinner			10	____
Plate, 13" sandwich	25		18	____
Relish dish			10	____
Salt & pepper			30	____
Saucer			2	____
Sherbet			10	____
Sugar			7	____

12" bowl on 13" sandwich plate. *Courtesy of Marie Talone.*

STARS & STRIPES

(1942   Anchor Hocking Glass Company)

Anchor Hocking produced Queen Mary from 1936-1939 whose similarities to the 1942 line of Stars & Stripes are obvious. Enthusiasm for Fire-King has spilled over into other Anchor Hocking glassware, and Stars & Stripes has benefited from this current trend.

There are only three crystal pieces in this patriotic pattern: a dinner plate, a sherbet, and a tumbler, which are rarely collected to actually use. Collectors usually want one of each Stars & Stripes pieces to compliment a Fire-King collection.

A mere twenty cents afforded a set of all three items in 1942. In September 2000 an eBay bidder paid $98.54 for a single tumbler!

Tumbler, 8" plate, sherbet. *Courtesy of Scott & Rhonda Hackenburg / Blue Jay Antiques & Collectibles.*

STARS & STRIPES	Crystal	Qty
Plate, 8"	35	____
Sherbet	20	____
Tumbler, 5"	45	____

STRAWBERRY

(Early 1930s   U.S. Glass Company)

7.5" deep berry bowl, 3.75" tumbler.

4.5" large creamer, 5.5" large sugar w/ lid, large creamer. *Courtesy of Vic & Jean Laermans.*

Strawberry is a pattern that is growing in popularity. Despite the fact that there are no dinner plates, the charming design and usable serving pieces are gaining favor with increasingly larger numbers of collectors. Sherbets are plentiful, but beyond them this becomes a challenge to find, and more individuals are rising to the challenge.

Many of the rims on Strawberry pieces have a ridged texture susceptible to damage. The rims need particular attention when choosing a selection to buy. An area that may appear to have damage might also be roughness from the time of manufacture.

Few people are interested in either crystal (clear) or iridescent. However, the butter dish and pitcher are desirable in any color.

If you like this pattern, you may want to consider the Cherryberry pattern, which is also by U.S. Glass Company. The molds are the same and the designs are quite similar. Pieces from the two patterns mix and match nicely.

Back row: 7.5" salad plate, pitcher; *front:* butter, 6" sherbet plate, 3.5" tumbler, 7.5" deep berry bowl. *Courtesy of Donna L. Cehlarik.*

STRAWBERRY	Pink, Green	Crystal, Iridescent	Qty
Bowl, 4" berry	35	6	____
Bowl, 6.25", 2" deep	130	20	____
Bowl, 6.5" deep salad	28	15	____
Bowl, 7.5" deep berry	40	20	____
Butter dish base	75	40	____
Butter dish lid	150	100	____
Butter complete	225	140	____
Comport, 5.75"	28	15	____
Creamer, small, 3.75"	30	10	____
Creamer, large, 4.5"	40	15	____
Olive dish, 5" w/1 handle	25	10	____
Pickle dish, 8.25" oval	25	10	____
Pitcher	250	175	____
Plate, 6" sherbet	14	5	____
Plate, 7.5" salad	20	5	____
Sherbet	8	6	____
Sugar, small	28	15	____
Sugar, large (5.5")	38	15	____
Sugar lid for 5.5" piece	62	15	____
Tumbler, 3.75"	38	10	____

Sherbet on 6" sherbet plate.
Courtesy of Donna L. Cehlarik.

SUNBURST

(Late 1930s   Jeannette Glass Company)

Jeannette Glass Company produced some of the most popular glassware of the Depression era. Sunburst, however, has fallen through the cracks and holds very little interest for most collectors perhaps because it is only available in crystal (clear).

Molds were often used and reused by manufacturers. Iris was made until 1932, Sunburst was a product of the late 1930s, and Anniversary was introduced in 1947. All three patterns have strong design similarities because of the recycling of old molds.

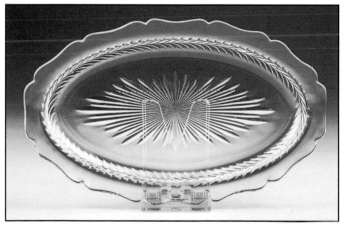

Far left: 5.25" x 8.75" oval tray. *Courtesy of Bettye S. James.*

Left: Candlestick.

Below: *Back row:* 9.25" dinner, 11" bowl; *front:* cup & saucer, 2-part relish, creamer & sugar.

SUNBURST	Crystal	Qty
Bowl, 4.75" berry	10	____
Bowl, 8.5" berry	22	____
Bowl, 11"	25	____
Candlestick, ea.	15	____
Creamer	12	____
Cup	8	____
Plate, 5.5"	10	____
Plate, 9.25" dinner	25	____
Plate, 11.75" sandwich	18	____
Relish, 2-part	15	____
Saucer	4	____
Sherbet	15	____
Sugar	12	____
Tray, 5.25" x 8.75" oval	15	____
Tumbler, 4"	25	____

SUNFLOWER

(1930s Jeannette Glass Company)

Giving glass away with a product or service was common practice in the 1930s. Jane Ray was free with gasoline, Royal Lace was distributed in movie houses, and Sunflower cake plates were placed inside bags of flour. This is why there are so many pink and green Sunflower cake plates today. It is important to note that the green cake plate is a darker shade of green than the rest of the Sunflower pieces.

Finding other pieces of Sunflower may be more difficult. There aren't many items from which to select and the 7" trivet is one of the most elusive pieces of Depression Glass of all. Both the cake plate and trivet are round with three feet. The surface of the trivet (as shown in the picture) curves upward at the edges while the cake plate is entirely flat and three inches larger.

Sunflower is not a particularly popular pattern despite its lovely design. For those who appreciate and collect it, the hunt goes on.

Back: 4.75" tumbler, 9" dinner plate; *front:* 10" cake plate, cup & saucer, sugar & creamer.

SUNFLOWER	Green	Pink	Qty
Ashtray	15	10	____
Cake plate, 10"	20	28	____
Creamer	30	25	____
Cup	18	15	____
Hot plate (Trivet), 7"	1000	1000	____
Plate, 9" dinner	30	25	____
Saucer	20	18	____
Sugar	30	25	____
Tumbler, 4.75"	45	40	____

Note: Opaque creamer, cup, & sugar, $85 each. Ultramarine Ashtray, $30, Delphite creamer, $100. Yellow creamer & sugar, $500 each. Caramel creamer & sugar, $500 each.

Hot plate (trivet).

SWIRL
(1937-1938 Jeannette Glass Company)

Although available in pink and Delphite ("Delfite"), Swirl is primarily collect in "Ultra-marine." This bluish-green color is used infrequently in Depression Glass so when a large quantity of ultramarine Swirl is on display many heads turn, even those of individuals not particularly interested in Depression Glass.

Swirl has a few peculiarities that need to be considered. First, in regard to the color, there were pieces made in a greenish blue variation that is an entirely different shade. Most collectors do not like or want pieces in this hue, which is believed to have been created by factory workers when blending colors together at the end of the day prior to closing the factory. If you are unable to discern the difference in the two shades, you may want to carry a small piece of true ultramarine with you when shopping. Once your eye is trained to recognize the difference in the colors it becomes unmistakable. Another thing to consider is the design of the plates as they were made in two styles. Some plates were finished with a narrow, scalloped rim, and some simply had the swirling pattern continue to the end with no finished treatment. Plates molded without the rim are often uneven. If you take a measurement from the center of one of these plates and measure the radius in one direction and then do the same in the opposite direction chances are good you will get entirely two different measurements. Some collectors have no problem with this, others do. Before you buy your first plate it is important to decide whether or not these irregularities really matter. Vases are also very likely to have been made in an uneven fashion.

Pink is harder to find than ultramarine. Perhaps if collectors were seeking pink, additional pieces would find their way to the marketplace. Interesting to note, the butter dish and open candy dish are much easier to find in pink than in ultramarine.

A new find is a second candy dish lid seen only in ultramarine at this time. Instead of the flat finial, this lid was made with the round "knob" finial seen on the butter dish lid.

Delphite Swirl continues to get little attention.

The values shown on the list are an excellent indication of availability. Pitchers are virtually impossible to find. Butter dishes and candy dishes will also pose a challenge as will the 5" flat tumbler that is pictured.

If you locate ribbed mixing bowls, refrigerator dishes, and measuring cups with tab handles in ultramarine, you are looking at Jennyware. This is a line of kitchen glassware produced by Jeannette Glass Company. Barbara shows examples of Jennyware in *The Complete Book of Kitchen Collecting*.

Salt & pepper. *Courtesy of Michael Rothenberger/ Mike's Collectibles.*

Back: 4.5" flat tumbler, 6.5" sherbet plate; *middle:* 9" salad bowl, open candy w/ 3 feet, double candlesticks; *front:* 4.75" berry bowl. *Courtesy of Marie Talone & Paul Reichwein.*

6.5" vase. *Courtesy of Jane O'Brien.*

5" flat tumbler. *Courtesy of Wes & Carla Davidson.*

Two candy dishes w/ lids, butter. *Courtesy of Diefenderfer's Collectibles & Antiques.*

Back: 9.25" dinner plate; *middle:* 10.5" console bowl, 9 oz. footed tumbler, 8.5" vase; *front:* lug soup bowl w/ 2 tab handles, cup & saucer, sherbet. *Courtesy of Marie Talone & Paul Reichwein.*

Coaster. *Courtesy of Charlie Diefenderfer.*

SWIRL	Ultramarine	Pink	Delphite	Qty
Bowl, 4.75" berry	18	14		____
Bowl, lug soup w/2 tab handles, 5"	50	35		____
Bowl, 5.25" cereal	18	14	15	____
Bowl, 9" salad	28	22	28	____
Bowl, 10" footed w/handles	35	35		____
Bowl, 10.5" console w/foot	35	35		____
Butter dish base	45	45		____
Butter dish lid	280	180		____
Butter complete	325	225		____
Candlestick, ea. (double)	25	30		____
Candlestick, ea. (single)			75	____
Candy dish, open w/3 feet	20	15		____
Candy dish w/lid	150	225		____
Coaster	20	15		____
Creamer	16	12		____
Cup	16	12	10	____
Pitcher	trtp*	trtp*		____
Plate, 6.5" sherbet	8	6	8	____
Plate, 7.25"	15	10		____
Plate, 8" salad	18	18	15	____
Plate, 9.25" dinner	20	24	15	____
Plate, 10.5"			25	____
Plate, 12.5" sandwich	35	25		____
Platter, 12"			40	____
Salt & pepper	50			____
Saucer	7	5	5	____
Sherbet	25	18		____
Sugar	16	12		____
Tray, 10.5", 2 handles			30	____
Tumbler, 4", flat	35	25		____
Tumbler, 4.5", flat		25		____
Tumbler, 5", flat	130	65		____
Tumbler, 9 oz., footed	50	25		____
Vase, 6.5"		30		____
Vase, 8.5", 2 styles	30			____

Note: Ultramarine candy lid with round finial, $450.

*trtp = too rare to price

SYLVAN (PARROT)
(1931-1932 Federal Glass Company)

Today Sylvan (or Parrot) is thought to be one of the most striking patterns of Depression Glass, although at the time of its production it was considered a mistake. Supposedly a Federal Glass Company employee designed the Sylvan motif after vacationing in the Bahamas. You can see that Caribbean influence in the palm fronds framing tropical birds. Federal executives were unhappy with the resulting dinnerware, due to large areas of blank, undecorated glass. There was concern that homemakers would be dissatisfied with the long-term durability of Sylvan because knife marks would be so easily visible. The decision was made to terminate production in 1932 and the molds were reworked for Madrid, introduced the same year.

Perhaps the short time of production resulting in limited quantities has helped to make it so popular. Not one piece of Sylvan is easy to find, and many items are a near impossibility. We stated in the first edition that a pitcher sold online for more that $5000 at the end of 1998. Since that sale we have been unaware of any other pitcher being in the marketplace. Hot dishes (also called coasters and trivets) are extremely rare, as are stemmed sherbets, butter dishes, sugar lids, shakers…do you get the picture? Only the most motivated collectors should tackle the task of collecting a service of eight with accessories in Sylvan.

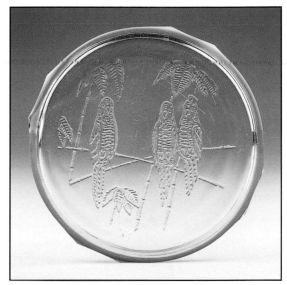

5" scalloped hot dish/coaster.

SYLVAN (PARROT)	Green	Amber	Qty
Bowl, 5" berry	35	25	____
Bowl, 7" soup	55	45	____
Bowl, 8" berry	100	85	____
Bowl, 10" vegetable	70	75	____
Butter dish base	75	200	____
Butter dish lid	375	1200	____
Butter complete	450	1400	____
Creamer	65	70	____
Cup	50	50	____
Hot dish/coaster, 5" scalloped	900	1000	____
Hot dish/coaster, 5" smooth	1000		____
Jam dish, 7"		50	____
Pitcher	trtp*		____
Plate, 5.75" sherbet	40	30	____
Plate, 7.5" salad	40		____
Plate, 9" dinner	60	50	____
Plate, 10.5" round grill	80		____
Plate, 10.5" square grill		60	____
Platter, 11.25"	65	75	____
Salt & pepper	325		____
Saucer	18	18	____
Sherbet, cone-shaped w/foot (Madrid style)	35	35	____
Sherbet, 4.25" tall w/stem	1500		____
Sugar base	45	45	____
Sugar lid	300	600	____
Tumbler, 4.25" flat	150	125	____
Tumbler, 5.5" flat	175	150	____
Tumbler, 5.5" w/foot		175	____
Tumbler, 5.75" w/foot	150	125	____

Note: Blue sherbet:, $250.

*trtp = too rare to price

Above: *Back row:* 7.5" salad plate, 9" dinner plate, 8" berry bowl; *middle:* sugar w/ lid, 5.5" tumbler w/ foot, 10" vegetable bowl sitting on 11.25" platter, butter; *front:* 5" berry bowl, creamer, salt & pepper, 5.5" sherbet plate, sherbet.

Left: Sherbet, 5.75" footed tumbler. *Courtesy of Debora & Paul Torsiello, Debzie's Glass.*

6" 11 oz. footed tumbler.

TEA ROOM
(1926-1931 Indiana Glass Company)

Tea Room was designed for use in ice cream parlors and soda fountains and the array of pieces is indicative of this. There are two banana splits, two glaces, a parfait, three sherbets, and five tumblers. Many of the other items would be useful in a restaurant setting: several creamers and sugars on trays, a variety of vases, a marmalade and a mustard each with lids, an ice bucket, and more.

So the dilemma with this dramatic pattern having many offerings is: Is it more difficult to find any Tea Room or perfect Tea Room? Collectors of this pattern have amazing stamina because after finding a creamer, sugar, and pickle dish the availability of pieces diminishes tremendously. The design, having many edges, is a magnet for damage. So, Tea Room collectors, take care and take heart!

Among the hardest to find Tea Room pieces is the pitcher. Like the Royal Lace straight-sided pitcher, the crystal (clear) pitcher is the most difficult pitcher to find. A green pitcher was offered on eBay in October 2000. The highest bid of $280 was still not at the seller's reserve.

Here are a few clarifications regarding Tea Room. A glace is a stemmed item similar to a goblet for use with sorbets and sundaes. The flat banana split resembles an oval relish dish and rests flat on the table. The footed banana split is on a pedestal. Both measure 7.5" across the longest part of the oval.

Above: *Back row:* creamer & sugar on center handled tray, 11" ruffled vase; *front:* low footed sherbet/ice cream on 6.5" sherbet plate, 8.5" pickle, tall sherbet/sundae, 5.25" footed tumbler. *Courtesy of Debora & Paul Torsiello, Debzie's Glass.*

Right: 3.25" creamers & sugars on 6.25" x 7" trays having one side handle. *Courtesy of Vic & Jean Laermans.*

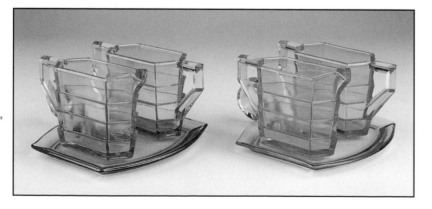

Back row: 8.5" pickle, 12 oz. footed tumbler. *front:* mustard w/ lid, 2-part relish, sugar base. *Courtesy of Debora & Paul Torsiello, Debzie's Glass.*

Creamers & sugars w/ lids. *Courtesy of Vic & Jean Laermans.*

TEA ROOM	Green	Pink	Crystal	Amber	Qty
Banana Split, 7.5" flat	120	100	65		____
Banana Split, 7.5" footed	80	70	50		____
Bowl, finger	65	50	35		____
Bowl, 8.5" w/2 handles	100	80	40		____
Bowl, 8.75" salad	100	80	40		____
Bowl, 9.5" oval	70	70	35		____
Candlestick, ea.	30	25	20		____
Creamer, 3.25" oval & flat	40	40	20		____
Creamer, 4.5" footed	25	25	10	80	____
Creamer, rectangular	30	25	10		____
Cup	60	60	40		____
Glace, 7 oz. & 6.5" ruffled	85	80	50		____
Goblet	85	80	50		____
Ice Bucket	70	70	45		____
Lamp	135	135	80		____
Marmalade w/lid	225	200	100		____
Mustard w/lid	200	175	90		____
Parfait	90	85	50		____
Pickle, 8.5"	30	25	15		____
Pitcher, 10"	220	175	trtp*	450	____
Plate, 6.5" sherbet	40	35	20		____
Plate, 8.25" luncheon	40	35	20		____
Plate, 10.5" w/2 handles	55	50	25		____
Plate, 10.5" sandwich w/center handle	55	50	25		____
Relish, 2-part	35	30	20		____
Salt & pepper	100	100	45		____
Saucer	40	35	20		____
Sherbet, low w/foot, ice cream	35	30	20		____
Sherbet, ruffled	45	40	25		____
Sherbet, tall, sundae, 5"	100	100	50		____
Sugar base 4.5" w/foot	25	25	10		____
Sugar lid (for 4.5")	200	200	50		____
Sugar, rectangular	30	35	10		____
Sugar base, 3.25", oval & flat	40	40	20		____
Sugar lid (for flat)	20	175	85		____
Tray, center handle	200	175	50		____
Tray for cream & sugar (center handle)	50	40	20		____
Tray for oval, flat cream & sugar (1 side handle), 6.25" x 7"	65	55	35		____
Tumbler, 4.25" flat	125	110	50		____
Tumbler, 6 oz. footed	45	40	20		____
Tumbler, 5.25" footed	40	35	15	100	____
Tumbler, 11 oz. footed	60	50	25		____
Tumbler, 12 oz. footed	75	65	35		____
Vase, 6.5"	100	90	50		____
Vase, 9.5" ruffled	125	115	15		____
Vase, 9.5" straight	80	75	45		____
Vase, 11" ruffled	275	325	150		____
Vase, 11" straight	150	125	75		____

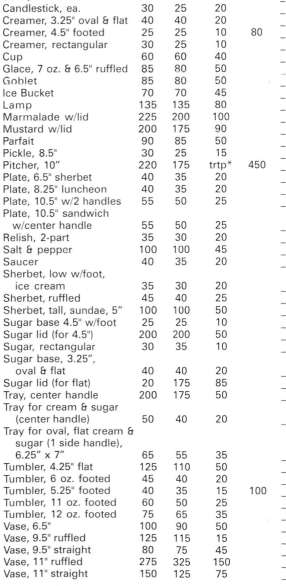

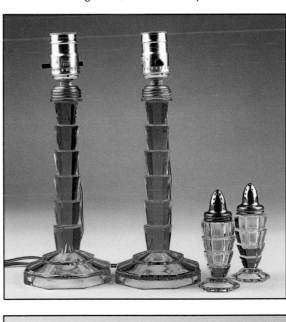

Pair of lamps, salt & pepper. *Courtesy of Debora & Paul Torsiello, Debzie's Glass.*

8.5" bowl w/ two handles having hand painted embellishment. *Courtesy of Charlie Diefenderfer.*

8" luncheon plate.

THISTLE
Reproduced
(1929-1930 Macbeth-Evans Glass Company)

One of Macbeth-Evan's earliest Depression Glass patterns is the delicate and elusive seven-item Thistle. Production was brief as Thistle was unpopular. The molds were reworked and the Dogwood pattern was introduced the same year Thistle was discontinued. Similarities are obvious as both patterns have thin glass with slightly uneven outer rims. The Thistle cup is like the thin cup in Dogwood.

THISTLE	Pink	Green	Qty
Bowl, 5.5" cereal	30	30	____
Bowl, 10.25" fruit	400	250	____
Cake plate, 13"	150	175	____
Cup	25	28	____
Plate, 8" luncheon	25	25	____
Plate, 10.25" grill			
w/pattern only on rim	35	40	____
Saucer	13	15	____

Reproduction information: These items are new & were never originally produced: butter dish, pitcher, & tumbler.

Back row: 10.25" grill plate; *front row:* 8" luncheon plate, 5.5" cereal bowl, cup & saucer. *Courtesy of Wes & Carla Davidson.*

13" cake plate. *Courtesy of Diefenderfer's Collectibles & Antiques.*

THUMBPRINT
(1927-1930 Federal Glass Company)

Thumbprint is another early Depression Glass pattern. Introduced in 1927, it predates mold etching, a technique used with later offerings. Made only in green, Thumbprint has a complete line of pieces needed to set a table and most everything to serve a meal. There is neither a butter dish nor platter.

We are looking for some help with this pattern. Shown is a pitcher that is unlike either pitcher from Federal's 1928 catalog. We would appreciate hearing from a Thumbprint collector, especially if you could get your glass to the studio so we can accurately document this pattern.

Collectors new to this pattern and to Depression Glass in general sometimes have difficulty discerning the differences between Thumbprint, Pebble Optic (Raindrops), and Hex Optic. All three patterns are pictured, but here are some additional points to consider. Thumbprint "indents" are longer than the round indents of Pebble Optic. The shape of the surface design on Hex Optic is more honeycomb-like or hexagonal (hence the name).

Vase, pitcher. *Courtesy of Marie Talone.*

THUMBPRINT	Green	Qty
Bowl, 4.75" berry	15	____
Bowl, 5" cereal	15	____
Bowl, 8" berry	25	____
Creamer	18	____
Cup	8	____
Pitcher, 7.25"	75	____
Plate, 6" sherbet	10	____
Plate, 8" luncheon	15	____
Plate, 9.25" dinner	25	____
Salt & pepper	80	____
Saucer	2	____
Sherbet	10	____
Sugar	18	____
Tumbler, 4"	20	____
Tumbler, 5"	25	____
Tumbler, 5.5"	30	____
Vase, 9"	60	____

8" luncheon plate, cup & saucer.

TULIP
(1930s Dell Glass Company)

The only Dell Glass Company pattern shown in this book is Tulip. It is quite unique for several reasons. First, are the colors. Tulip was made in ice blue, amethyst, amber, and a green that is a deeper shade than other transparent green Depression Glass. Many of the pieces were produced in two variations: with stippled texture and without stippled texture. (Collectors seem to have no preference.) Finally, the shapes and proportions are unlike other patterns. The pieces are reminiscent of the blossom for which the pattern was named.

Tulip was made in New Jersey but is rarely seen in neighboring Pennsylvania. In fact, we find very little Tulip in our travels. Few people are collecting Tulip as it has received little exposure and is not readily available in the marketplace.

The edges of Tulip were not carefully finished and one will find roughness and extra glass. Be aware that the kind of unevenness that might be considered damage on another pattern is normal for Tulip.

2.75" juice tumbler/cigarette holder. *Courtesy of Charlie Diefenderfer.*

Cup. *Courtesy of Neil McCurdy - Hoosier Kubboard Glass.*

Back row: Candle holder, 10.5" plate; *front row:* creamer, candle holder, 1.75" whiskey tumbler, 2.5" candle holder, creamer.

Dell sticker.

TULIP *by* DELL HAND MADE IN AMERICA

Creamers & sugars in various colors. *Courtesy of Vic & Jean Laermans.*

TULIP	Amethyst & Blue	Green & Amber	Crystal	Qty
Bowl, 6"	20	18	15	____
Bowl, 13.25"	100	90	40	____
Candle holder, ea., 3.75" diam., 2" tall, resembles a blossom bowl	35	30	25	____
Candle holder, ea., 5.25" diam. 3" tall, regular candlestick design	25	20	15	____
Candy jar, complete	100	75	40	____
Cigarette holder (same as juice)	30	25	15	____
Creamer, 2"	30	18	15	____
Cup	20	18	12	____
Decanter w/stopper	trtp*	trtp*	trtp*	____
Goblet, 7" water	trtp*	trtp*	trtp*	____
Ice tub	70	60	30	____
Plate, 6"	12	10	5	____
Plate, 7.25"	15	12	7	____
Plate, 9"	20	18	12	____
Plate 10.5"	45	35	20	____
Saucer	10	8	5	____
Sherbet	25	20	10	____
Sugar, 2"	30	18	15	____
Tumbler, 1.75" whiskey	30	25	15	____
Tumbler, 2.75" juice (Same as cig. holder)	30	25	15	____

*trtp = too rare to price

TWISTED OPTIC
(1927-1930 Imperial Glass Company)

One of Imperial Glass Company's earliest Depression Glass patterns was Twisted Optic. Like other early patterns this pre-dates mold etching, a technique used with later offerings. Many of these simpler patterns are less popular with today's collectors.

Twisted Optic was made in a palette of colors but today's favorites are pink ("Rose Marie") and green. There are two shades of green: "Imperial Green" and "Golden Green."

Cups, saucers, and smaller plates are so common that many dealers are disinterested in adding them to their inventories. The other pieces get progressively difficult to locate. In another pattern, some of the elusive Twisted Optic items would be a lot more expensive. The relatively low demand negatively impacts the values of this glassware.

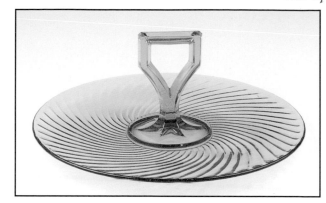

Rack: sandwich server w/ two handles; *front:* two creamers, 3" candlestick, two cups.

TWISTED OPTIC	Pink	Green	Amber	Blue & Yellow	Qty
Basket	45	40	40	90	____
Bowl, cream soup	15	12	10	25	____
Bowl, 5" cereal	10	8	6	25	____
Bowl, 7" salad	15	12	10	25	____
Bowl, 9"	20	18	12	30	____
Bowl, 10.5" console w/rolled edge	40	35	25	65	____
Bowl, 11.5" console (Base in black 100)	40	35	25	65	____
Candlestick, 3.5" ea.	20	18	15	25	____
Candlestick, 8.25" ea.	25	22	20	35	____
Candy jar w/lid (5 sizes)	50	45	40	75	____
Cologne bottle w/stopper	55	50	50	85	____
Condiment w/lid	35	35	30		____
Creamer	12	12	8	15	____
Cup	7	7	5	12	____
Mayonnaise	25	20	20	40	____
Pitcher	50	40	35		____
Plate, 6" sherbet	5	4	3	8	____
Plate, 7" salad	7	6	5	10	____
Plate, 8" luncheon	8	7	6	12	____
Plate, 10" sandwich	12	12	10	18	____
Platter, 9" x 7.5" oval w/ indent	8	7	6	12	____
Powder jar w/lid	40	40	35	65	____
Sandwich server w/center handle	20	18	18	35	____
Sandwich server w/2 handles	15	15	12	25	____
Saucer	5	4	3	8	____
Sherbet	10	10	8	15	____
Sugar	12	12	8	15	____
Tumbler, 4.5"	12	10	10		____
Tumbler, 5.25"	14	12	12		____
Vase, 7.25",	25	25	25	65	____
Vase, 8", 2 styles	30	30	30	75	____

3.5" candlesticks & 4" powder jar w/lid.

Sherbet. *Courtesy of Charlie Diefenderfer.*

U.S. SWIRL

(Late 1920s U.S. Glass Company)

Hocking made Spiral, Imperial made Twisted Optic, and U.S. Glass made U.S. Swirl. All are early Depression Glass patterns with simple spiraling designs. All are available in at least green, and none are particularly popular with today's collectors who generally prefer patterns that are mold etched.

Presented are two pieces that still have original stickers. Imagine, seventy-five years and no one thought to pull them off!

U.S. Glass Company created a "generic" butter bottom that fits several other patterns including Aunt Polly, Cherryberry, Floral and Diamond Band, and Strawberry. The center of the base has only the definitive starburst, and is without other embellishments or designs. Additional similarities between the U.S. Glass Company patterns do exist. The 3.5" tumbler is only one example of an Aunt Polly mold being shared with U.S. Swirl. The 8" pitcher is the same mold used for Floral and Diamond Band. Cherryberry, Strawberry, Aunt Polly, and U.S. Swirl all share an 8.25" oval bowl.

The use and reuse of molds was a clever way to maximize production and minimize cost.

For the sake of providing clarification, two pieces of Federal Twisted Optic are shown. The goblet has a capacity of 7.5 ounces and the bowl has a Federal shield in the bottom.

U.S. SWIRL	Green	Pink	Qty
Bowl, 4.5" berry	8	10	____
Bowl, 5.5" w/1 handle	12	14	____
Bowl, 7.75" round	15	20	____
Bowl, 8.25" oval 2.75" deep	50	50	____
Bowl, 8.25" oval, 1.75" deep	75	75	____
Butter dish base	75	75	____
Butter dish lid	100	110	____
Butter complete	175	185	____
Candy w/lid	35	40	____
Comport, 5" diam., 2.75" tall	40	40	____
Creamer	15	18	____
Pitcher, 8"	60	65	____
Plate, 6.25" sherbet	5	5	____
Plate, 7.75" salad	7	8	____
Salt & pepper	60	65	____
Sherbet	5	8	____
Sugar base	12	14	____
Sugar lid	28	31	____
Tumbler, 3.5"	10	12	____
Tumbler, 4.75"	15	18	____
Vase, 6.5"	25	25	____

Note: Iridescent & Crystal items ½ the value of green.

2.75" tall comport (5.25" diameter) & 5.5" bowl w/1 handle.

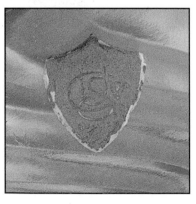

U.S. Glass Company sticker.

Federal Twisted Optic, not U.S. Swirl. 5.5" goblet & 6" bowl.

VERNON

(1931 Indiana Glass Company)

This lovely pattern was manufactured for one year, yet its legacy continues on with strength. There are many collectors of Vernon in both green and yellow ("Topaz"); although, yellow is a bit more popular. Often Depression Glass yellow is amber or apricot, but Vernon's yellow is a true, cheerful, bright color. Crystal (clear) gets far less attention, even though the delicate Vernon detail is still easily evident and quite attractive.

Vernon is an abbreviated line with only luncheon items. Either the 8" or the 11" plate can be used as a dinner plate since Vernon has no true dinner plate.

11" sandwich plate.

VERNON	Green & Yellow	Crystal	Qty
Creamer	35	12	____
Cup	25	10	____
Plate, 8" luncheon	15	5	____
Plate, 11" sandwich	35	12	____
Saucer	10	5	____
Sugar	35	12	____
Tumbler, 5"	45	15	____

Creamers & sugars in various colors. *Courtesy of Vic & Jean Laermans.*

5" tumbler.

VICTORY

(1929-1931 Diamond Glass-Ware Company)

Victory is available in a variety of colors: amber, black, cobalt blue, green, and, the color most commonly seen, pink. The fact that Victory is usually found in pink is of particular interest as black is a signature color of Diamond Glass-Ware Company. Actually, black as well as blue are quite difficult to find! Victory was made both plain (undecorated) and embellished with gold or silver overlays. Pink items may have hand painted flowers.

As with all glassware, condition is very important. Because Victory has so much plain glass even the slightest wear is obvious. Any scratching is very noticeable, particularly on black glass. Embellishments must have survived in excellent condition.

The gravy boat and under plate are the most elusive pieces. Although made in Pennsylvania, Victory is not often seen in the eastern states.

Mayonnaise comport, 8.5" indented under plate both w/ gold trim. *Courtesy of Charlie Diefenderfer.*

Back row: 12" platter, 8" luncheon plate. *Courtesy of Kelly O'Brien-Hoch.*

Above: 12.5" bowl w/ flat rim, 6" comport, 11" sandwich server w/ center handle.

Right: 3.25" candlestick w/ gold trim. *Courtesy of Charlie Diefenderfer.*

Below: Creamers & sugars in various colors. *Courtesy of Vic & Jean Laermans.*

VICTORY	Blue	Black	Other Colors	Qty
Bon bon, 7" hi-footed	30	20	15	____
Bowl, 6.5" cereal	40	35	15	____
Bowl, 8.5" flat soup	60	50	25	____
Bowl, 9" oval vegetable	120	100	35	____
Bowl, 11" rolled edge	65	50	30	____
Bowl, 12" console	75	65	38	____
Bowl, 12.5" flat rim	75	65	38	____
Candlestick, ea., 3.25" tall	65	55	20	____
Cheese & cracker set (12" indented plate & comport)			55	____
Comport, 6" tall			20	____
Creamer	55	50	18	____
Cup	40	35	10	____
Goblet, 5"	100	85	25	____
Gravy boat	275	250	125	____
Gravy under plate	125	100	100	____
Mayonnaise 3-piece set	115	90	60	____
Mayo. comport, 3.75" tall	50	40	30	
Mayo. ladle	25	25	15	
Mayo 7.5" under plate, w/indent	40	25	15	
Plate, 6" bread & butter	20	18	8	____
Plate, 7" salad	20	18	8	____
Plate, 8" luncheon	40	35	10	____
Plate, 9" dinner	55	45	25	____
Platter, 12"	90	75	35	____
Sandwich server, 11" w/center handle	90	80	35	____
Saucer	18	15	5	____
Sherbet	35	30	15	____
Sugar	55	50	18	____

VITROCK

(1934-1937 Hocking Glass Company)

Recent interest in Fire-King has resulted in a renewed enthusiasm for Hocking Glass, and Vitrock has benefited from this phenomenon. Vitrock is a white glassware that often had the word "Vitrock" imprinted on the underside. It was used in a variety of glassware including Lake Como Depression Glass and a line of kitchen glass. However, this presentation concerns the pattern named "Vitrock."

All the pieces needed to set a table and serve a meal are available in Vitrock dinnerware. Thus, although the pattern is limited, it meets the needs for which it was intended. As with many Fire-King patterns, the 9" flat soup bowl and 11.5" platter are the hardest pieces to locate.

It is much easier to find white Vitrock than fired-on pieces, which is reflected in the pricing. Fired-on glass is subject to damage from abrasive cleaning and modern dishwashers, so those pieces that survived unscathed are more costly than their white counterparts.

10" dinner. (Note the slight design difference with the dinner plate in the following picture.) *Courtesy of Michael Rothenberger/Mike's Collectibles.*

VITROCK	White	Fired-on colors & striped trim	Qty
Bowl, 4" dessert	6	10	____
Bowl, cream soup, 4.75"	18	25	____
Bowl, 6" fruit	8	12	____
Bowl, 7.5" cereal	10	12	____
Bowl, 9" flat soup (soup plate)	35	50	____
Bowl, 9.5" vegetable	18	25	____
Creamer	8	12	____
Cup	5	8	____
Plate, 7.5" bread	5	8	____
Plate, 8.75" luncheon	5	8	____
Plate, 10" dinner	12	15	____
Platter, 11.5"	35	50	____
Saucer	5	8	____
Sugar	8	12	____

Back row: 10" dinner, 6" fruit bowl, 4" dessert bowl; *front row:* cup & saucer, creamer & sugar.

Cream soup bowl.

Sugar w/ lid. *Courtesy Of Vic & Jean Laermans.*

WATERFORD
(1938-1944 Hocking Glass Company)

Initially, Depression Glass was most popular in colors. As tastes changed glass companies attempted to regain consumer interest by offering the alternative of crystal (clear) glass. Today's collectors favor the earlier, colorful offerings and crystal Depression is often overlooked.

In its day, crystal Waterford was very successful. Pink ("Rose") was first issued in 1938 with crystal following one year later and continuing until 1944. This was so popular, Hocking made additional pieces in crystal that were not made in pink. Likewise, crystal Waterford was integrated into some Royal Ruby and Forest Green sets. There are two different salt and pepper shakers in crystal and none in pink. As a note, the goblet was made in 1959.

Today, pink Waterford commands the attention of collectors. No piece in pink is particularly common, and the pitcher, butter dish, and juice tumbler are scarce.

We have had crystal sherbets that were found in Canada having etching in alternating diamonds, a bit like a chess board. Often American Depression Glass received interesting embellishments when pieces traveled north.

80 oz. tilted water pitcher. *Courtesy of Michael Rothenberger/Mike's Collectibles.*

Back row: 9.5" dinner plate, 10.25" cake plate w/ two closed handles; *front:* sherbet, 4.75" berry bowl, cup & saucer, 5.5" cereal bowl. *Courtesy of Diefenderfer's Collectibles & Antiques.*

Back row: saucer, 7.25"
salad plate, 6" sherbet
plate; *front:* sherbet, 8.25"
berry bowl. *Courtesy of
Charlie Diefenderfer.*

WATERFORD	Pink	Crystal	Qty
Ash tray		8	____
Bowl, 4.75" berry	20	8	____
Bowl, 5.5" cereal	40	20	____
Bowl, 8.25" berry	28	10	____
Butter dish base	40	8	____
Butter dish lid	210	25	____
Butter complete	250	33	____
Coaster		5	____
Creamer, oval	15	5	____
Creamer, ftd.		45	____
Cup	20	8	____
Goblet, 5.25" & 5.5"		18	____
Lamp, 4" round base		45	____
Lazy Susan, 14"		35	____
Pitcher, juice (tilted), 42 oz.		30	____
Pitcher, water (tilted), 80 oz.	200	50	____
Plate, 6" sherbet	12	5	____
Plate, 7.25" salad	15	8	____
Plate, 9.5" dinner	30	15	____
Plate, 10.25" cake w/2 closed handles	35	15	____
Plate, 13.75" sandwich	50	15	____
Relish, 13.75" round w/5 parts		20	____
Salt & pepper, narrow		12	____
Salt & pepper, wide (flared bottom)		8	____
Saucer	10	5	____
Sherbet, smooth foot & smooth rim	20	5	____
Sherbet, scalloped		25	____
Sugar base	18	7	____
Sugar lid	100	20	____
Tumbler, 3.5" juice	120		____
Tumbler, 4.75" footed	30	10	____
Tumbler, 5.25" footed		12	____

Wide, flared bottom salt & pepper, narrow
salt & pepper. *Courtesy of Michael
Rothenberger/Mike's Collectibles.*

Note: Ashtray w/advertisement in center, $20.
Amber goblet: $20. Yellow goblet: too rare to
price. Forest Green, 13.75" round relish plate, $35;
smooth inserts for relish, $12; center insert, $20.

WHITE SHIP
(Late 1930s Hazel-Atlas Glass Company)

This pattern has been moved from "Ships" to restore the original name, "White Ship."

The bold statement made by pieces of White Ship often entrances even people who do not collect Depression Glass. The white sailboats contrasted on the cobalt blue glass create a unique and appealing design. Then there are the pieces themselves, as White Ship has a huge array of tumblers and pieces rarely seen in other patterns: a covered box, a cocktail mixer and shaker, an ice bowl and tub, and trays, real trays as opposed to all glass ones.

Condition is quite important when buying White Ship or any of the variations such as Windmills, Fish, Hunt Scenes ("Tally Ho"), etc. If the white is not truly white, pass unless you are satisfied with what you are seeing. There is no way to correct stains, fading, or discoloration.

Now some clarifications. The ice tub has thin, straight sides and was designed to hold ice cubes. The cocktail stirrer is smaller, has thicker, sloping sides, and was created as a container for one to stir a cocktail. The cocktail shaker should have a metal lid found in several styles with either a metal or plastic plug. White Ship dinnerware comes from Moderntone molds. Plates will have a white ship in the center, but the cup has no decoration of any kind and is actually the Moderntone cup.

Pictured is clear Hazel-Atlas cocktail shaker with an oasis motif. Although not "White Ship" many collectors enjoy assembling a variety of shakers. Also shown is a grouping of aluminum coasters with a ship motif that would surely be a great "go-along."

Back row: 8" salad plate, 9" dinner plate, 6" sherbet plate; *front:* cup & saucer. (Note: this is also the Moderntone cup and has no details.) *Courtesy of Bob & Cindy Bentley.*

Pitcher w/ ice lip, pitcher w/ ice lip and ribs at neck, pitcher w/ no ice lip. *Courtesy of Bob & Cindy Bentley.*

Cocktail mixer, cocktail shaker, ice tub. *Courtesy of Bob & Cindy Bentley.*

Tray. *Courtesy of Bob & Cindy Bentley.*

Ashtray w/ metal sailboat, blotter ("go along" item $50), box w/ 3 sections & lid. *Courtesy of Bob & Cindy Bentley.*

Hazel Atlas cocktail shaker. *Courtesy of Steve Wasko & Jeaneen Heiskell.*

"Go-along" 3" aluminum coasters. *Courtesy of Marie Talone.*

Tumblers: sailboat w/out clouds, (+4.75" tall, 2.75" diameter); Atlantic City (+4.75" tall, 2.75" diameter); "Tally Ho" & Flamenco dancers, (4.75" tall, 2.75" diameter); small tumbler shown with fish & ship, (3.75" tall, 2.5" diameter); old-fashioned w/ship, (3.25" tall, 3" diameter); heavy bottom shown with windmill, (3.25" tall, 2.5" diameter); roly poly w/ship, (2.25" tall, 2.5" diameter). *Courtesy of Steve Wasko & Jeaneen Heiskell.*

Two Hazel Atlas pitchers w/ fish motif & Flamenco dancer motif. *Courtesy of Steve Wasko & Jeaneen Heiskell.*

Five Hazel Atlas cocktail shakers. *Courtesy of Steve Wasko & Jeaneen Heiskell.*

Ice bucket w/ sailor motif & cocktail mixer w/windmill motif. *Courtesy of Steve Wasko & Jeaneen Heiskell.*

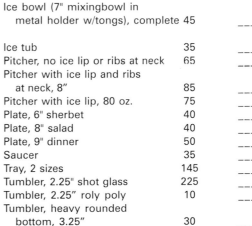

SHIPS	Blue glass w/white details	Qty
Ashtray, 2 styles	65	____
Ashtray w/metal sailboat	125	____
Box, 3 sections	250	____
Cocktail mixer	45	____
Cocktail shaker	60	____
Cup (no details)	15	____
Ice bowl (7" mixingbowl in metal holder w/tongs), complete	45	____
Ice tub	35	____
Pitcher, no ice lip or ribs at neck	65	____
Pitcher with ice lip and ribs at neck, 8"	85	____
Pitcher with ice lip, 80 oz.	75	____
Plate, 6" sherbet	40	____
Plate, 8" salad	40	____
Plate, 9" dinner	50	____
Saucer	35	____
Tray, 2 sizes	145	____
Tumbler, 2.25" shot glass	225	____
Tumbler, 2.25" roly poly	10	____
Tumbler, heavy rounded bottom, 3.25"	30	____
Tumbler, 3.25" old fashion	22	____
Tumbler, 3.5" whiskey	45	____
Tumbler, 3.75" juice	15	____
Tumbler, 4.75" straight water	18	____
Tumbler, 4.75", 10 oz. iced tea	18	____
Tumbler, 12 oz. iced tea, 5"	25	____
Tumbler, 5" no clouds	28	____

WINDSOR
(1932-1946 Jeannette Glass Company)

In an attempt to simplify the listing of Windsor items we have used the abbreviation "zz" to indicate a zigzag or pointy rim. Keep in mind that the prices are for perfect pieces and locating perfect Windsor takes time because each surface needs examination.

Production of Windsor began in 1932 when colored glassware was considered very fashionable. As tastes changed crystal (clear) became more popular than the colors, and crystal Windsor production continued until 1946. Like Hocking Glass Company's Waterford, Jeannette Glass Company's Windsor has more pieces in crystal than in either pink or green. Today collectors are interested in colored Windsor.

This pattern enjoyed a long period of production, and many different pieces were created. There are thirteen different bowls with the "boat" bowl being the most recognizable. It has two pointy ends along the 11.75" side and is 7" wide. The bowl does resemble a boat. In pink the 8" and 10.5" bowls with zigzag rims and the 12.5" fruit bowl are the most difficult bowls to find. Fewer bowls were produced in green and crystal. The green butter dish is the hardest one to find, and the crystal one is quite common. The pink powder jar is extremely rare and we are pleased to picture one. The three-part platter is elusive in crystal and almost nonexistent in pink. The 6.75" pitcher in pink is common, but the 4.5" milk pitcher is rare. Two 4.5" milk pitchers were sold on eBay in October 2000 for $401 and $412. Note the differences in the sugar lids and their respective prices.

Added to the list is a 5" crystal finger light.

The ice blue cup and plate had been advertised and sold as crystal. Just imagine the surprised delight when the buyer opened the package and discovered ice blue!

Powder jar w/ lid. *Courtesy of Michael Rothenberger/Mike's Collectibles.*

5" flat tumbler, 4" flat tumbler, 3.25" tumbler. *Courtesy of Diefenderfer's Collectibles & Antiques*.

5" finger light. *Courtesy of Mike Rothenberger / Mike's Collectibles.*

Back: 9" dinner plate, 6.75" pitcher; *middle:* 5.5" deep cereal bowl, 11.5" platter, cream soup bowl; *front:* cup & saucer, creamer, sugar w/ lid. *Courtesy of Diefenderfer's Collectibles & Antiques.*

WINDSOR	Pink	Green	Crystal	Qty
Ash tray	42	45	15	____
Bowl, 4.75" berry	12	12	5	____
Bowl, 5" zz*	45		5	____
Bowl, cream soup	25	30	7	____
Bowl, 5.5" deep cereal	35	35	9	____
Bowl, 7.25" w/3 feet	38		10	____
Bowl, 8" zz*	125		15	____
Bowl, 8" w/handles	25	25	7	____
Bowl, 8.5" berry	25	25	7	____
Bowl, 9.5" oval vegetable	25	30	8	____
Bowl, 10.5" salad	15			____
Bowl, 10.5" zz*	225		30	____
Bowl, 12.5" fruit	140		30	____
Bowl, 7"x 11.75" "boat"	40	45	26	____
Butter dish base	20	40	10	____
Butter dish lid	40	60	20	____
Butter complete	60	100	30	____
Cake plate, 10.75"	35	35	10	____
Candlestick, ea.	45		12	____
Candy jar w/lid			30	____
Coaster, 3.25"	20	20	5	____
Comport			20	____
Creamer (2 styles in Crystal)	15	15	7	____
Cup	12	12	4	____
Finger light, 5"			45	____
Pitcher, 4.5", milk	150		25	____
Pitcher, 6.75"	40	70	15	____
Plate, 6" sherbet	8	8	3	____
Plate, 7" salad	20	25	4	____
Plate, 9" dinner	25	35	8	____
Plate, 10" sandwich w/closed handles	25		10	____
Plate, 10.5" zz*			10	____
Plate, 10.25" w/open handles	20	20	8	____
Plate, 13.5" chop	40	40	15	____
Platter, 11.5"	30	30	8	____
Platter, 3-part	400		30	____
Powder jar complete	350		20	____
Relish, 11.5", 2-part			15	____
Salt & pepper, 3"	45	65	20	____
Saucer	10	10	3	____
Sherbet	18	20	4	____
Sugar base, 3" w/smooth rim	30	40	15	____
Sugar base, 3.25" w/scalloped rim	15	20	7	____
Sugar lid w/pointy knob	20	30	8	____
Sugar lid w/small knob	120		10	____
Tray, 4" sq. w/handles	10	15	5	____
Tray, 4" sq. no handles	50		10	____
Tray, 4" x 9" w/handles	10	15	5	____
Tray, 4" x 9" no handles	60		12	____
Tray, 8.5" x 9.75" w/handles	25	35	10	____
Tray, 8.5" x 9.75" no handles	95		15	____
Tumbler, 3.25" flat	30	35	10	____
Tumbler, 4" flat	18	35	10	____
Tumbler, 4.25" w/foot			10	____
Tumbler, 4.5" flat		60	10	____
Tumbler, 5" w/foot	35	60	10	____
Tumbler, 5" flat			10	____
Tumbler, 7.25" w/foot			10	____

*zz = zigzag or pointed edges

Note: Delphite ashtray, $65. Blue creamer, cup, 9" dinner, 10.5" plate, 3.25" flat tumbler, & 4" flat tumbler: $75 each; powder jar, $375; red pitcher, $500. Yellow powder jar, $375. Crystal one-handled candleholder, $20.

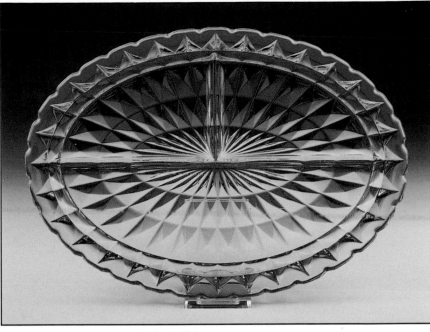

3-part platter. *Courtesy of Marie Talone.*

Ashtray. *Courtesy of Mike Rothenberger / Mike's Collectibles.*

Salt & pepper. *Courtesy of Vic & Jean Laermans.*

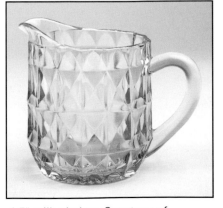

4.5" milk pitcher. *Courtesy of Vic & Jean Laermans.*

Windsor

Back: 9" dinner plate, 10.25" plate w/ open handles; *middle:* 5" footed tumbler, 7.25" footed tumbler, 7" x 11.75" "boat" bowl, 8" bowl; *front:* 4" flat tumbler, butter, sugar base, creamer. *Courtesy of Marie Talone & Paul Reichwein.*

4.5" flat tumbler. *Courtesy of Mark Fors / Marwig Glass Store.*

10.5" plate w/zigzag edges & cup in ice blue. *Courtesy of Mark Fors / Marwig Glass Store.*

Candlesticks.

10.5" bowl, 7.25" bowl w/ 3 feet. *Courtesy of Michael Rothenberger/Mike's Collectibles.*

7" footed tumbler, 5" footed tumbler, 4.25" footed tumbler, 3.25" flat tumbler. *Courtesy of Vic & Jean Laermans.*

Bibliography

Antique & Collectors Reproduction News, *Depression Glass Reproductions.* Des Moines, IA: 1994.

Florence, Gene. *Anchor Hocking's Fire-King & More*. Paducah, KY: Collector Books, 1998.

Florence, Gene. *Collectible Glassware from the 40s 50s 60s...* Paducah, KY: Collector Books, 1998.

Florence, Gene. *Collector's Encyclopedia of Depression Glass.* Paducah, KY: Collector Books, 1998.

Florence, Gene. *Pocket Guide to Depression Glass and More.* Paducah, KY: Collector Books, 1999.

Goshe, Ed, Ruth Hemminger, and Leslie Piña. *Depression Era Stems & Tableware: Tiffin.* Atglen, PA: Schiffer Publishing Ltd., 1998.

Hopper, Philip. *Forest Green Glass*. Atglen, PA: Schiffer Publishing, 2000.

Hopper, Philip. *More Royal Ruby*. Atglen, PA: Schiffer Publishing, 1999.

Hopper, Philip. *Royal Ruby*. Atglen, PA: Schiffer Publishing, 1998.

Keller, Joe & David Ross. *Jadite: An Identification and Price Guide.* Atglen, PA: Schiffer Publishing, 1999.

Kilgo, Garry & Dale, and Wilkins, Jerry & Gail. *Anchor Hocking's Fire -King Glassware*. Addison, Alabama: K & W Collectibles Publisher, 1997.

Piña, Leslie, and Paula Ockner. *Depression Era Art Deco Glass.* Atglen, PA: Schiffer Publishing Ltd., 1999.

Snyder, Jeffery B. *Morgantown Glass: From Depression Glass through the 1960s.* Atglen, PA: Schiffer Publishing Ltd., 1998.

Weatherman, Hazel Marie. *Colored Glassware of the Depression Era.* Ozark, MO: Weatherman Glassbooks, 1970.

Weatherman, Hazel Marie. *Colored Glassware of the Depression Era 2.* Ozark, MO: Weatherman Glassbooks, 1974.

Yeske, Doris. *Depression Glass, 3rd Edition.* Atglen, PA: Schiffer Publishing Ltd., 1999.

Websiste:http://www.dgshopperonline.com
Website:http://www.justglass.com

Dealer Directory

The following is partial listing of the fine dealers whose inventory and personal collections were instrumental in creating this reference. Several generous souls chose to remain anonymous, but the others are shown. We can not thank them enough for their assistance. We invite you to contact them for any Depression Glass or Elegant Glass needs. Their integrity is outstanding and all are just down right great people!

DAVID G. BAKER / DAVIDS DISHES
Specializing in Franciscan, Fiesta, & Depression Glass "I ship anywhere!"
Found at Renninger's in Adamstown, PA selling with the Mauzys.
E-mail: DGBaker69@aol.com
eBay selling as: davidsdishes
Phone: (717) 896-3197
Halifax, PA 19607

WES & CARLA DAVIDSON / D AND D ANTIQUES
Located at the Ozark Antiques
200 S. 20th Street
Ozark, MO 65721
Phone: (417) 581-5233

CHARLIE DIEFENDERFER / WEST WALL AUCTION
Specialty auctions held throughout the year. Depression Era glassware, China, and pottery; Carnival Glass, Fiesta, Hall, and Blue Ridge; antiques, collectibles, furniture, and more.
Web Site: www.westwall.com
E-mail: westwall@westwall.com
Phone: (610) 929-3802

SCOTT & RHONDA HACKENBURG / BLUE JAY ANTIQUES & COLLECTIBLES
E-mail: bluejay@innernet.net
eBay selling as: bluejay16
Found at all Shupp's Grove Extravaganzas in Adamstown, PA

DOTTIE & DOUG HEVENER/
THE QUACKER CONNECTION
Shop location:
The Pirate's Quay Shops
MP 11 Route 158 Bypass
Nags Head, NC 27959
Shop phone: (252) 441-2811
Web Site: http://www.thequackerconnection.com

RICK HIRTE & SUSIE THOMPSON/ SPARKLE PLENTY GLASSWARE
9 Pleasant Street
Bar Harbor, ME 04609
Web Sites: http://www.spglass.com & http://www.fire-king.net
E-mail: rick@spglass.com & susie@spglass.com
Phone: (800) 409-7577

JANICE JOHNSTON / BEHIND THE GREEN DOOR
640 Haig Blvd.
Reading, PA 19607
Phone: (610) 777-1477

WALTER LEMISKI /WALTZ TIME ANTIQUES
Web Site: www.members.home.net/wlemiski
E-mail: wlemiski@home.com
Phone: (905) 846-2835
Found at: DG Shopper Online & Mega Show
Promoter of: Toronto Depression Glass Shows that are scheduled for the last Sunday in May and the first Sunday in November. Please call for more information!

NEIL McCURDY - HOOSIER KUBBOARD GLASS
Phone: (610) 346-7946
Found at the following shows:
* Liberty Bell Depression Glass Show
* Kutztown, PA Renninger's Extravaganza every April, June, September
* Brimfield, MA J & J Shows every May, July, September
* Hillsville, VA Labor Day Gun Show every Labor Day weekend

* Fisherville, VA every May and October
* Valley Forge, PA Renninger's Midwinter Show every February
* Schnecksvilled, PA Lehigh Valley Dep. Glass Show Thanksgiving Weekend
* Mt. Dora, FL Renninger's January Show

PAUL REICHWEIN
Selling in Booth 12 at Black Angus Antique Mall, Adamstown, PA (just north of Renninger's Antique Market) every Sunday. Also selling on line:
*www.collectoronline.com (Booth 115)
*www.hwcantiques.com (Booth 1)
Selling each Spring at Antlantique City Show
2321 Hershey Avenue
East Petersburg, PA 17520
Phone: (717) 569-7637
E-mail: PaulRDG@aol.com

MICHAEL ROTHENBERGER / MIKE'S COLLECTIBLES
Found at: Rt. 272 Adamstown, PA Antiques Capital USA (just off exit 21 of the PA Turnpike) in Adams's Annex Antiques, booth J-2 & Glennwood Antique Center, showcases EMT.
Collector Online, booth 30 (www.collectoronline.com)
E-mail: miker@talon.net

STACI AND JEFF SHUCK/GRAY GOOSE ANTIQUES
Also a big part of Gray Goose Antiques:
Jerome and Donna Leamer
Phone: (814) 643-2588 and (814) 627-2639
E-mail: jjshuck@vicom.net
"Visit us on the Internet at Mega Show" www.glassshow.com - Aisle 6
Found at: Dairyland Antiques
    (Sundays noon-5:00/ Wed.-Sat. 10:00-5:00)
    Route 655
    Reedsville, PA

MARIE TALONE/MARIE'S ANTIQUES
Found at:
* Renninger's Antique Market in Adamstown, PA off exit 21 of the PA Turnpike, north ½ mile on Route 272 in booth D - 14 every Sunday
* Renninger's Shows in Kutztown, PA annually in April, June, and September
* Renninger's Show at Valley Forge Convention Center in King of Prussia, PA annually in February
Phone: (610) 868-3702 for show dates or to transact business
E-mail: martal@sprynet.com

JO TIMKO / SNOWFLAKE58 COLLECTIBLES
420 Garrison Road
Millville, NJ 08332
E-mail: xcskier@worldnett.att.net
Phone: (856) 453-3686
eBay selling as: Snowflake58

DEBORA & PAUL TORSIELLO, DEBZIE'S GLASS
Also known as Paden City Glass Guild & Quality Glass Repair
E-mail debglas@idt.net & debglas-2@idt.net
Phone: (973) 428-4885

Collector Note:
Vic & Jean Laermans
Always looking for unusual or rare creamers and sugars to buy, sell, or trade.
E-mail: vjdep1@aol.com
Phone: (309) 755-9082

2200 Line, 169-170
Adam, 9-10
Alice, 84
American Pioneer, 11-12
American Sweetheart, 13-15
Anniversary, 16-17
Apple Blossom, 74-75
Aunt Polly, 18
Aurora, 19
Avocado, 19-20
Ballerina, 32-37
Banded Rings, 202-204
Banded Rib, 59
Basket, 139
Beaded Block, 21-23
Block, 24-28
Block Optic, 24-28
Bouquet and Lattice, 173
Bowknot, 29
Bubble, 29-31
Bullseye, 29-31
Butterflies and Roses, 110-111
Buttons and Bows, 122-123
Cabbage Rose, 224-225
Cameo, 32-37
Canadian Swirl, 38-39
Chain Daisy, 9-10
Charm, 85-86
Cherry Blossom, 40-44
Cherryberry, 45
Chinex Classic, 46-47
Christmas Candy, 47
Circle, 48-49
Clover, 49-50
Cloverleaf, 49-50
Colonial, 51-53
Colonial Block, 54-55
Colonial Fluted, 55-56
Colonial "Knife and Fork," 51-53
Columbia, 56-57
Corex, 58
Coronation, 59
Cremax, 60-61
Crown, 64
Crow's Foot, 62-63
Cube, 65-66
Cubist, 65-66
Cupid, 67
Daisy, 68-69
Dancing Girl, 32-37
Della Robbia, 69-70
Diamond Pattern, 153-156
Diamond Quilted, 71-72
Diana, 73-74
Dogwood, 74-75

Doric, 76-77
Doric and Pansy, 77-78
Double Shield, 168-169
Dutch Rose, 208-209
Early American Rock Crystal, 205-207
Emerald Crest, 79-80
English Hobnail, 81-84
Fan and Feather, 9-10
Fine Rib, 124-125
Fire-King Alice, 84
Fire-King Breakfast Set, 85
Fire-King Charm, 85-86
Fire-King Jane Ray, 87
Fire-King Laurel, 88
Fire-King Oven Glass, 93
Fire-King Misc. Jade-ite, 89-90
Fire-King Philbe Dinnerware, 190
Fire-King Restaurantware, 91-92
Fire-King Sapphire Blue, 93
Fire-King Sapphire Oven Ware, 93
Fire-King 1700 Line, 94
Fire-King Sheaves of Wheat, 94
Fire-King Shell, 95
Fire-King Sunrise, 96
Fire-King Swirl, 96
Fire-King Turquoise Blue, 96-97
Flat Diamond, 71-72
Floragold, 98-99
Floral, 100-104
Floral and Diamond Band, 105-106
Florentine No. 1, 106-107
Florentine No. 2, 108-109
Flower Garden with Butterflies, 110-111
Flower and Leaf Band, 127
Flower Rim, 110-111
Forest Green, 112-114
Fortune, 114
Frosted Block, 21-23
Fruits, 114-115
Georgian, 115-116
Georgian Lovebirds, 115-116
Gray Laurel, 88
Green Crest, 79-80
Gothic Arches, 207
Hairpin, 171-172
Harp, 117
Heritage, 118
Herringbone, 128-130
Hex Optic, 118-119
Hiawatha, 120
Hobnail, 121
Holiday, 122-123
Homespun, 124-125

Honeycomb, 118-119
Horizontal Ribbed, 142-144
Horseshoe, 126
Indiana Custard, 127
Iris, 128-130
Iris and Herringbone, 128-130
Jane Ray, 87
Jubilee, 131-132
Katy, 133
Katy Blue, 133
Knife and Fork, 51-53
La Furiste, 134
Lace Edge, 175-176
Laced Edge, 133
Lake Como, 135
Laurel, 136-137
Lincoln Inn, 138
Lorain, 139
Louisa, 98-99
Lovebirds, 115-116
Madrid, 140-142
Manhattan, 142-144
Many Windows, 209-210
Mayfair "Federal," 145-146
Mayfair (Hocking), 146-152
Mayfair "Open Rose," 146-152
Miss America, 153-156
Moderntone, 157-160
Moderntone Platonite, 157-160
Moondrops, 161-163
Moonstone, 164-165
Moroccan, 166-167
Moroccan Amethyst, 166-167
Mt. Pleasant, 168-169
National, 169-170
New Century, 170-171
Newport, 171-172
Normandie, 173
No. 601, Indiana, 19-20
No. 610, Indiana, 196
No. 612, Indiana, 126
No. 616, Indiana, 229
No. 618, Indiana, 192
No. 620, Indiana, 68-69
No. 622, Indiana, 193
No. 624, Indiana, 47
Old Cafe, 174
Old Colony, 175-176
Old English, 177
Old Florentine, 106-107
Open Lace, 175-176
Open Rose, 146-152
Optic Design, 187
Orchid, 178
Ovide, 179

Oyster and Pearl, 180-181
Paneled Aster, 193-194
Park Avenue, 181
Parrot, 235
Patrician, 182
Patrician Spoke, 182
Patrick, 183
Peach Lustre, 88
Peacock and Rose, 184-185
Peacock and Wild Rose, 186
Peacock Reverse, 186
Pear Optic, 239
Pebble Optic, 187
Petal Swirl, 233-234
Petalware, 188-189
Philbe, 190
Piecrust, 191
Pineapple and Floral, 192
Pinwheel, 226-227
Platonite, 157-160
Poinsettia, 100-104
Poppy No. 1, 106-107
Poppy No. 2, 108-109
Pretzel, 193
Primo, 193-194
Princess, 194-195
Pinwheel, 226-227
Prismatic Line, 196-198
Provincial, 29-31
Pyramid, 196
Queen Mary, 196-198
Radiance, 199-201
Raindrops, 187
Restaurantware, 91-92
Ribbon, 202
Ring, 202-204
Rock Crystal, 205-207
Rock Crystal Flower, 205-207
Romanesque, 207
Rope, 55-56
Rose Cameo, 208
Rose of Sharon, 224-225
Rosemary, 208-209
Roulette, 209-210
Round Robin, 210
Roxana, 211

Royal Lace, 211-215
Royal Ruby, 216-217
"S" Pattern, 218
Sailboat, 248-249
Sandwich (Anchor Hocking),
   220-222
Sandwich (Indiana), 223
Sandwich Glass (Anchor Hocking),
   220-222
Sandwich Glass (Indiana), 223
Sanguenay, 219
Saxon, 56
Shamrock, 49-50
Sharon, 224-225
Ships, 248-249
Sierra, 226-227
Spiral, 228
Spoke, 182
Sportsman Series, 248-249
Starlight, 229
Stars and Stripes, 230
Stippled Rose Band, 218
Strawberry, 230-231
Sunburst, 231
Sunflower, 232
Swirl, 233-234
Sylvan, 235
Tea Room, 236-237
Thistle, 238
Threading, 177
Thumbprint, 239
Tulip, 239-240
Turquoise Blue, 96-97
Twisted Optic, 241
U.S. Swirl, 242
Vernon, 243
Vertical Ribbed, 196-198
Victory, 243-244
Vitrock, 245
Waffle, 246-247
Waterford, 246-247
White Ship, 248-249
Wild Rose, 74-75
Windsor, 250-252
Windsor Diamond, 250-252